MW00710709

CHANNELS
A Basic Writer's Workbook

CHANNELS
A Basic Writer's Workbook

Marjolyn Verspoor
University of Missouri at Kansas City

Linda Hart
Northeast Louisiana University

Mona Oliver
Northeast Louisiana University

SCOTT, FORESMAN/LITTLE, BROWN HIGHER EDUCATION
A Division of Scott, Foresman and Company
Glenview, Illinois   London, England

A separate Instructor's Edition of *Channels: A Basic Writer's Workbook* is available through a Scott, Foresman sales representative or by writing the Scott, Foresman English Editor, Scott, Foresman/Little, Brown Higher Education Division, 1900 East Lake Avenue, Glenview, IL 60025.

Acknowledgments

Cover photo: COMSTOCK INC./Russe Kinne

Acknowledgments for copyrighted materials not credited on the page where they appear are listed in the Acknowledgments section at the back of the book. This section is to be considered a legal extension of the copyright page.

Library of Congress Cataloging-in-Publication Data

Verspoor, Marjolyn.
    Channels: a basic writer's workbook / Marjolyn Verspoor, Linda
Hart, Mona Oliver.
        p.   cm.
    ISBN 0-673-39853-6
    1. English language—Rhetoric—Problems, exercises, etc.
2. English language—Grammar—1950–   —Problems, exercises, etc.
I. Hart, Linda.   II. Oliver, Mona.   III. Title.
PE1413.S666   1990
428′.076—dc20   89-28693
                                                                      CIP

ISBN 0-673-47874-2, Instructor's Edition

Copyright © 1990 Scott, Foresman and Company.
All Rights Reserved.
Printed in the United States of America.

1 2 3 4 5 6—GBC—94 93 92 91 90 89

To the Teacher

Channels: A Basic Writer's Workbook is intended for the grammar component of a developmental English writing program. Its objective is to improve students' writing skills by stressing the connection between grammar, reading, and writing. Although we strongly believe that students learn to write better through reading and writing, we also feel that studying the differences between everyday, spoken English and formal, written English helps students to avoid common errors in their own writing.

To encourage students to read, we include exercises that cover a variety of interesting and informative subjects, with an emphasis on unusual facts. We combine the contemporary with the classic, aiming to increase students' general knowledge. Many of the exercises are thematically related, a subtle way of lobbying for well-developed, specific, and interesting paragraphs. We encourage teachers to incorporate outside readings, in addition to the readings in the text, so students have a variety of source material from which to draw.

The organization of the text easily adapts to self-study, group work, or the traditional lecture approach. Each chapter begins with a brief transition relating old material to new. New material is introduced, one principle at a time, through clear, simple explanations that stress understanding of concepts as well as correct application. The exercises that follow the introductory matter reinforce the ideas presented. At the end of the new material, students are asked to summarize and illustrate the chapter's key principles, then to write on topics related to what has been read in the exercises. The Writing Practice sections are intended to encourage students to write and practice what they have just learned about correct writing.

Once students have worked through the explanations and exercises emphasizing the correct way to write, a review section following either a chapter or a series of related chapters points out problem areas by contrasting incorrect and correct examples. Editing exercises then help students acquire proofreading skills.

The text consists of five units. Units 1 through 3 help students understand basic sentence structure and avoid major errors: subject–verb agreement, verb tense, sentence fragments, comma splices, and fused sentences. Unit 4 explains the correct use of adjectives, adverbs, pronouns, and other troublesome or confusing words. Unit 5 presents techniques for combining words, phrases, and clauses that can make sentences more varied and more effective.

At the end of each of the first four units is a "Writing Process" section that explains one of the various stages of writing to the student: the basics of composing a rough draft, selecting and developing details, polishing, and, finally, proofreading.

Following Unit 5 is a discussion called "Writing an Essay," which explains the essay form and reviews the steps involved in writing an essay. The writing assignments stress clear, interesting communication and involve grammar as only one aspect of the writing process.

Acknowledgments

We are grateful to our colleagues, particularly Louise Harris, David K. Jeffrey, Fleming McClelland, Nancy Rethard, and Martha Wickelhaus, for their support, constructive criticism, and help in field testing *Channels*.

We also welcomed the numerous suggestions made by the following reviewers:

Karen Patty, *Southern Illinois University*;

C. Jeriel Howard, *Northeastern Illinois University*;

Jean Forman, *Kent State University*;

Audrey J. Roth, *Miami Dade Community College*;

Roslyn J. Harper, *Trident Technical College*;

Ellen W. Stukenberg, *Columbus State Community College*;

Laurance J. Riley, *Milwaukee Area Technical College*;

and Judy Stanford, *Rivier College*.

Thanks also to Ron Newcomer for handling the production, and to our copy editor, Elliot Simon. We owe a special debt of gratitude to Fae Dremock, who contributed the first four "Writing Process" sections and gave valuable feedback on early drafts.

We also thank our families for their patience and support.

M. V.
L. H.
M. O.

To the Student

If you are like many students we have met in our classes, you may feel insecure about your English grammar skills. How can you be bad at English, you wonder, when you use it every day to communicate with your family and friends? You think in English. People understand you; you understand them. Why, then, might you feel self-conscious when beginning to write?

English, which like every language is a system of sound symbols used to communicate ideas, feelings, and desires, is continually changing. People invent new words and drop other words that are no longer needed. They change the pronunciation of words slightly. They adopt new rules of grammar or shed old ones. For example, today people wouldn't say, "Our Father, who art in heaven, hallowed be thy name," but "Our Father, who is in heaven, we hope that your name will be respected."

Written English is different from spoken English—because it is more formal, more conservative. When speaking informally to one another, many people say *ain't* instead of *isn't*, probably because this is easier. When they write to one another, however, these same people use the more formal *isn't*, and that's because *written* language changes only when enough people accept the change. We assume the following:

> If enough people say it wrong, it will become correct.
>
> And if even an English teacher says it wrong, it probably has become correct!

In other words, what students refer to as the "rules" of English are actually just widely accepted practices or conventions.

Of course, in college you are expected to write in language that is accepted by educated speakers and writers. This same language probably will also help you obtain a higher-level job.

How can you become more familiar with formal written English? Actually, it is not difficult at all. Just as you learned to understand and use spoken English by hearing people around you speak (no one taught you the "rules" of grammar—you acquired the language naturally because you were surrounded by people who spoke it), so will you learn to use conventional written language. If you want to learn to write, you must be exposed to writing. In other words, you must read. By reading, you "naturally" learn how to spell words, how to use commas and periods correctly, and how to write sentences that follow the currently accepted conventions of good English usage. You also acquire new words through reading.

Of course, it took several years for you to acquire spoken language, so don't expect miracles after reading two or three pages. Start by reading thirty minutes a day. Find an interesting magazine, a good comic book, or an exciting novel, and take it wherever you go. Read while waiting for a class, or riding the bus, or waiting for a friend. If at first you don't enjoy the reading, then find material that really interests you.

If you can gain confidence in recognizing the conventions of written English by reading, why do you need this grammar book? Well, it points out major differences between spoken language and written English, so when you proofread your writing you'll be able to pinpoint the trouble spots. It also explains the general structure of the English sentence, so if you write a complicated sentence, you can examine it and make sure all necessary parts are there and are used correctly. This book will also familiarize you with some of the vocabulary used to describe the English language, so when you write papers for other courses, you'll be able to easily find the needed guidelines, for instance, on using verbs logically or on proper punctuation. (Even professional writers have to look up the conventions sometimes!)

The best way to learn how to use the more conservative written language and how to improve sentence structure, spelling, vocabulary, and punctuation in your writing is to read extensively. Along with reading, an understanding of the material in this grammar book will help you edit your work. Properly edited writing will be visible proof that you are, indeed, a writer.

Contents

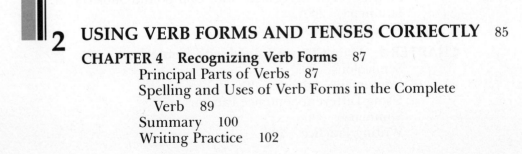

CHANNELS
A Basic Writer's Workbook

Making Subjects and Verbs Agree

UNIT **1**

The first unit of this text will help you understand a major problem that students may have in their writing: making the subject of a sentence and the verb agree. To make the subject and verb agree, you have to be able to recognize two main sentence parts: the subject and the predicate.

THE SUBJECT AND THE PREDICATE

As you probably know, a **subject** (bracketed in the following sentences) is a word or group of words that tells *who* or *what* does something or is something. It is usually located at the beginning of the sentence. The **predicate** (underlined) tells what the subject is, has, feels, or does.

[Linda] is typing a term paper.

Who is typing a term paper? [Linda]
Linda *is doing* what? She is typing a term paper.

[Her last paper] took forever to complete.

What took forever to complete? [Her last paper]
Her last paper *did* what? It took forever to complete.

Exercise 1

As in the previous discussion, bracket the subject part and underline the predicate part.

1. No one walked down Main Street at noon.

2. Every business shut its doors.

3. The police officer was standing on the corner, leaning on the mailbox, and whistling.

4. The waitresses were sleeping at Kay's Place with their elbows on the tables.

5. The bums were lying on park benches, snoring.

6. No buses were arriving from Montgomery.

7. The traffic lights blinked in almost empty streets.

8. An Irish setter was dreaming outside the butcher shop.

9. The pawn shop closed.

10. Old Ezra Jackson had aptly named this place Sleepy Hollow.

Exercise 2

The following sentences are incomplete because they lack either a subject or a predicate. Complete them in your own words.

1. _____ was bustling at midnight.

2. Teenagers in red convertibles _____.

3. _____ was barking.

4. The bums _____.

5. _____ probably didn't know that Sleepy Hollow wasn't sleepy at midnight.

CHAPTER 1
Recognizing Verbs

Now that you can separate the subject from the predicate, you will learn to recognize the most important part of the predicate: the verb. First we will look at the kinds of verbs that may be found in the verb part: main verbs and helping verbs.

MAIN VERBS

Main verbs express an action, such as *walk, sing,* or *see*; a state of being, such as *be, appear,* or *seem*; a state of possession, such as *have, belong,* or *possess*; or a state of emotion, such as *love, hate,* or *enjoy*.

One simple way to tell whether or not a word can function as a main verb is to see if it makes sense when you apply the following test:

"Someone/something can _____."
Someone can <u>walk</u>.
Something can <u>belong</u>.

Note: You may have to change the word somewhat to apply this test. For example, in the sentence "She walked," *walked* is a verb, but you must remove the *-ed* ending to apply the test.

The verb part of the predicate almost always has a main verb. When you compare the following sentences, notice that a sentence becomes either meaningless or changes its meaning when the main verb (with the M over it) is taken out.

M
John <u>was writing</u> a letter to his friend.

John <u>was</u> a letter to his friend.

M
John <u>has written</u> a letter to his friend.

John <u>has</u> a letter to his friend.

M
John <u>wrote</u> a letter to his friend.

John a letter to his friend.

Note: The main verb is typically the last one in the verb part.

Exercise 3

As in the previous examples, place an *M* over each main verb. Remember that there must be one main verb and that it is typically the last word in the verb part.

1. Mary <u>has been studying</u> Greek mythology this semester.

2. She <u>has found</u> many interesting facts in her studies.

3. The goddess Athena <u>had sprung</u> full-grown from her father's head.

4. Gods and goddesses <u>played</u> important roles in the lives of ancient people.

5. Many occurrences in nature <u>were explained</u> through myths.

6. Early Greeks <u>worshipped</u> Zeus as a rain god.

7. Zeus, the king of the gods, <u>could cause</u> thunder and lightning by throwing his thunderbolt.

8. He <u>would provide</u> the rain necessary for their crops as reward for their worship of him.

9. Droughts <u>were caused</u> when Zeus <u>was</u> angry at his worshippers.

10. The powers of the gods <u>were</u> very great.

HELPING VERBS

Helping verbs are verbs such as *can, will, do, be,* and *have* that come before the main verb. As you can see in the following examples, some main verbs are—but others are not—preceded by one, two, or three helping verbs (with an *H* over them).

      M
John <u>wrote</u> a letter to his friend.

    H **M**
He <u>didn't</u> <u>tell</u> him about his job situation.

    H **H** **M**
He <u>has been fired</u> from his old job.

 H   **H** **H** **M**
<u>Should</u> he <u>have been telling</u> the truth?

Learn to recognize the following list of common helping verbs.

Common Helping Verbs			
Be	**Have**	**Do**	**Helping Verbs of Mood**
am	have	do	will
is	has	does	would
are	had	did	can
was			could
were			shall
will/can/ . . . be			should
has/have/had been			may
			might
			must

Note: The verbs *be, have,* and *do* are helping verbs when they are used together with a main verb, as in the following left-hand column. But they are main verbs when they are used by themselves, as in the right-hand column:

  H **M**
He <u>is walking</u>.

  H **M**
He <u>has written</u> a letter.

  H **M**
He <u>didn't</u> <u>help</u> his friend.

    M
He <u>is</u> a student.

    M
He <u>has</u> a new car.

    M
He <u>did</u> his homework.

Exercise 4

As in the previous examples, place an *M* over each main verb and an *H* over each helping verb.

1. Myths <u>have</u> often <u>been used</u> to explain the existence of many things.

2. A maiden's love of a Greek god <u>created</u> the sunflower.

3. Clytie, an ancient maiden, <u>had fallen</u> madly in love with Apollo, the

   Sun-god.

4. Apollo <u>did</u> not <u>return</u> her love.

5. Apollo <u>could find</u> nothing to love about Clytie.

6. She <u>spent</u> all her days sadly wishing for his love.

7. She <u>was</u> constantly <u>watching</u> the sky to see his bright chariot.

8. Her face <u>was</u> always <u>turned</u> toward the sun.

9. One day she <u>was changed</u> into a flower.

10. Like Clytie, the sunflower <u>points</u> its face always to the sun.

THE COMPLETE VERB

The main verb together with its helping verbs (if there are any) is called
the **complete verb** (underlined here).

complete verb

Linda <u>is typing</u> a term paper.

She <u>has been working</u> for two hours.

The term paper <u>has</u> fifteen pages.

6. Have you ever said "God bless you" to someone sneezing?

7. This phrase originated during an epidemic in the sixth century.

8. The blessing was intended to help prevent the spread of the dreaded

disease.

9. Even scientists cannot always explain the casue of sneezes.

10. Have you ever sneezed for no reason at all?

Exercise 10

Write five sentences about the things you do to have good luck or to avoid bad luck. Use the words given to interrupt your verbs; then underline the complete verb in each of your sentences.

1. _____ often _____.

2. _____ usually _____.

3. _____ never _____.

4. _____ not _____.

5. _____ always _____.

SUMMARY

Fill in the blanks with the appropriate response, to show your understanding of the principles in this chapter. Where indicated, write a sentence of your own to illustrate those principles.

1. What is a complete verb? _____

   Example sentence: _____

2. a. What is a main verb? _____

   _____

   b. Where does it occur in the complete verb? _____

   _____

   c. What is its importance in the sentence? _____

   _____

3. a. Where do helping verbs occur in relation to the main verb? _____

   _____

   b. If there is only one verb in the complete verb, is it a helping verb or

   a main verb? _____

4. Usually the helping verbs and main verb are grouped together. Certain words, however, may split the complete verb. Write a sentence with one of these interrupters in the middle of the complete verb.

   _____

   _____

5. In questions and sentences beginning with *there*, the complete verb may also be split. Rewrite the following sentence twice, beginning with the indicated word. Underline the complete verb.

   Many people <u>are waiting</u> in line.

   There _____.

   Are _____?

Summary Exercise

Underline the complete verb in each of the following sentences.

   [1]Are you aware of the many different things available in your library?

[2]Libraries are much more than just places to check out books. [3]There are

many services provided for the community by a library. [4]For example, local libraries can usually enlist the help of other libraries by borrowing from their collections. [5]Just knowing about the services of your library can often save you a great deal of time in trying to locate information.

[6]Specific information about your community and other communities is found in the library. [7]Vertical files often contain pamphlets and articles about your area. [8]Out-of-town telephone directories and newspapers offer information about other areas. [9]College catalogues can usually be found in libraries. [10]Also, have you ever heard about a library's archive collection? [11]These collections, where available, provide historical information about your community.

[12]Things other than books can be checked out of libraries in most areas. [13]Checking out art is possible in many libraries. [14]With this service, individuals are given the opportunity to enjoy art in their own homes. [15]Records and tapes are also checked out for home use. [16]In addition, video cassettes have become some of the most requested items for some libraries.

[17]Computers are now important parts of larger libraries. [18]What do these modern machines have to do with the world of books?[19]The computer can quickly allow the patron to reach valuable information available in the library. [20]Providing information swiftly helps save valuable time for the library patron. [21]Children's rooms may even contain computers for hands-on learning experience.

22No longer is the library only a place to find books to read. 23To find out about your library is easy. 24A visit or a phone call will quickly provide you with the services available. 25What are you waiting for?

WRITING PRACTICE

Write ten sentences or a short passage about one or more of the following topics, using the guidelines of your teacher. Underline each complete verb in your sentences.

1. one odd character or place in your town

2. the best story or book you have read

3. how you imagine your area looked about 500 years ago

4. something you are superstitious about

5. services your local library offers

CHAPTER 2
Forming the First Verb

So far you have learned that sentences consist of subjects and predicates, and you have learned to recognize the complete verb. Now you will see that the first verb in the complete verb must have a specific form in order to match the subject.

THE FIRST VERB

In the following examples notice that only the first verb (circled) in the complete verb changes when the subject of the sentence (in brackets) changes. When the subject is [John], the verb is *writes*. When the subject changes to [sisters], the verb is *write*. This change in spelling of the verb is done to make the subject and verb match. This matching of the subject with the first verb is called **subject–verb agreement**.

first verb

John (writes) many letters.

His five sisters (write) him every week.

John (has) written about ten letters this month.

His sisters (have) written about fifty letters to him.

Exercise 1

As in the previous examples, underline the complete verb and circle the first verb.

1. More people are known to drink tea than any other beverage except

   water.

2. This popular drink was invented about 4000 years ago.

3. A Chinese emperor's cook accidentally dropped some leaves from a tea branch into boiling water.

4. The smell carried into the emperor's room.

5. Curious, he demanded to taste the water.

6. Tea was born!

7. Tea leaves are harvested from an evergreen tree that sometimes reaches heights of thirty feet.

8. In 1896, tea was first placed in the bags familiar to us today.

9. Have you ever heard the phrase "for all the tea in China"?

10. That amount would be about 600 million pounds a year.

Exercise 2

Write five sentences of your own about a popular beverage. In each of your sentences, underline the complete verb and circle the first verb.

1. _____

_____

2. _____

_____

3. _____

_____

4. _____

_____

5. _____

_____

Now that you have learned to identify the first verb, notice that a first verb may have either a present form or a past form. You will first study the present and past forms of the verb *be*, the most frequently used verb in English.

THE PRESENT FORMS OF *BE*

The verb *be* causes many subject–verb agreement problems because it has many forms. Examine in the following box the changing verb forms that agree with each subject.

Present Forms of *be*			
Singular Subjects	I	<u>am</u>	unique.
	You	<u>are</u>	unique.
	He She It	<u>is</u>	unique.
Plural Subjects	We You They	<u>are</u>	unique.

When a noun such as *boy, girl, dog,* or *people* is the subject of a sentence (bracketed here), you can mentally substitute for it *he, she, it,* or *they* (whichever is appropriate) to decide on the right form of the verb.

he
[The boy] is unique.

she
[His sister] is unique.

it
[The dog] is unique.

they
[Many people] are unique.

Exercise 3

To decide the correct present form of the verb *be* that is needed, bracket the subject part of each omitted verb and write above it the appropriate pronoun substitute (*he, she, it,* or *they*). Then, using the box on present forms, fill in the blank. The first sentence has been done for you as an example.

1. [Shoplifting] *is* a costly expense for many merchants.

2. This crime _____ estimated to cost storeowners over $3 billion a year.

3. About 4 million shoplifters _____ caught each year, but millions _____ getting away.

4. Some shoplifters _____ professionals.

5. There _____ schools training people to shoplift in some parts of the world.

6. Then these "educated" thieves _____ shipped all over the world.

7. In some cases, a child _____ trained to be a shoplifter.

8. Children _____ less likely to be punished severely.

9. One shoplifting "school" _____ known to charge a tuition of $1500 for its course.

10. Shop owners _____ using sophisticated equipment to help prevent shoplifting.

THE PAST FORMS OF *BE*

The verb *be* also has different past forms. Examine in the following box
the past form that agrees with each subject.

Past Forms of *be*			
Singular Subjects	I	<u>was</u>	curious.
	You	<u>were</u>	curious.
	He		
	She	<u>was</u>	curious.
	It		
Plural Subjects	We		
	You	<u>were</u>	curious.
	They		

Exercise 4

To practice contrasting present and past forms, go back to Exercise 3.
This time begin the first sentence with the phrase "Last year . . ." Then,
using the box on past forms, write the correct past form over each present form of the verb *be* in the blank.

Exercise 5

To decide the correct past form of the verb *be* needed, identify the subject of each omitted verb and write above it the appropriate pronoun
substitute (*he/she/it* or *they*). Then, using the box on past forms, fill in the
blank. The first sentence has been done for you as an example.

[1]During World War I, a young British doctor, Alexander Fleming,
he

_____*was*_____ appalled by the number of deaths he saw from infection.

[2]His research _____ started as a result of his desire to fight the

infection-causing bacteria. [3]In 1928, while he _____ working

in his laboratory, this doctor discovered a mold he called *Penicillium*

notatum. [4]Because other doctors _____ uninterested in his work, his findings _____ lost for many years in stacks of papers. [5]Ten years later his papers _____ discovered by Dr. Howard Florey and Dr. Ernst Chain. [6]Believing the mold had great possibilities, these scientists continued the studies, thinking Fleming _____ dead. [7]They found that the mold _____ very unstable and still needed a great deal of work. [8]The doctors _____ willing to continue the study but needed help. [9]Large drug companies in the United States helped them to stabilize the mold, and in 1940 it _____ purified for use on patients. [10]Penicillin _____ the first substance made from molds to be used for treating infectious diseases in humans. [11]Even though Fleming _____ credited with the discovery of the mold, the drug now in use is actually the result of Florey's and Chain's research.

PRESENT VERB FORMS

In contrast to the verb *be*, almost all English verbs have only two present forms, one with and one without an *-s* ending. *I, you, we,* and *they* subjects match the form without the *-s* ending. Only *he, she,* and *it* require an *-s* ending on the verb.

Present Forms of *Work* and *Write*				
Singular	I		I	
Subjects	You	work every day.	You	write every day.
Only he, she, it subjects take verbs with an -s ending.	He She It	works every day.	He She It	writes every day.
Plural	We		We	
Subjects	You They	work every day.	You They	write every day.

Note: Some *he/she/it* forms have unusual spellings. Compare the following forms with and without the *-s* ending.

I/you/we/they form	he/she/it form
have	has
do	does
go	goes
pass	passes
study	studies

Exercise 6

To decide the correct present form of the verb in parentheses, identify the subject of each omitted verb and replace it with the appropriate pronoun (*he/she/it* or *they*). Then, using the previous charts as a guide, fill in the blank. The first one is done for you.

[1]Divorce customs *~~they~~ differ* (differ) throughout the world. [2]While Americans usually ___ end ___ (end) their marriages in courts of law, other countries ___ have ___ (have) widely varying practices. [3]An Arab man ___ divorce ___ (divorce) his wife by saying "I divorce thee" in front of two witnesses. [4]Eskimos simply ___ live ___ (live) apart, preferably with someone else. [5]In Australia, an Aborigine woman ___ starting ___ (start) divorce proceedings by eloping with another man. [6]In some cultures an annulment ___ says ___ (say) a marriage never even existed and ___ replaces ___ (replace) divorce. [7]In the United States, divorce ___ is ___ (be) a growing problem. [8]Some researchers ___ estimates ___ (estimate) that almost half of all American marriages ___ end ___ (end)

in divorce. [9]This problem _____does_____ (do) not exist in all countries.
[10]A few countries, such as Argentina and Ireland, ___prohibit__ (pro-
hibit) divorce in any case. [11]There ___are___ (be) no easy answers to
the problem, but one thing is certain: As long as marriages _exist_
(exist), some people will rely on divorce to end them.

Exercise 7

Answer the following questions in your own words, in complete sentences. Make sure the subject and verb agree.

1. What is the main idea of the preceding passage?

   The main idea of the preceding passage is the different divorces in the world.

2. In which country can one simply elope to divorce?

   In Australia, one can simple elope to divorce.

3. What is an annulment?

   An annulment is

4. How many marriages in America end in divorce?

   Half of all marriages in America end in divorce.

5. In which countries can one not divorce under any circumstance?

   In Argentina and Ireland, one can not divorce under any circumstance.

PAST VERB FORMS

As you can see from the following boxed examples, the past form does
not change its ending when the subject is *he, she,* or *it.*

Past Forms of *Work* and *Write*			
Singular Subjects	I You He She It	worked every day.	I You He She It	wrote every day.
Plural Subjects	We You They	worked every day.	We You They	wrote every day.

Note: To form the past tense, a verb either adds an *-ed* ending or has an irregular spelling, such as "write" changing to "wrote." (For a list of common irregular verbs and their changing forms, see Appendix 1.)

Exercise 8

To decide the correct past form of the verb in parentheses, identify the subject of each omitted verb and write above it the appropriate pronoun (*he/she/it* or *they*). Then fill in the blank. Remember what you have learned about the past tense of the verb *be*, and use the preceding box as your guide with other verbs. We have done the first one for you.

¹While visiting President Lincoln, Governor *he* Curtin of Pennsylvania

_____*was*_____ (be) disturbed to see how depressed Lincoln _____

(be) about the continuation of the Civil War. ²The governor _____

(express) his desire to help. ³In response, Lincoln _____ (tell)

Curtin the story of two Illinois farm boys. ⁴The amusing but pointed tale

_____ (go) like this.

⁵One day an old farmer out in Illinois _____ (decide) to raise

hogs. ⁶So, he _____ (order) the finest breed of hogs available

from Europe. ⁷He even _____ (give) the biggest prize hog a special pen. ⁸Then the farmer _____ (tell) his two mischievous sons

not to let the hog out. ⁹Naturally, the next day the worse boy of the two

_____ (disobey) and in the resulting chase _____ (find) it

difficult to hang on to the animal's tail. ¹⁰His quick-thinking brother

swiftly _____ (climb) the very tree that the hog _____ (be)

circling furiously. ¹¹So the boy holding on for dear life _____

(shout), "I say, John, come down quick and help me to let the hog

go!" ¹²Why _____ (do) Lincoln relate this story when Curtin

_____ (offer) to help?

Exercise 9

When you write about literature or when you want to make an event sound more lively, you can write about it in the present tense, even though it happened in the past. To practice contrasting present and past forms, go back to Exercise 8. Then, remembering what you have learned about the present forms of the verb *be* and other verbs, write the correct present form over each past form of the verb in the blank.

Exercise 10

In a paragraph tell a story (or anecdote) that someone told you. Check for correct subject–verb agreement.

PRESENT AND PAST FORMS OF THE HELPING VERBS OF MOOD

The **helping verbs of mood** (*will/would, can/could, shall/should, may/might,* and *must*) are different from all other verbs, for several reasons:

1. They are always helping verbs.

   helping verb and main verb
   I <u>can help</u>.

2. The past forms *would, could, should,* and *might* actually usually indicate that the *future*—not the past—is being referred to.

   past helper with future meaning
   I <u>could help</u> you tomorrow.

3. And most important, the present form has no *-s* ending when the subject is *he/she/it*.

Present Forms

Singular *Subjects*	I You He She It	can work every day.	I You He She It	may write every day.
Plural *Subjects*	We You They	can work every day.	We You They	may write every day.

[handwritten:] He, she, it subjects take no -s ending on the verb.

Note: Many inexperienced writers tend to overuse the helping verbs of mood. These helping verbs of mood are ordinarily used *only* when we want to express doubt or uncertainty about something or when we want to make our statement less direct. Compare the examples:

We <u>can work</u> every day.

We <u>work</u> every day.

Exercise 11

[handwritten: list of helping verbs of mood]

Using the <u>preceding box on present forms</u>, replace each past form of a helping verb of mood with its present counterpart. Note that this change doesn't affect the meaning of the sentence much. The first one has been done for you.

1. You ~~might~~ *may* do several things to improve your health.

2. You would *[will]* try to stay fit.

3. You could *[can]* work out every day in a gym.

4. You might *[may]* jog five miles a day if you could.

5. You could *[can]* also try to have a healthier diet because good food helps

   maintain your health.

Exercise 12

Rewrite the sentences in Exercise 11 without a helping verb of mood. The first one has been done for you. Notice that they sound more direct without this helping verb.

1. *You do several things to improve your health.*

2. _____

3. _____

4. _____

5. _____

_____

SUMMARY

Fill in each blank with the appropriate response, to show your understanding of the principles in this chapter.

1. Why is the first verb in the complete verb important in the sentence?

   _____

2. The verb *be* is quite irregular. Write down the appropriate forms to match each subject.

	Present		Past
I	_____	I	_____
you	_____	you	_____
he	_____	he	_____
she	_____	she	_____
it	_____	it	_____
we	_____	we	_____
they	_____	they	_____

3. Give the present and past forms for the following verbs. The first one has been done for you.

Present		Past
I/you/we/they form	he/she/it form	I/you/he/she/it/ we/they form
say	*says*	*said*
walk		
	tries	
go		
		did
have		
	sees	
find		
	can	
ask		
		might

Summary Exercise

To make the following passage sound more lively, and to practice subject–verb agreement, change all the first verbs (which have been underlined) to present forms. The first sentence has been done for you.

1. <u>Did</u> *Do* you know how Chief Telegrapher Thomas Eckert <u>described</u> *describes* Lincoln's writing habits?

2. Lincoln often <u>visited</u> the cipher room, where the latest news from the battlefield <u>was</u> received.

3. Lincoln, while waiting for messages, usually <u>scribbled</u> notes on borrowed sheets of paper.

4. During one of these frequent visits, while rereading what he <u>had</u> just written, Lincoln <u>glanced</u> at a large spiderweb nearby.

5. Spiderwebs <u>were</u> a common sight in the cipher room, so common in fact that one cabinet member <u>had</u> named this large community of spiders "Major Eckert's Lieutenants."

6. Eckert <u>noticed</u> that the spiders <u>were</u> diverting Mr. Lincoln and <u>joked</u> that these lieutenants <u>would</u> probably soon "pay their respects to the president."

7. Oddly, there <u>was</u> eerie prophetic truth to this claim, for one of the big spiders suddenly <u>appeared</u> at the crossroads of the web and <u>tapped</u> on the strands, summoning five or six others from all directions.

8. But when the spiders <u>did</u> nothing but hold a conference, Lincoln <u>turned</u> his attention back to his task.

9. The president, after another look at the web, <u>resettled</u> in his chair, <u>looked</u> out the window, and <u>began</u> to work slowly and seriously.

10. Lincoln, a cautious writer, <u>considered</u> every word carefully before writing it down and slowly <u>filled</u> his page.

11. He <u>was writing</u> an important document in that spider-filled room: The Emancipation Proclamation.

WRITING PRACTICE

Write ten sentences or a short passage about one or more of the following topics, using the guidelines of your teacher. In each of your sentences, circle the first verbs within your complete verbs.

1. what shop owners can do to catch shoplifters

2. some of the things that medical drugs have *not* been able to cure

3. your favorite humorous story

4. what you do to stay in shape

5. your own writing habits

CHAPTER 3
Recognizing Subjects

So far you have learned that the first verb in the complete verb must match the subject. In this chapter you will learn to locate the main word in the subject part, find subjects in unusual places, and recognize some special kinds of subjects.

Why are we spending so many lessons talking about subjects and first verbs? In spoken English, we often do not take much time to think, and even very educated speakers do not always make the subject and verb agree. However, in academic writing, when we have time to proofread and think about what is customary in educated English, we should make sure that the subject and the verb agree.

Actually, it is not very difficult to make the subject and verb agree. You already know what the verb should be when the subject is a pronoun, such as *I, you, he, she, it, we,* or *they.* But if the subject is a group of words, you simply ask yourself this question: Could the main word in the subject part be replaced by (1) *he/she/it* or (2) *they*? If the answer is (1), the first verb will normally get an *-s* ending. If the answer is (2), the verb will not get an *-s* ending. Usually the answer is easy to discover. For example, *shoe* could be replaced by *it,* and *socks* by *they.* However, finding the main word in the subject part can be tricky when the main word is surrounded by descriptive words or when it is in an unusual place. First we will look at subjects surrounded by descriptive words, called **modifiers**.

THE SIMPLE SUBJECT
AND THE COMPLETE SUBJECT

As you saw in the earlier examples and exercises, the subject part often consists of several words. In this group of words, there is usually one main word that names the *who* or *what*. This word is called the **simple subject** (circled in the following examples).

The simple subject together with all of its describing words is called the **complete subject** (bracketed).

complete subject

simple subject

[The (man) wearing the gray overcoat] is a secret agent.

[This (agent) , with the CIA for five years,] <u>does</u> not <u>look</u> like James Bond.

[The (CIA) , the Central Intelligence Agency,] <u>has</u> secret agents all over the world.

Exercise 1

As in the foregoing examples, underline the complete verb. Then circle the simple subject and bracket the complete subject.

1. Old men in white suits shouldn't sit in the parks.

2. Busy people hurrying past resent them.

3. Children playing on the swings like to scare them.

4. Long-haired dogs with fleas try to bite them.

5. Pickpockets in the area rifle their coats.

6. Police officers on the beat try to protect them.

7. While running past, joggers plugged into Walkman radios stumble over them.

8. Young mothers with five toddlers in tow want them to baby-sit.

9. Young and cocky baseball players from city leagues trade insults with them.

10. Joe, the hot dog vendor on the corner, gossips with them.

11. Lawyers in Brooks Brothers suits want to make out their wills.

12. Middle-aged tourists from Nebraska take their pictures.

13. Filmmakers from New York want to make documentaries about them.

14. Old women in white suits want to hold their hands.

Exercise 2

Make the following sentences more interesting and specific by adding describing words *before* or *after* the simple subject. Try to make them humorous! The first one has been done for you.

1. Women like to sit on park benches.
Middle - aged women in blue jeans like to sit on park benches.

2. People talk to them.

3. Dogs wag their tails at them.

4. Pickpockets feel guilty about taking their purses.

5. Joggers jump over their feet.

6. Mothers ask their advice.

7. Lawyers give them free legal counsel.

8. Tourists take their pictures.

9. Advertising agents make them stars of television commercials.

10. Men are a little jealous of them.

ISOLATING MODIFIERS TO FIND THE SIMPLE SUBJECT

As you can see from the previous exercises, there may be different kinds of describing words (modifiers) before and after the simple subject. In the next few sections, you will learn to recognize some different types of modifiers—adjectives, prepositional and other adjective phrases, and adjective clauses—so that you can isolate the simple subject more easily.

Adjectives

The separate words that usually come before the simple subject (circled here) to make it clearer are called **adjectives**. They include *the, a, an*, and many other words. Look at the following examples.

[A baby (elephant)] <u>suckles</u> with its mouth, not its trunk.

[The first telegraphic (communication) between New York City and Chicago] <u>was established</u> June 10, 1848.

[A recent scientific (survey)] <u>shows</u> that millions of Americans are both uncomfortable and unhappy with the names their parents have given them.

Exercise 3

As in the preceding examples, circle the simple subject. (Make sure you do *not* circle a modifier.) Then fill in the blank with the correct form of the verb given in parentheses.

Note: Remember to replace the simple subject mentally with *he/she/it* or *they* to help you correctly form the verb.

1. [Another Abe Lincoln story] _____ (*illustrate*, present) the

   President's unusual ability to handle people.

2. [The wily, down-to-earth Lincoln] _____ (*be*, past) once over-

   heard telling this tale to people seeking a political appointment from

   him.

3. [Superstitious kings] _____ (*employ*, past) people to tell them

   of future events.

4. Therefore, [a far-sighted, accurate astrologer] _____ (*be*,

   past) usually in demand.

5. One day, [one advisor's astrological weather forecast] _____ (*be*, past) that the sun would shine for his king's proposed hunting trip.

6. On the road that morning, [the king's hunting party] _____ (*be*, past) greeted by a farmer, who warned them that [rain] _____ (*be*, past) coming.

7. Later, [the drenched and angry monarch] _____ (*return*, past) to his palace and _____ (*cut*, past) off the head of his chief astrologer.

8. When sent for to replace the astrologer, [the same outspoken farmer] quickly _____ (*credit*, past) his donkey's ears for the accurate prediction of rain.

9. Thus, [the new court astrologer's job] _____ (*be*, past) to go to a donkey.

10. Soon [every donkey in the land] _____ (*be*, past) standing in front of the palace asking for an office.

Exercise 4

In no more than five sentences explain the point that Lincoln was trying to make with this anecdote. Make sure that your subjects and verbs agree.

_____

_____

_____

_____

_____

_____

_____

_____

_____

_____

Phrases

Sometimes the simple subject (circled here) is made clearer by a group of words following it. When such a group of words functions as a unit but does not contain a complete verb, it is called a **phrase** (in parentheses here).

he   *phrase modifying the simple subject*

[(Antley Donald,) (a famous pitcher for the New York Yankees,)] once <u>threw</u> a baseball at the rate of 94.7 miles per hour.

[The longest human (beard) (ever recorded)] <u>was</u> eleven feet, six inches, grown by Hans N. Lanoseth in 1912.

[The longest (mustache) (to be recorded)] <u>measured</u> seventy-six inches.

Exercise 5

As in the preceding examples, circle the simple subject. (Make sure you do not circle any part of a phrase that might follow the subject to make it clearer.) Then fill in the blank with the correct form of the verb given in parentheses.

1. "Mrs. Lincoln, my dear wife, _____ (*have*, present) got a no-

   tion into her head that I shall be assassinated," Lincoln once said.

2. His attempt to reassure her _____ (*be*, past) to carry a cane on

   his nightly walks to the War Department.

3. Any person plotting to kill him _____ (*be*, past) going to find a way to do it anyway, he believed.

4. Lincoln, a very public figure, simply _____ (*be*, past) not willing to live in fear despite this ever-present threat.

5. Lincoln's assassination, April 14, 1865, now _____ (*seem*, present) to take on an ironic meaning.

6. Certainly, stories such as this one _____ (*give*, present) us clues about a person's character.

7. Lincoln, the man and the President, _____ (*be*, present) a remarkable figure in American history.

8. In fact, the stories concerning President Lincoln's courage and humor _____ (*have*, present) made him a legend.

9. A legend, growing steadily with every year, often _____ (*pick*, present) up some "facts" that aren't necessarily accurate.

10. Thus, not all anecdotes reported about Lincoln _____ (*be*, present) true.

Prepositional Phrases

The most common type of phrase that follows the subject and modifies it is a **prepositional phrase**, which is a phrase that starts with a preposition and ends with a *whom* or *what* word. For example:

prep.	*what?*		prep.	*whom?*
on	the desk		for	the boy

The simple subject *never* occurs inside a prepositional phrase! Therefore, setting off the prepositional phrases (in parentheses here) in the complete subject (bracketed) can help you find the simple subject (circled) more easily.

it   prepositional phrase modifying the simple subject

[The inside (of cucumbers)] is often twenty degrees hotter than the surrounding air.

[The most prevalent infection (in the world)] today is malaria.

[The dimensions (of a regulation football field)] are 360 feet long and 160 feet wide.

The following list of common prepositions will help you recognize prepositions. Remember, though, that some words have more than one function, so these words are only used as prepositions if they have a *whom* or *what* word following them.

Common Prepositions

about	but ("except")	outside
above	by	over
across	despite	past
according to	down	round
after	during	since
against	except	through
along	for	throughout
amid	from	till
among	in	to
around	inside	toward
at	in spite of	towards
because of	into	under
before	like	underneath
below	near	until
beneath	of	up
beside	off	upon
besides	on	with
between	on account of	within
beyond	out	without

Exercise 9

In the following sentences, circle the simple subjects. (Make sure you do *not* circle one of its modifiers.) Then circle the correct form of the verb.

1. Walt Whitman, a well-respected poet, (describe, describes) President Lincoln's daily journey down Vermont Avenue with these details.

2. A company of thirty cavalry with drawn swords held upright over their shoulders (ride, rides) with the President.

3. The men in this guard (accompany, accompanies) Lincoln at the insistence of his advisors, but against his own wishes.

4. However, this procession, in spite of the uniforms and horses, (is, are) not a great spectacle.

5. Mr. Lincoln, who (is, are) dressed in plain black clothes, (ride, rides) to work on a large, ambling gray horse.

6. The dust on his suit and stiff hat (show, shows) the effects of the ride into town.

7. But Whitman, who daily (exchange, exchanges) bows with Lincoln, hardly (notice, notices) Mr. Lincoln's dusty clothes.

8. Lincoln's dark-complexioned face with its deep lines and expressive, sad eyes (draw, draws) all attention away from his dress and attendants.

Exercise 10

Write five sentences about your impressions of Lincoln. Make sure your subjects and verbs agree.

1. _____

   _____

2. _____

   _____

3. _____

   _____

4. _____

   _____

5. _____

   _____

Exercise 11

The first verbs in the following passage have been underlined for you. Change each of these past verb forms to its present form. The first sentence has been done for you.

1. One day, a man who ~~had~~ *has* an intimidating look about him ~~entered~~ *enters* the President's office and ~~pushed~~ *pushes* a gun into Lincoln's face.

2. The self-possessed commander-in-chief <u>asked</u> calmly if there <u>was</u> a problem.

3. The equally calm stranger <u>responded</u> that he <u>had</u> sworn an oath that if he ever <u>came</u> across an uglier man than himself he <u>would</u> shoot him on the spot.

4. The amused Lincoln, whose face <u>transformed</u> immediately with obvious relief, <u>told</u> the stranger to shoot.

5. Then he <u>added</u> that if he <u>were</u> an uglier man than the stranger he <u>didn</u>'t want to live.

6. Another humorous anecdote about Lincoln as a young lawyer <u>illustrated</u> his horse-trading skill.

7. An appointment at 9:00 o'clock <u>was</u> set between Lincoln and a judge who <u>claimed</u> to be the better horse trader.

8. Neither man <u>was</u> supposed to look at the other's horse before the appointed time.

9. Leading his own sorry excuse for a horse, the judge <u>was</u> surprised to see Lincoln carrying a wooden sawhorse over his shoulder.

10. Walking away with the judge's horse, Lincoln <u>claimed</u> that this <u>was</u> the first time he <u>had</u> ever gotten the raw end of a deal.

Exercise 12

Complete the following sentences in your own words. As you can see, Sentence 1 needs adjectives, Sentence 2 needs an adjective phrase, Sentence 3 needs a prepositional phrase, and Sentence 4 needs an adjective clause.

1. The _____ and _____ president obviously had a good sense of humor.

2. The president, always _____, obviously had a good sense of humor.

3. The president with _____ obviously had a good sense of humor.

4. The president, who _____, obviously had a good sense of humor.

DIFFERENT SUBJECT POSITIONS

In most of the sentences you have seen so far, the subject comes at the beginning of the sentence, before the complete verb. However, in some cases the subject does not occur at the beginning of the sentence, and in other cases it does not occur before the complete verb. In this section, you will practice making subjects in unusual positions agree with the first verb.

The Subject After Introductory Words

Subjects often occur at the beginning of a sentence, but sometimes single words or groups of words telling *why, where, when, how,* or *in spite of* come before the subject (in brackets here). These are not considered part of the complete subject because they do not answer the *who* or *what* question.

Where?
From his room, [John] <u>was talking</u> to Cindy on the phone.

When?
While talking, [John] <u>dropped</u> the phone on his toe.

Why?
Because of this mishap, [the connection] <u>was broken</u>.

How?
Angrily, [Cindy] <u>hung up</u>.

In spite of what?
Although he kept trying, [John] <u>could</u> not <u>reach</u> Cindy again.

In spite of his clumsiness, [this lucky young man] <u>didn't</u> <u>break</u> anything but the connection.

Exercise 13

As in the preceding examples, underline the complete verb and bracket the complete subject of each sentence. Make sure your subject brackets do *not* include introductory words like those in the examples.

1. This morning the police officer wasn't working very hard on his beat.

2. Because of the lull he seemed to be asleep on his horse.

3. In fact, his eyes were closed.

4. His hands were resting on the saddle.

5. Sliding from his grip, the reins fell by the horse's mane.

6. The horse also looked sleepy, standing there with its head down.

7. Suddenly a man ran from the store.

8. Ironically, the robber couldn't get away.

9. While looking behind him, he tripped over the horse's back leg.

10. Startled by the jolt, the officer leaped from his horse to arrest the

    thief.

Subjects in Questions

As you saw in Chapter 1, the subject in a question (circled here) usually splits the complete verb (underlined).

Why <u>did</u> the (phone) <u>fall</u> on the floor?

Whom <u>does</u> the (world) of the secret service <u>intrigue</u>?

Note: If the question word is the subject, then the subject comes at the beginning of the question.

(What) <u>intrigues</u> him?

Exercise 14

As in the preceding examples, circle the simple subject of each question and fill in the blank with the correct form of the verb given in parentheses.

1. Why _____ (*do*, present) people fear strange sights and sounds, especially at night?

2. _____ (*have*, present) "things that go bump in the night" really inspired stories in every part of the world?

3. How _____ (*do*, past) legends concerning mysterious lights originate?

4. _____ (*be*, present) "will-o'-the-wisp" indeed a common name for such mysterious lights?

5. How often _____ (*have*, present) people traveling at night been misled by such lights?

6. _____ (*do*, past) the wandering spirits of murderers actually return to the scene of the crime and turn into jack-o'-lanterns?

7. Why _____ (*be*, present) strange sobbing, wailing sounds at night the subject of another old world legend?

8. _____ (*be*, present) such sounds called "the cry of the Banshee" in Ireland?

9. What _____ (*do*, past) these cries mean?

10. _____ (*be*, past) the death of someone in an old, noble family really foreshadowed by the Banshee's cry?

Subjects in Sentences Starting with *there*

The word *there* is not a *who* or *what* word and can *never* be a subject. Remember, when a sentence begins with *there*, the subject (circled) occurs after the first verb.

There <u>are</u> seventeen (people) <u>enjoying</u> the picnic.

There <u>is</u> a (storm) <u>approaching</u>.

There <u>are</u> many (people) <u>waiting</u> in line at the food table.

There <u>is</u> a (man) who looks like my grandfather <u>watching</u> the kids.

Note: Especially in speaking, we often start a sentence with the word *there*, and we usually contract the verb after it—for example, "there's" or "there're." However, we often say "There's . . . ," even if the subject is plural. In writing, we must make sure that the verb and the subject agree.

Exercise 15

Circle the simple subject. Then fill in the blank with the correct form of the verb.

1. There _____ (*be*, present) people of all ages enjoying Aesop's

   fables.

2. There _____ (*be*, present) moral and political lessons taught

   in his fables.

3. There _____ (*be*, present) ordinary human weaknesses such

   as greed and envy pointed out in a simple, humorous way.

4. There _____ (*be*, present) usually a moral point at the end of

   each fable.

5. There _____ (*have*, present) come many common sayings from Aesop's fables.

6. For example, there _____ (*be*, present) the saying "acting like a wolf in sheep's clothing," which refers to an enemy posing as a friend.

7. There _____ (*be*, present) many lessons that we can learn from Aesop's fables which are as valuable today as in 500 B.C.

8. However, there _____ (*be*, present) many tales attributed to Aesop that he may not have created himself.

9. There _____ (*be*, present) a possibility that Aesop may have heard ancient legends and retold them.

10. There _____ (*be*, present) many other tales that have been kept alive for centuries.

Avoiding Sentences Beginning with *there*

Many writers avoid sentences beginning with *there* because they consider them wordy and vague. Starting a sentence with the subject is usually more effective.

vague and wordy

There <u>were</u> seventeen (people) <u>enjoying</u> the picnic.

There <u>was</u> a (storm) <u>approaching</u>.

There <u>were</u> many (people) <u>waiting</u> in line at the food table.

more effective

Seventeen (people) <u>were enjoying</u> the picnic.

A (storm) <u>was approaching</u>.

Many (people) <u>were waiting</u> in line at the food table.

Exercise 16

To practice making the sentences in Exercise 15 more effective, rewrite the first five starting with the subject, as in the preceding examples. The first one has been done for you.

1. *People of all ages enjoy Aesop's fables.*

2. _____

3. _____

   _____

4. _____

5. _____

Other Subjects That Appear After the First Verb

Just like sentences beginning with *there*, sentences beginning with a negative word, such as *hardly, never, seldom, only,* or *scarcely,* have subjects (circled) after the first verb.

   Never had Ⓘ seen such a strange sky.

   Scarcely had Ⓘ put a spoonful of potato salad in my mouth when I heard loud thunder.

   Also, to add sentence variety, writers may turn a sentence around so that the subject comes at the end of the sentence.

   A (man) cried "Help!"

   "Help!" cried a (man).

   The (remains) of the picnic were scattered around the park.

   Scattered around the park were the (remains) of the picnic.

Exercise 17

In the following sentences, the complete verb has been underlined for you. Circle the simple subject.

1. In ancient legends <u>are</u> the roots of fairy tales beloved by children.

2. In other words, there <u>are</u> many modern fairy tales <u>connected</u> closely to ancient folk tales.

3. Never <u>are</u> the contemporary versions as frightening and grim as the source material.

4. In contrast to the modern good-fairy image, there <u>were</u> evil, lying, deceitful fairies in ancient folk tales.

5. <u>Have</u> you ever <u>heard</u> about the "real" effects of elf or fairy music?

6. Never <u>could</u> a person reproducing such a tune <u>stop</u> playing it.

7. <u>Dancing</u> in the street, all day and all night, <u>were</u> his enchanted listeners.

8. Only by playing the tune backwards <u>could</u> the musician <u>break</u> the spell.

9. There <u>was</u> little opportunity for the frantic musician to do so.

10. Only on a few occasions <u>did</u> people who were in this situation <u>survive</u>.

Exercise 18

To practice writing sentences with different patterns, rewrite the following sentences by starting them with the subject.

1. In ancient legends are the roots of fairy tales beloved by children.

_____

2. There are many modern fairy tales connected closely to ancient folk
    tales.

    _____

3. Never are the contemporary versions as frightening and grim as the
    source material.

    _____

4. Punished with terrible consequences were any musicians reproduc-
    ing elf music.

    _____

5. There existed only one remedy to break the spell.

    _____

Exercise 19

In the following statements and questions, the complete verb is underlined for you and the complete subject is given in brackets. With a
caret (∧), indicate where the subject should occur in the sentence. Do *not*
begin any sentence with the subject. The first one has been done for you
as an example.

1. <u>Aren't</u> a major tool of the American shopper? [credit cards]
      ∧

2. <u>Haven't</u> <u>used</u> at least one kind of credit card? [most shoppers]

3. Today there <u>are</u>. [cards for buying everything from gas to airline
   tickets, as well as clothes, groceries, and medical services]

4. <u>Can't</u> <u>be purchased</u> with a credit card? [almost anything for sale]

5. However, <u>is</u> overuse. [one major problem with credit cards]

6. Sometimes <u>spend</u> too much and <u>can't</u> <u>pay</u> the bill. [we]

7. Also, for the privilege of being able to charge an item with the card, <u>pay</u> interest. [we]

8. Seldom <u>do carry</u> a low interest rate. [credit cards]

9. Therefore, <u>can make</u> the cost much higher than the original price of the item. [paying for an item with a credit card]

10. <u>Don't</u> <u>become</u> compulsive shoppers? [some people with credit cards]

11. To help people curb their spending, <u>have been formed</u>. [certain organizations]

12. As one such support group for compulsive shoppers there <u>is</u>. [Shoppers Anonymous]

13. To help each other, <u>come</u> together. [people with compulsive shopping problems]

14. However, <u>is</u> bad. [not all credit card use]

15. To avoid spending too much, <u>should</u> simply <u>understand</u> the disadvantages of using these cards. [we]

SPECIAL SUBJECTS

In the preceding sections, you learned to find the simple subject by isolating the modifiers and saw that some subjects occur in unusual positions. Most of the subjects you have seen so far have been nouns, such as *man* and *Lincoln*. However, some subjects are pronouns, such as *everybody* and *all*; or actions, such as *walking* and *to go*; or clauses with their own subject and verb. In this section you will learn to recognize such special kinds of subjects.

Pronouns

All pronouns ending in *-body*, *-one*, or *-thing* and other pronouns in which *one* is understood are singular; some pronouns are always plural; and some may be either singular or plural depending on whether there is a singular or plural word in the prepositional phrase that follows.

Pronouns That Are Always Singular				
anyone	anybody	anything	one	much
everyone	everybody	everything	each (one)	less
no one	nobody	nothing	either (one)	little
someone	somebody	something	another (one)	

he/she
Almost (everybody) in the class <u>has passed</u> the test.

he/she
(Each) of the students <u>has studied</u> very hard.

Pronouns That Are Always Plural	
both	others
few	several
fewer	many
a few	

They
(Many) of the students <u>are smiling</u> now.

They
(Few) <u>are laughing</u> out loud.

They
(Fewer) than ten lunches <u>were ordered</u>.

Pronouns That May Be Singular or Plural	
all	none
any	some
most	

they
(Most) of the students <u>are pouting</u>.

it
(Most) of the class <u>is</u> unhappy.

Exercise 20

Circle the simple subject. Then fill in the blank with the correct form of the verb given in parentheses.

1. Almost everyone _____ (*recognize*, present) the name Walt Disney.

2. Since the 1920s, all of the people in the United States _____ (*have*, present) been affected by the art of Disney in some way.

3. Nothing _____ (*have*, present) been the same for children since Mickey Mouse first made his appearance in 1928.

4. Each of Disney's subsequent characters _____ (*be*, past) equally well received.

5. What child _____ (*do*, present) not have fond memories of Mickey, Donald Duck, Goofy, and Bambi?

6. Many of the innovations brought to cartoons _____ (*be*, past) the creations of Disney and his talented staff.

7. One of his greatest ideas _____ (*be*, past) the theme park.

8. Both of the theme parks, Disneyland and Disney World, _____ (*be*, present) attractions that never seem to lose their appeal.

9. There _____ (*be*, present) many "firsts" attributed to Disney.

10. Some of them _____ (*be*, present) the first full-length cartoon film (*Snow White and the Seven Dwarfs*) and the first "true-life" adventure series, which showed animals living in their natural habitats.

11. Some of the achievements of Disney and his staff _____ (*have*, present) had a tremendous effect on the techniques of the motion picture industry.

12. Whether through movies, cartoon characters, or a visit to Disneyland, no one _____ (*have*, present) totally escaped the influence of Walt Disney in his or her life.

13. Most of us _____ (*have*, present) enough child in us to appreciate the talents of this famous American.

Exercise 21

Write sentences about your favorite cartoon. Use *present* verb forms with the following troublesome pronouns as the simple subjects. Then circle the first verbs that match each of these subjects.

1. No one _____

_____

2. Every _____

_____

3. Few _____

_____

4. Both _____

_____

5. Any _____

_____

6. All _____

_____

Sometimes words like *and, both . . . and, or, either . . . or, neither . . . nor* (called **conjunctions**) connect two parts of the subject. To determine which pronoun replaces the subject, we must look at the meaning of the conjunctions.

Compound Subjects

When two or more simple subjects are added together by conjunctions such as *and* or *both . . . and,* the subject is replaceable by *they.*

he + he = they
(Abraham Lincoln) and (Charles Darwin) were the children of cousin marriages.

it   it = they
The minimal (composition) of the human body and the (composition) of seven gallons of seawater are the same.

Note: Sometimes two or more items joined by *and* are regarded as one unit.

it   (one dish)
(Red beans and rice) is my favorite dish.

he/she   (same person)
(My best friend and roommate) has the measles.

Also, when *each* or *every* precedes a subject, the subject is always singular.

he/she
Each man, woman, and child is issued a life jacket.

On the other hand, conjunctions like *or* indicate a choice between two items. (In the examples, we will use the slash mark (/) to indicate choice.

When two items are joined with *or, nor, either . . . or,* or *neither . . . nor,* the item nearer the verb determines the form of the verb.

he / he
(John) or (Peter) is going to the store.

he / they
(Peter) or his (friends) want to go.

he + he / he
Either (John) and (Peter) or (Mark) is going to the store.

they / she
Are either your (parents) or your (sister) going to attend your graduation?

Exercise 22

As in the preceding examples, write a plus sign or a slash mark above the conjunction in the complete subject. Then fill in the blank with the correct form of the verb given in parentheses.

1. Government and history _____ (*provide*, present) important attractions in Washington, D.C.

2. Politicians, tourists, foreign officials, and spies _____ (*move*, present) in this exciting city.

3. The workings of our government or the historical sites in Washington _____ (*attract*, present) all types of people.

4. Every adult and child _____ (*be*, present) able to find something he or she likes among the many sights that Washington has to offer.

5. Historical sites and museums of technology and art _____ (*be*, present) available for view—most at little or no cost.

6. The Smithsonian Institution and the National Gallery _____ (*be*, present) favorite tourist attractions, for example.

7. Across the Potomac River _____ (*lie*, present) the Tomb of the Unknown Soldier and the graves of many American heroes in Arlington National Cemetery.

8. Both the Washington Monument and the Lincoln Memorial _____ _____ (*stand*, present) as tributes to two famous United States leaders.

9. The Capitol and the White House _____ (*be*, present) focal

points of the city.

10. Neither powerful politicians nor the average citizen_____ (*be*,

present) immune to the aura of power that is ever-present in Wash-

ington, D.C.

Exercise 23

Write sentences of your own about historical places. Use compound
subjects joined with the conjunctions given, and only *present* verb forms.
Make sure your subjects and verbs agree.

1. Both _____ and _____

   _____

2. _____ or _____

   _____

3. Either _____ or _____

   _____

4. Neither _____ nor _____

   _____

5. _____ and _____

   _____

6. Each _____, _____, and _____

   _____

Gerund and *to*-infinitive Subjects

Simple subjects arc not always persons or things. They can be **gerunds** (verb forms that end in *-ing*) or ***to*-infinitives** (verb forms that are preceded by *to*). Gerunds and *to*-infinitives can also be followed by other words that make the simple subject more specific.

Since a gerund or *to*-infinitive subject can be replaced by *it*, the first verb takes an *-s* ending in the present tense.

to - infinitive
(To walk) is good for you.

it
(To walk) along the beach <u>is</u> Pete's favorite pastime.

gerund
But (seeing) a dead crab in the bathroom sink <u>disgusted</u> him.

it
(Finding) the prankster <u>is</u> important.

Exercise 24

As in the previous examples, circle the gerund or *to*-infinitive subject. Then fill in the blank with the verb in parentheses in the present form.

1. To eat _____ (be) everything.

2. Sleeping _____ (be) not as fulfilling.

3. Watching Rambo in a theater _____ (tire) me out.

4. Even sitting in front of the TV after work _____ (do) not help.

5. But to sit down at a table covered with pastry and roast chicken ____

    _____ (be) living.

6. Unfortunately, cooking a four-course meal _____ (be) not possible every day.

7. Buying hamburgers at a fast-food outlet _____ (seem) barely

    tolerable.

8. So to make beans and rice _____ (have) become a habit.

9. Yet to dream of eating spareribs _____ (be) to visit heaven.

10. Dreaming of TV dinners _____ (be) like going to jail.

Clause Subjects

Sometimes a whole **clause** (a group of words with its own subject and predicate) serves as the subject of the sentence (bracketed here), because it answers the *who* or *what* question. In such a case, since we can substitute *he*, *she*, or *it* for the whole clause, the first verb takes an *-s* ending in the present tense.

        it
[What you said] <u>makes a lot of sense to me</u>.

What makes a lot of sense to me? [What ⟨you⟩ said]

        it
[That we have to keep on trying] <u>is obvious</u>.

What is obvious? [That ⟨we⟩ have to keep on trying]

        he/she
[Whoever arrives first] <u>should turn on the lights</u>.

                      he/she
Who should turn on the lights? [⟨Whoever⟩ arrives first]

Exercise 25

As in the examples, bracket the complete subject and write *he, she*, or *it* above it. Then fill in the blank with the correct form of the verb.

1. Whoever drove the car on the sidewalk _____ (*have*, present) to report to John's office.

2. What John has in mind _____ (*be*, present) unclear.

3. That he is angry, on the other hand, _____ (*be*, present) apparent.

4. Whatever the driver damaged _____ (*have*, present) to be re-
paired by the school.

5. That no one was injured _____ (*be*, present) miraculous.

6. Whatever will happen to the driver _____ (*be*, present) unclear.

7. After all, whoever did it _____ (*be*, past) probably just not
thinking.

8. That the sidewalk wasn't marked "pedestrians only" _____
(*be*, present) also to be noted.

9. Of course, warning cars off sidewalks _____ (*do*, present) not
seem necessary.

10. _____ (*do*, present) to come forward to admit one's error seem
the decent thing to do?

Exercise 26

Fill in the blank with the correct form of the verb.

1. Walking on the sidewalk at midnight _____ (*do*, present) not
appeal to too many people.

2. Somehow to chance it _____ (*seem*, present) dangerous.

3. On a clear night, however, strolling alone in the moonlight
_____ (*be*, present) not so bad.

4. Only a few shadows _____ (*darken*, present) the alleyways.

5. That there are fewer dark entryways _____ (*be*, present) also
comforting.

6. Of course, to worry too much about lurking shadows _____
(*be*, present) silly.

7. Excessive worrying about hidden dangers _____ (*be*, present)
not wise either.

8. Anyway, whoever is afraid to that extent _____ (*be*, present) a
victim of his own fear.

9. Friday-the-Thirteenth nights _____ (*do*, present) not occur
very frequently either.

10. After all, there _____ (*be*, present) not that many killers in
Putnam, Arkansas.

Exercise 27

Complete the following sentences in your own words. Make sure that the
subjects and verbs agree.

1. Whoever goes to the fair at night _____

_____

2. Watching the midway light up _____

_____

3. To see the lights blinking in the dark _____

_____

4. Deciding what to ride _____

_____

5. To visit the "Haunted House" _____

_____

SUMMARY

Fill in the blanks with the appropriate response, to show your understanding of the principles in this chapter. Where indicated, write a sentence of your own to illustrate those principles. Underline the complete verb and circle the simple subject in each of your sentences.

1. A subject answers the *who* or *what* question.

   Example sentence: _____

   _____

2. a. What is a simple subject? _____

   Example sentence: _____

   _____

   b. Why is it important to find it in the complete subject? _____

   _____

3. a. What are modifiers? _____

   Example sentence: _____

   _____

   b. Why should they be isolated in the complete subject? _____

   _____

4. Write a sentence with a simple subject modified by one or more adjectives.

   _____

   _____

5. Write a sentence with a simple subject modified by a prepositional phrase.

_____

_____

6. Write a sentence with a simple subject modified by another kind of adjective phrase.

_____

_____

7. Write a sentence with a simple subject modified by an adjective clause.

_____

_____

8. A subject is usually at the beginning of a sentence, but it may be preceded by introductory word(s), telling *why, where, when,* or *how,* that are not part of the subject. Write sentences illustrating two of these.

Example: _____

_____

Example: _____

_____

9. In the following types of sentences, the subject either splits the complete verb or follows it. Complete the sentences and give an example of each.

a. In most questions, _____

Example: _____

_____

b. In sentences beginning with *there*, _____

Example: _____

_____

c. In sentences beginning with a negative word, _____

Example: _____

_____

d. In sentences with the subject at the end, _____

Example: _____

_____

10. Some subjects are unusual because they are not simply nouns. Write a sentence to illustrate each of the following special kinds of subjects.

a. a compound subject joined by *and*: _____

_____

b. a compound subject joined by *or*: _____

_____

c. a *to*-infinitive subject: _____

_____

d. a gerund subject: _____

_____

e. a clause subject: _____

_____

11. Pronouns used as subjects can also be considered special. Write a sentence using each of the following pronouns as a subject.

a. All _____

_____

b. Everyone _____

_____

c. A few _____

_____

d. Something _____

_____

e. None _____

_____

Summary Exercise 1

Fill in the blank with the correct form of the verb given in parentheses.

1. Everyone _____ (*have*, present) helped to paint the office.

2. Painting it _____ (*be*, past) not too difficult.

3. After all, anyone _____ (*be*, present) able to hold a brush.

4. What happened _____ (*be*, past) hard to foresee.

5. The paint store _____ (*have*, past) mixed several cans of paint.

6. Whoever blended the cans _____ (*be*, past) not using the same formula for each.

7. In daylight, each wall _____ (*seem*, past) a different shade of brown.

8. Needless to say, the new boss _____ (*be*, past) very upset.

9. He _____ (*demand*, past) an explanation.

10. To err _____ (*be*, present) human.

11. Nevertheless, convincing us to paint it all again _____ (*be*, present) going to be difficult.

12. Some of us _____ (*be*, present) still finding brown paint in our hair.

13. Speckled on my eyeglasses _____ (*be*, present) millions of tiny brown spots.

14. Never _____ (*be*, present) we going to get rid of these side effects.

15. Unfortunately, there _____ (*be*, present) not enough money to hire a professional painting crew.

Summary Exercise 2

Fill in the blank with the correct form of the verb given in parentheses.

1. Collecting matchbooks _____ (*have*, present) always been my hobby.

2. Whoever convinced me to start _____ (*have*, present) my gratitude.

3. Naturally, very few people actually _____ (*understand*, present).

4. A matchbook, whether small and ornate or large and plain, _____ *do*, present) not take up much space.

5. My oldest sister, the one with three boyfriends, _____ (*worry*, past) about fires.

6. "How can these things be safe?" _____ (*be*, past) her question.

7. To her there _____ (*appear*, present) to be several thousand in my closet.

8. People like my sister _____ (*tend*, present) to exaggerate.

9. So to frighten me, she _____ (*buy*, past) a fire extinguisher and _____ (*put*, past) it in my closet.

10. But a girl with three boyfriends _____ (*be*, present) not supposed to worry about matchbooks.

11. That she has her own explosion brewing _____ (*be*, present) evident to me.

12. Because of her interference, I now _____ (*feel*, present) guilty about adding to my collection.

13. However, it _____ (*do*, present) not stop me.

14. In fact, her boyfriends _____ (*pick*, present) up attractive matchbooks for me.

15. Luckily for me all of them _____ (*travel*, present) a lot.

16. Luckily for her they _____ (*be*, present) seldom in town at the same time.

WRITING PRACTICE

Write ten sentences or a short passage about one or more of the following topics, using the guidelines of your teacher. Make sure all subjects and verbs agree.

1. the trouble you once got into with a parent, a coach, a teacher, or a boss

2. someone you admire, using an anecdote

3. a time you or someone you know got the better of a practical joker

4. a hobby or activity you enjoyed that someone else didn't appreciate

5. an imaginative story about a superstition that affected someone

REVIEW
Avoiding Subject–Verb Agreement Errors

So far, you have learned to find the complete subject and its simple subject, to find the complete verb and its first verb, and to mentally replace the subject with a pronoun (*he, she, it*, or *they*) in order to determine the correct form of the first verb. Now you will learn to recognize some common errors.

COMMON ERRORS

Leaving Off the *-s* Endings

Probably the most common error is caused by leaving the *-s* ending off a present verb form when the subject is *he, she*, or *it*. (Note also that regular past verb forms have an *-ed* ending; don't leave that off either.)

Incorrect: He ~~walk~~ to school every day.
Correct: He walks to school every day.
Correct: He walked to school every day.

Incorrect: He ~~write~~ many letters.
Correct: He writes many letters.
Correct: He wrote many letters.

Incorrect: He ~~ask~~ and answers a lot of questions.
Correct: He asks and answers a lot of questions.

Incorrect: He ~~ask~~ and answered a lot of questions.
Correct: He asked and answered a lot of questions.

Using the Wrong Form of the Verb *be*

The verb *be* is especially confusing because it has many different forms.

Incorrect: He ~~be~~ walking.
Correct: He is walking.

73

Incorrect: You X walking.
Correct: You are walking.

Incorrect: They was here.
Correct: They were here.

Putting An *-s* Ending on the Second Verb

Remember that only the first verb uses an *-s* ending.

Incorrect: Does he often asks questions?
Correct: Does he often ask questions?

Incorrect: Can he walks very fast?
Correct: Can he walk very fast?

Forgetting That Subject Placement May Vary

The subject is not always in front of the verb.

Incorrect: There X many people in this room.
Correct: There are many people in this room.

Incorrect: Scattered around the park X the remains of the picnic.
Correct: Scattered around the park are the remains of the
                picnic.

Incorrect: Where X the scissors?
Correct: Where are the scissors?

Having the First Verb Agree with the Wrong Subject

The first verb must agree with the simple subject, which is not always the word nearest the verb.

Incorrect: The strongest of human senses are sight.
Correct: The strongest of human senses is sight.

Incorrect: Each year, approximately one person out of a million
                are injured or killed by lightning.
Correct: Each year, approximately one person out of a million is
                injured or killed by lightning.

Incorrect: Horatio Alger, one of the most prolific American authors, ~~were~~ able to write and publish 119 novels in thirty years.

Correct: Horatio Alger, one of the most prolific American authors, was able to write and publish 119 novels in thirty years.

Incorrect: The home, along with the state, the church, and the school, ~~are~~ fundamental units of society.

Correct: The home, along with the state, the church, and the school, is a fundamental unit of society.

Correct: The home, the state, and the church are fundamental units of society.

Incorrect: Each of our physical characteristics ~~are~~ determined by the genes we inherit from our parents.

Correct: Each of our physical characteristics is determined by the genes we inherit from our parents.

Confusing Singular and Plural

Remember that some subject pronouns are always singular, some are always plural, and some may be either singular or plural depending upon what they refer to.

Incorrect: Everyone ~~use their~~ imagination to see animals and shapes in the clouds.

Correct: Everyone uses his or her imagination to see animals and shapes in the clouds.

Incorrect: Few of us ~~recognizes~~ the constellations.
Correct: Few of us recognize the constellations.

Incorrect: All of the night sky ~~become~~ a picture book for those with knowledge of the stars.

Correct: All of the night sky becomes a picture book for those with knowledge of the stars.

Incorrect: Most of the historical material given to the library ~~are~~ kept in the rare book room.

Correct: Most of the historical material given to the library is kept in the rare book room.

Correct: Most of the historical documents have been well preserved.

Using a Clause, Gerund, or *to*-infinitive with a Plural Verb

Clause, gerund, and *to*-infinitive subjects are singular.

Incorrect: When you want the books a̶r̶e̶ not clear.
Correct: When you want the books is not clear.

Incorrect: Slamming oven doors c̶a̶u̶s̶e̶ a cake to fall because it breaks the tiny air cells that make the cake rise.
Correct: Slamming oven doors causes a cake to fall because it breaks the tiny air cells that make the cake rise.

Incorrect: To believe in Santa Claus and his elves a̶r̶e̶ to believe in magic.
Correct: To believe in Santa Claus and his elves is to believe in magic.

Confusion over a Compound Subject

Compound subjects joined by *and* are usually plural, unless the items joined by the *and* are regarded as one unit. When two items are joined by *or* or *nor*, the first verb agrees with the nearer subject.

Incorrect: Cement and concrete i̶s̶ not synonymous. Cement is merely one of the several ingredients of concrete.
Correct: Cement and concrete are not synonymous. Cement is merely one of the several ingredients of concrete.

Incorrect: Red beans and rice a̶r̶e̶ a popular dish in Louisiana.
Correct: Red beans and rice is a popular dish in Louisiana.

Incorrect: Neither a fly nor a glowworm a̶r̶e̶ named correctly. Both are beetles.
Correct: Neither a fly nor a glowworm is named correctly. Both are beetles.

Incorrect: Either my parents or my sister a̶r̶e̶ going to attend his wedding.
Correct: Either my parents or my sister is going to attend his wedding.

EDITING EXERCISE

Find and correct the twenty subject–verb agreement errors in the following passage. (*Note:* A sentence may have *only one* error.)

[1]After having studied the United States population for almost fifty years, Paul Glick, former chief demographer for the U.S. Census Bureau, has made some interesting observations.

[2]Studying changes in United States families have been Glick's specialty. [3]Although neither he nor any other expert know what the future will bring, he predicts that many trends that have molded American society since the '40s may soon end.

[4]Following World War II, millions of men left the armed services, married, and settled down. [5]This period of prosperity and family building that followed are known as the "baby boom." [6]Among the effects of the postwar years and its shortage of men due to the casualties of war have been "the marriage squeeze."

[7]According to sociologists, there is many results predictable from this imbalance. [8]When women outnumber men and men believe that they can easily find another mate, there is usually more divorce cases. [9]Unmarried women are forced into the job market, and equality—socially and on the job—become another issue.

[10]Now one sweeping change are in the offering. [11]The "squeeze" may be headed the other way. [12]That males outnumber females are soon to

be a possibility. [13]As fewer of the women are available, perhaps "Stand

By Your Woman—Not Man" is going to be the new motto. [14]The result

could be one social change almost everybody support, a reverse in the
                                            supports

divorce rate.

[15]Information derived from census reports have revealed other shift-
                                              has

ing social trends in America. [16]For example, there is more households
                                                         are

maintained by unmarried couples. [17]Also, the composition of major so-

cial and ethnic groups are changing. [18]Many of these statistics, in turn,
                                is

forms the basis for many of our laws.
form

[19]The shifting of social trends also cause changes in language. [20]For
                                        causes

instance, the term "head of household" used to refer mainly to men, but

now there is many families headed by women. [21]Determining who is the
              are

"head" when both spouses work and earn equal incomes is also difficult.

[22]Some of us may not realize how vital, and sometimes controversial,

the census information is. [23]Federal funding for state and local govern-

ments have become dependent on population statistics. [24]Politicians is
        has   *are*

also affected by the census. [25]Probably every group that has something

to lose or gain by challenging the accuracy of the latest census have done
                                                                  has

so. [26]"People who don't cooperate with the census loses," Glick says.

[27]"Really, what it is all about is money."

WRITING ASSIGNMENTS

Write at least two pages about one or both of the following topics, using the guidelines of your teacher. Check your paper for items listed under number 1 in the proofreading checklist at the end of Unit 4 (p. 322).

1. Imagine that it is twenty years in the future, the twenty-first century. Write about what society is like. How has it changed from today?

2. Re-create an incident you (or someone close to you) was involved in when you discovered that "Really, money is only money."

The Writing Process
Basics

Throughout this book we encourage you to practice the grammatical structures you have learned, by writing short pieces on a variety of topics. Now we will talk about writing as a process, a way of talking on paper that you can revise and improve. Most writers, even professional ones, are somewhat fearful of starting to write, or putting those first few words on paper. But all learn to do it, not by making that first phrase or sentence or paragraph perfect, but by assuming that much of those first few lines, paragraphs, and sometimes even pages will be thrown away—or filed for use in some other work. Writing is really a process of revision, and in this book we will talk about writing as a four-step procedure: composing a rough draft, selecting and developing details, polishing beginnings and endings, and proofreading.

The primary purpose of writing is to transmit information from writer to reader in a clear, thoughtful, and interesting way. But first you need to have information to transmit.

Suppose you are talking about a party you went to. To a stranger you might simply say that you were there. To parents or employers, or employees and acquaintances, you might mention that you had a lot of fun—dancing, singing, staying up until four o'clock in the morning. But to your friends you might mention that Joe got so drunk he locked his keys in his car, and that when he came back with a coat hanger, he tried to break into the wrong Chevette and was nearly arrested. You might also mention that the taxi you took back to your cousin's house brought you to Center Street instead of Center Avenue, and you didn't even notice until after the taxi had left.

Well, telling a story about a party is probably more fun and "easier" than writing about some of the topics you are assigned in your classes, but the process is the same. When you are finished, the essay should have good, interesting detail, clear language, and a logical structure. But you need some place to start.

Let's take the topic "The Definition of Friendship." You might think you need to look up friendship in every dictionary in town, but what is really wanted is *your* idea of friendship. So what do you do? Start writing. Think of times when friendship was important, or when being a friend was difficult, or when some friend meant a lot to you for one reason or another. Don't worry about grammar or sentence structure or style; just write. Talk about memories and situations, real or imagined, that deal with real or imagined people, real or imagined events. Keep writing until you have described several incidents. This is your rough draft. (With a less subjective topic, you would follow the same process and write down all the information at hand. Again, you would not worry about grammar or style; your job initially would be to get the material on paper.)

Next, take a break. Go outside if you can, walk around, get some food or a drink, watch TV, look out the window, stretch. Now reread what you have written and pick three or four (or as many as you need) of the most interesting anecdotes or memories. Perhaps there was a time you had a flat tire on your way back to town at 3:00 A.M. and you called your friend Henry collect because you had no spare and no money, and he got out of bed and drove thirty miles to rescue you. What does this show about friendship? Perhaps that friendship means being able to help even when it's inconvenient.

What about your next anecdote? Maybe there was a time you were going to lend money to a new acquaintance and your old friend Mark insisted the woman was a con artist, convinced you even though you thought you were falling in love. You were angry, until she left town two weeks later owing other friends nearly a thousand dollars, which she never paid back. Again what does this say about friendship? Perhaps this means that a friend sometimes tells you the truth even when it makes you angry.

Continue until you have as many points as you need for your essay. Again stop, take a break, go for a walk. When you get back, you are ready for the next step: adding or selecting details.

Exercise 1

Write three pages of memories associated with any (or each) of the following topics.

1. windows

2. desks

3. two people you know well

4. two bars or restaurants you frequent

5. times when your car broke down

6. examples of bad driving

7. reasons to stay home all day

8. reasons not to make money

9. reasons sports are bad for you

10. reasons watching television is good for you

Exercise 2

From any of the foregoing written exercises pick three anecdotes and try to summarize each in one sentence. (Example of summary: Friendship means helping someone even when it's inconvenient.)

1: _____

_____

2: _____

_____

3: _____

_____

Exercise 3

Write a letter to a friend about your life at the present. List several topics from your letter that could be used as subjects for later papers.

UNIT 2 Using Verb Forms and Tenses Correctly

In Chapter 1, you saw that the complete verb may have several verb parts and that the first part, which is either a present or a past verb form, agrees with the simple subject. You also saw that the complete verb may contain one or more helping verbs.

Look at the following examples. Notice that, by changing the form of the main verb or by adding helping verbs, you can show *when* an action, a state, or an event occurs.

usually
John <u>writes</u> many letters.

earlier
John <u>wrote</u> many letters.

later
John <u>will write</u> many letters.

already
John <u>has written</u> many letters.

now
John <u>is writing</u> many letters.

The relation to time expressed by the complete verb is called **tense**. There are three basic tenses: present, past, and future. These tenses also have perfect and progressive forms. In this unit you will first learn about the forms of the verb and then how they are combined to create different tenses.

CHAPTER 4
Recognizing Verb Forms

In this chapter you will learn to recognize and form the principal parts of different verbs, and then you will see how these parts are combined to make complete verbs.

PRINCIPAL PARTS OF VERBS

A verb has three principal parts—(1) the base form, (2) the past form, and (3) the past participle form.

	Base Form	Past Form	Past Participle Form
Regular verbs	talk	talked	talked
	listen	listened	listened
	move	moved	moved
	try	tried	tried
Irregular verbs	go	went	gone
	see	saw	seen
	write	wrote	written
	find	found	found

As the table shows, there are two patterns, regular and irregular. **Regular verbs** simply add *-ed* to the base in the past and past participle forms (as in *talked/talked*). **Irregular verbs**, on the other hand, have irregular spellings in the past and past participle forms. (Remember, Appendix 1 lists common irregular verbs.)

Exercise 1

Fill in the blanks with the correct regular verb forms.

Base Form	Past Form	Past Participle Form
1. smile		
2. laugh		
3. caution		
4. call		
5. ask		

Exercise 2

Fill in the blanks with the correct irregular verb forms.

Base Form	Past Form	Past Participle Form
1. blow		
2. teach		
3. drive		
4. rise		
5. sit		
6. fly		
7. know		
8. go		

9. ___run___   _____   _____

10. ___take___   _____   _____

SPELLINGS AND USES OF VERB FORMS IN THE COMPLETE VERB

Now you will see how the principal parts (base, past, and past participle) of verbs and the verb forms created from the base (the present and the -*ing* form) are spelled and used in the complete verb.

Base Form

The **base form** of a verb is the form without any special ending. It is the one found in the dictionary. For example, if you didn't know the meaning of *seen*, you would have to look up *see*.

The base occurs after the helping verbs of mood (*will, would, can, could,* and so on) and *do*. For example, we say, "They will see," not "They will seeing," or "They will sees," or "They will seen."

will + base

We <u>will see</u> you tomorrow.

We <u>could see</u> you tomorrow.

do + base

<u>Do</u> they <u>see</u> him often?

<u>Did</u> we <u>see</u> you yesterday?

Exercise 3

Give the base form of the following verbs.

1. traveled   _____   2. being   _____

3. led   _____   4. flown   _____

5. scheduling _____   6. done   _____

7. wanted   _____   8. overlook   _____

9. receiving   _____   10. rose   _____

11. met   _____   12. study   _____

13. had   _____   14. reaching   _____

15. used   _____   16. makes   _____

17. headed   _____   18. providing _____

19. respected   _____   20. becomes   _____

Exercise 4

In the following sentences, underline each complete verb. Then circle each first verb and put a *B* over each base form. The first one has been done for you.

1. The mating habits of the black widow spider (could) inspire **B** fear in the

   human male if copied by the human female.

2. The male spider, much smaller than the female, must approach the

   edge of the female's web.

3. Then his feet, placed on the edge of the web, will cause the web to

   vibrate.

4. If she is ready to breed, she should respond.

5. The male then can make his way to her in the web.

6. The mating process takes several hours, during which the male will wrap the female in a loose sack of silk.

7. After mating, the male may not always exit the web.

8. If the female is hungry, she will stop him and make a tasty meal of him.

9. According to scientists, we should consider the female spider neither romantic nor sadistic—only practical.

Present Form

Except for the verb *be*, the **present form** and the base form are identical when the subject is *I, you, we,* or *they*. Only by looking at the verb's place in the complete verb can you tell whether it is a base form or a present form. Remember, the present form (circled) is always the first verb.

     present form
We (see) him every day.

       base form
We (will) see him tomorrow.

An *-s* ending is added to the base to make the present form only when the subject is *he, she,* or *it*.

     present form
She (sees) him every day.

Spelling Changes That May Occur When -s Is Added

I/you/we/they Form	he/she/it Form	Spelling Rules
write read	writes reads	Usually when the subject is *he, she,* or *it,* an -s is added.
miss push	misses pushes	When the base ends in an -s sound, an -es is added.
do go	does goes	An -es is added to the verbs *do* and *go.*
have	has	*Has* is an irregular spelling because the -ve is dropped.
carry study try	carries studies tries	A final *y* preceded by a consonant is changed to *ie* before the -s ending.
say play	says plays	A final *y* preceded by a vowel does not change.
be/am/are/	is	*Be* is very irregular.
will can must may	will can must may	*Remember:* The helping verbs of mood do not add an -s when the subject is *he, she,* or *it.*

Exercise 5

Give the *he/she/it* present form for the following verbs. The first one has been done for you.

I/you/we/they Form	he/she/it Form	I/you/we/they Form	he/she/it Form
1. write	*writes*	2. call	_____
3. do	_____	4. have	_____
5. can	_____	6. study	_____
7. say	_____	8. wish	_____
9. hurry	_____	10. rush	_____

Exercise 6

Rewrite the following sentences (from Exercise 4) by taking out the help-ing verbs of mood and changing the base form to a present form. The first one has been done for you. Note that in some cases you need to add an -s ending to the base form and in some you need not.

1. The male spider, much smaller than the female, must approach the

   edge of the female's web.

   approaches (handwritten, replacing "must approach")

2. Then his feet, placed on the edge of the web, <u>will cause</u> the web to

   vibrate.

3. If she <u>is</u> ready to breed, she <u>will respond</u>.

4. The male then <u>can make</u> his way to her in the web.

5. The mating process <u>takes</u> several hours, during which the male <u>will</u>

   <u>wrap</u> the female in a loose sack of silk.

6. After mating, the male <u>may</u> not always <u>exit</u> the web.

7. If the female <u>is</u> hungry, she <u>will stop</u> him and <u>make</u> of him a tasty

   meal.

Past Form

Like the present form, the **past form** (circled) is always the first verb.

past form

We (wrote) him a letter.

The letter (was) written a few weeks ago.

She (walked) to school yesterday.

She (had) never (walked) to school before.

As you already know, the past forms of some verbs have irregular spellings (*write/wrote, see/saw, buy/bought*). In the case of regular verbs, however, an -ed ending is simply added to the base form (*walk/walked*).

Spelling Changes That May Occur When -ed Is Added

Base	Past Form	Spelling Rules
talk	talked	Usually an -ed is added to the base.
help	helped	
miss	missed	
hope	hoped	If the base ends in silent e, only a d is added.
schedule	scheduled	
suppose	supposed	
drop	dropped	After a short stressed vowel, the consonant is doubled.
omit	omitted	
pot	potted	
whisper	whispered	After an unstressed vowel, the consonant is not doubled.
discover	discovered	
travel	traveled	
carry	carried	A final y preceded by a consonant is changed to i before the -ed ending.
apply	applied	
study	studied	
play	played	A final y preceded by a vowel does not change.
stay	stayed	
say	said	The verbs say, lay, and pay are exceptions.
lay	laid	
pay	paid	

Exercise 7

Write the past forms of the following verbs. Remember, the verb *be* has two past forms.

1. be _____ _____   2. stop _____

3. rake _____   4. develop _____

5. lay _____   6. bury _____

7. beat _____   8. decay _____

9. differ _____   10. try _____

11. call _____   12. hurry _____

Past Participle Form

The past participle form is used after the helping verbs *have* and *be* (circled).

have + past participle
John (has) written a novel.

be + past participle
The novel (was) written a few years ago.

Remember that regular verbs have identical past participle and past forms, so only by looking at the verb's place in the complete verb can you tell which form it is.

past form
We (talked) to him yesterday.

have + past participle
We (have) not talked to him today.

In the case of irregular verbs, however, past and past participle forms are not always the same, so you must make sure that you use the past participle (*not* the past) form after the helping verbs *have* and *be*.

past form
We (wrote) to him yesterday.

have + past participle
We (had) not written to him before.

be + past participle
No letters (were) written by him.

Exercise 10

Fill in the blanks with the past participle form.

1. throw	_____		2. prove	_____
3. designing	_____		4. become	_____
5. use	_____		6. find	_____
7. grow	_____		8. arises	_____
9. are	_____		10. keep	_____
11. building	_____		12. has	_____
13. fly	_____		14. know	_____

Exercise 11

Place an *H* over each *have* and *be* helping verb, and fill in the blank with the past participle form of the verb. An example has been done for you.

[1] Have you ever __seen__ (see) an almond tree? [2]It is a tree that grows in warm climates, and it is __related__ (relate) to the peach tree. [3]Many almonds are __grown__ (grow) in the warm valleys of California. [4]After an almond tree has __matured__ (mature), it produces a fruit that looks like a peach. [5]However, the outside of the fruit cannot be __eaten__ (eat). [6]Inside each fruit is a nut that is __covered__ (cover) by a shell. [7]Unlike the peach, whose pit is __thrown__ (throw) away, the almond's true fruit is the nut. [8]So far, two kinds of almonds are __known__ (know) to exist. [9]One is bitter and the other is sweet. [10]It is the sweet almond that is of value to the almond grower. [11]The bitter one is like the pit that is __found__ (find) inside the peach. [12]It should not be __eaten__ (eat).

The *-ing* Form

The *-ing* form of the verb is made by adding *-ing* to the base form. It follows the *be* (circled) helping verb.

be + ing form

When a person (is) shivering, his muscles tighten and relax very quickly over and over again.

While his muscles (are) working hard, he (is) warming up.

2. Verbs may be either regular or irregular. *Smile* is a regular verb be-

   cause _____.

   Fly is an irregular verb because _____.

3. When is the base form not identical to the present form? _____

   _____

4. Present and past forms are always _____ verbs in the complete

   verb.

5. The helpers _____ and _____ are used with the past

   participle form of the verb.

6. Why is the following sentence incorrect?

   "I have wrote a letter."

   _____

   _____

7. The helping verb _____ is used before the *-ing* form of the verb.

Summary Exercise

Create short example sentences using each of the following verb forms
correctly.

   1. write (base form): _____

   _____

   2. to write: _____

   3. writing: _____

   4. written: _____

5. write (present, first verb): _____

6. wrote: _____

7. be (base form): _____

8. to be: _____

9. being: _____

10. been: _____

11. am: _____

12. is: _____

13. are: _____

14. was: _____

15. were: _____

WRITING PRACTICE

Write ten sentences or a short passage about one or more of the following topics, using the guidelines of your teacher. Make sure you have formed each verb correctly.

1. a trick your pet does and how he learned to do it

2. the unusual habits of an insect or animal you have observed

3. a monument that has special meaning for you

4. a historical place you would like to visit

5. your favorite cold weather activity

CHAPTER 5
Forming and Using Tenses

In Chapter 4 you learned to recognize the principal parts of verbs and other distinctive verb forms and saw how some of them must be combined with helping verbs to form complete verbs. You also learned that present and past forms are always first verbs. When a main verb by itself has a present or a past form, it is called present tense or past tense, respectively. There are several tenses other than present tense and past tense. In this chapter, you will see how these tenses are formed and used.

FORMATION OF PRESENT, PAST, AND FUTURE TENSES

The **present tense** is created from the first principal verb part—the base form of the verb. Remember that any present verb also includes a form with an -s ending.

Base	Present Tense (*I*/*you*/*we*/*they*)	Present Tense (*he*/*she*/*it*)
walk	walk	walks
write	write	writes

The **past tense** is identical to the second principal verb part—the past form of the verb.

Past Tense
walked
wrote

The **future tense** is created by adding the helping verb *will* (or *shall*) before the base form of the main verb.

present form of *will* + base = **future tense**

will + walk   will walk
will + write   will write

Exercise 1

Fill in the blanks with the tenses given. Assume the subject is *it*. The first one has been done for you.

base: _____walk_____

present tense: *it walks*

past tense: *it walked*

future tense: *it will walk*

1. base: _____drive_____

   present tense: *it drives*

   past tense: *it drove*

   future tense: *it will drive*

2. base: _____go_____

   present tense: *it goes*

   past tense: *it went*

   future tense: *it will go*

3. base: _____see_____

   present tense: *it sees*

   past tense: *it saw*

   future tense: *it will see*

4. base: _____do_____

   present tense: *it does*

   past tense: *it did*

   future tense: *it will do*

5. base: _____try_____

   present tense: *it tries*

   past tense: *it tried*

   future tense: *it will try*

Meanings of Present, Past, and Future Tenses

The present tense is used for a current situation, an action that takes place regularly, or something that is always true.

current situation
I <u>live</u> in an apartment.

regularly
He <u>drives</u> to work every day.

always true
The sun <u>rises</u> in the east.

The past tense is used for situations or actions that took place in the past.

situation finished

I <u>lived</u> in the dorm.

He <u>drove</u> to work yesterday.

She <u>worked</u> at the post office.

The future tense is used for situations or actions that will take place in the future.

future situation

I <u>will live</u> in the dorm next year.

He <u>will drive</u> to work tomorrow.

She <u>will work</u> at the post office next month.

Exercise 2

Fill in the blanks with an appropriate tense of the verb given in paren-theses. The first one has been done for you. (*Note:* Because the passage describes mostly present, general situations, you will need mostly pres-ent tense verbs, but in a few cases you may need a future tense.)

¹Actors, who **believe** (believe) in many things as signs of good

and bad luck, often ___*see*___ (see) their luck directly related to

whether they ___*follow*___ (follow) certain rules established by tradi-

tion. ²An actor who ___*sends*___ (send) a good luck message to another

actor must word that message just right. ³Otherwise he *will jinx* ___

to make bad luck
(jinx) his fellow actor's performance. ⁴When an actor ___*leaves*___

(leave) a dressing room at the end of a run, he must make sure not to

leave anything behind. ⁵If he ___*leaves*___ (leave) soap behind, for instance, he ___will bring___ (bring) bad luck on himself and may never work

again. ⁶Actors also ___believe___ (believe) that if someone ___knits___

(knit) anywhere near the stage, the actors must beware. ⁷An actor who

___reads___ (read) lines during rehearsal never ___reads___ (read)

the last line of the play aloud. ⁸To do so ___causes___ (cause) him to

forget some of his lines. ⁹Also, dress rehearsals that ___run___ (run)

smoothly are considered unlucky.

Exercise 3

Fill in the blanks with an appropriate tense of the verb given in parentheses, as in the first one done for you. (*Note*: Because the passage describes past events, you will need mostly past tense verbs, but at least one situation is still true today and needs present tense.)

¹Because the Pilgrims ___felt___ (feel) that traditional Christmas

celebrations ___were___ (be) associated with pagan festivals inspired

by Satan, they ___banned___ (ban) all frivolities. ²Even the color green

___was___ (be) outlawed, and preachers ___denounced___ (denounce)

holly-and-ivy decorations as signs of the devil at work. ³Also, these fer

vently religious people ___interpreted___ (interpret) the Bible literally, and

since it ___did___ (do) not mention that people ___should___ (shall)

have a good time while celebrating Christmas, they ___felt___ (feel) it

was improper to do so. ⁴Their first Christmas in a new land, December

25, 1620, the Mayflower Pilgrims ___did___ (do) their usual work,

cutting down trees. ⁵Governor William Bradford ___issued___ (issue)

past form of *have* + past participle = **past perfect tense**

had	walked	had walked
had	written	had written

future form of *have* + past participle = **future perfect tense**

will have	walked	will have walked
will have	written	will have written

Exercise 5

Fill in the blanks with the tense given. Assume the subject is *he*. The first one has been done for you.

base: walk

present perfect tense: *he has walked*

past perfect tense: *he had walked*

future perfect tense: *he will have walked*

1. base: drive

    present perfect tense: he has driven.

    past perfect tense: he had driven

    future perfect tense: he will have driven

2. base: go

    present perfect tense: _____

    past perfect tense: _____

    future perfect tense: _____

3. base: see

    present perfect tense: _____

    past perfect tense: _____

    future perfect tense: _____

4. base: do
   _____

   present perfect tense: _____

   past perfect tense: _____

   future perfect tense: _____

5. base: try
   _____

   present perfect tense: _____

   past perfect tense: _____

   future perfect tense: _____

Meanings of the Perfect Tenses

To express that something took place in the past, we can use either a past tense or a present perfect tense, but these tenses have different meanings.

he no longer is

John <u>was</u> my friend for five years.

he still is

John <u>has been</u> my friend for five years.

As you can see, the present perfect shows that something that began in the past is still related to the present.

studying began in the past and relates to today

I <u>have studied</u> very hard for the test today.

The past perfect tense emphasizes that one past event took place before, and is related to, another past event.

dieting was before and is related to weighing

After Mona <u>had dieted</u> for three months, she <u>weighed</u> only 118 pounds.

Meanings of Progressive Tenses

In contrast to the present tense, which is used to express a current situation, an action that takes place regularly, or something that is always true, we use **progressive tenses** for *temporary* situations, to emphasize that an action is in progress at a specific point in time or during a limited period of time.

action in progress

He is studying in the library.

action during limited time period

He was studying when I went to visit him.

He will be studying all day tomorrow for finals.

Note: Progressive tenses are used most commonly in speaking, because they describe specific actions that are or were or will be going on at a certain moment. In writing, however, simple tenses are more common because they describe general situations.

"usually" is understood

He studies a lot.

"at this moment" is understood

He is studying.

Exercise 12

Change the verbs in parentheses to the simple past or past progressive tense. Remember to use the progressive sparingly.

¹One day, while he _____ (stay) at Campobello, Franklin

Delano Roosevelt _____ (go) sailing with his wife and sons in a

small boat. ²While he _____ (teach) his boys to sail the boat, a for-

est fire _____ (break out) on a nearby beach, and the whole

family _____ (go) to help put out the fire. ³The fire, however,

_____ (prove) to be more serious than they had first supposed.

⁴For three hours they _____ (work on) putting it out. ⁵Later, to

cool off, they _____ (go) for a swim in a nearby lake. ⁶On their way home, Roosevelt and his sons _____ (run) part of the way—a distance of about a mile and a half. [7]Then Mr. Roosevelt _____ (decide) to go swimming again, even though the water in the bay was ice cold all year round. [8]Next, while he _____ (read) through his mail, he _____ (sit) for a half an hour in his wet bathing suit. [9]It _____ (be) then that he _____ (feel) a bad chill. [10]His wife, Eleanor, finally _____ (persuade) him to go to bed, but by this time he _____ (feel) so weak that his sons _____ (have) to help him upstairs. [11]The next day, Roosevelt _____ (have) a high temperature. [12]Because his left leg _____ (feel) uncomfortably heavy and _____ (hurt) him, the family _____ (call) a local doctor.[13]As Roosevelt _____ (get) worse, they _____ (consult) other doctors. [14]After two weeks, the diagnosis _____ (be) that Roosevelt _____ (have) poliomyelitis. [15]Despite this debilitating disease, the 39-year-old Roosevelt still _____ (lead) an active life, and he _____ (become) the thirty-second president of the United States at the age of 51.

Exercise 13

Describe an important event in your own or someone else's life. Use the past tense consistently and the past progressive sparingly.

_____

_____

_____

_____

_____

_____

_____

_____

_____

SEQUENCE OF TENSES

Some sentences contain more than one complete verb. Usually the form (present or past) of the first verb in the main clause (circled here) and the form of the first verb in a dependent clause have to agree. This is called the **sequence-of-tense rule**.

    present   *present*
  Charles (says) that he (is)hungry.
    past   *past*
  Charles (said) that he (was) hungry.
  present *present form*
  He (says) he (will) give us a quiz today.
  past *past form*
  He (said) he (would) give us a quiz today.

 Sometimes the tenses don't match, to show that one situation happened before the other.

  present   *past*
  I believe that he worked here last year.

   past   *past perfect*
  They understood that he had worked here last year.

The tenses also don't match if something that was mentioned earlier is still true today.

  past   *present*
  He said that water freezes at 32° Fahrenheit.

Exercise 14

Using the preceding sequence-of-tense examples as a guide, change the following sentences to dependent clauses to follow the phrase "He said . . ." (Do not change the tense if the dependent clause states something that is still true today.) The first one has been done for you.

1. They have already painted the house.

   He said that they had already painted the house.

2. The sun rises in the east and sets in the west.

   _____

3. Construction on the house will begin next week.

   _____

4. Thor Heyerdahl recorded his historical sea journey in the book *Kon-Tiki*.

   _____

   _____

5. You can leave now.

   _____

6. Jack has never arrived on time.

   _____

7. Honesty is the best policy.

   _____

8. She wanted to be the new senator from this district.

   _____

9. We will have a fund-raiser for her.

_____

10. Jane Goodall discovered that much of the social behavior of apes resembles that of humans.

_____

_____

11. The Mississippi River serves as a natural boundary for Louisiana.

_____

12. Rats desert a sinking ship.

_____

13. The capital of Texas changed fifteen times before it became Austin.

_____

14. The director does not want Karen to leave.

_____

15. His father took a nap yesterday afternoon.

_____

SUMMARY

Fill in the blanks with the appropriate response, to show your understanding of the principles in this chapter.

1. There are three basic tenses: present, _____, and _____.

2. Each of these three tenses has a corresponding perfect form. These

    are _____, _____, and _____.

3. The perfect tense is made with a form of the helping verb _____

    followed by the _____ form of the main verb.

4. Give the perfect tense forms of the verb *read*.

    a. present perfect: _____

    b. past perfect: _____

    c. future perfect: _____

5. The progressive tenses are made with a form of the _____

    helping verb followed by the _____ form of the main verb.

6. Give the progressive tenses of *read*.

    a. present progressive   _____

    b. past progressive   _____

    c. future progressive   _____

    d. present perfect progressive _____

    e. past perfect progressive   _____

    f. future perfect progressive   _____

7. The sequence-of-tense rule requires that the form of the first verb in

    the dependent clause typically agree with the form of the first verb in

    the _____ clause. For example, the statement "I am talking on

    the phone" changes to "He said that he _____

    _____" because the verb *said* in the main clause is

_____

_____

_____

WRITING PRACTICE

Write ten sentences or a short passage about one or more of the following topics, using the guidelines of your teacher. Make sure you have used verb tenses correctly and consistently.

1. a world record you would like to accomplish

2. the events that led up to a major happening in your life

3. an insect you hate

4. a holiday tradition you would like to see created

5. a competition you took part in

CHAPTER 6
Active Voice and Passive Voice

The English language has a way to show whether the subject of a sentence (bracketed here) is the performer of the action indicated by the verb or the receiver of the action indicated by the verb. This is called **voice**. The *active voice* indicates that the subject *performs* the action; the *passive voice* tells that the subject *receives* the action.

Active voice: [John] <u>writes</u> a letter.

Passive voice: [The letter] <u>is written</u> by John.

In both of the preceding sentences, the action indicated by the verb is *write*. But in the first sentence, the subject (John) performs the action; in the second sentence, the subject (the letter) receives the action. Most of the sentences we have studied thus far have been in the active voice. In this chapter you will see how the passive voice is formed and used, and you will contrast the passive voice with the active voice.

FORMATION OF THE PASSIVE VOICE

When you compare active and passive sentences, you can see that they are closely related.

John writes many letters.

Many letters are written by John.

John saw Mary.

Mary was seen by John.

Notice that the *who* or *what* word after the verb becomes the subject of the new sentence. But we cannot simply turn the sentence around because the meaning would change.

John performs the action
John <u>saw</u> Mary.

Mary performs the action
Mary <u>saw</u> John.

Mary does not perform the action
Mary <u>was seen</u> by John.

We must add the *be* helping verb to indicate that the subject doesn't perform the action.

Note: In a passive sentence, the *by* phrase can be left off.

All the letters were written (~~by John~~).

Exercise 1

Change the following active sentences to passive ones. You must start each sentence with the *who* or *what* word(s) underlined after the verb.

1. People harvest <u>flax</u> once in seven years.

   _____

2. Except in self-defense, alligators seldom viciously attack <u>a person</u>.

   _____

   _____

3. Gypsies speak <u>the Romany language</u>.

   _____

4. A banana stalk produces <u>only one bunch of bananas</u> in a season.

   _____

5. People can make <u>approximately 400 dresses</u> from an average bale of cotton.

_____

_____

TENSES IN THE PASSIVE VOICE

Passive voice verbs are made with the _be_ helping verb followed by the past participle of the main verb. The following examples match the subject _it_.

a present form of _be_ + past participle = **present passive tense**
      is + written   is written

a past form of _be_ + past participle = **past passive tense**
      was + written   was written

the future
form of _be_ + past participle = **future passive**
      will be + written   will be written

a present perfect
form of _be_ + past participle = **present perfect passive**
      has been + written   has been written

the past perfect
form of _be_ + past participle = **past perfect passive**
      had been + written   had been written

the future perfect
form of _be_ + past participle = **future perfect passive**
      will have been + written   will have been written

Note: The passive voice can be used even in some progressive tenses.

The letter <u>is being written</u>.
The letter <u>was being written</u>.

Exercise 2

Take the following present passive verb through all the passive tenses listed. Assume the subject is *it*. One has been done for you as an example.

present: *it is seen*

past: *it was seen*

future: *it will be seen*

present perfect: *it has been seen*

past perfect: *it had been seen*

future perfect: *it will have been seen*

present: *it is tried*

past: _____

future: _____

present perfect: _____

past perfect: _____

future perfect: _____

Exercise 3

In the following passage identify the voice of each underlined complete verb. Put a *P* over each passive verb and an *A* over each active complete verb. Remember that passive voice always has a *be* helping verb.

[1]The tarot is a deck of cards which <u>are used</u> for fortune-telling. [2]They <u>were introduced</u> in Europe by gypsies during the fourteenth century.

[3]People who <u>believe</u> in tarot think that the pack <u>represents</u> a certain phi-

losophy embracing the true nature of the human being, the universe, and God. [4]They _feel_ insight _can be gained_ into these mysteries when the cards _are laid out_.

[5]Most often, however, the cards _are used_ for fortune-telling. [6]They _are shuffled_ and _set out_ in the Tree of Life pattern. [7]The cards _are placed_ in ten piles of seven. [8]The rest _are set_ aside. [9]Each pile _represents_ a certain aspect of life—intelligence, creativity, virtue, strength, love, imagination, and so on. [10]When each card _is turned over_, it _is interpreted_ according to the cards around it, and a person's fortune _unfolds_.

Exercise 4

Change the verbs in parentheses to the present tense in the active or the passive voice.

[1]The more people (learn) about weather, the more fully they (realize) how complex it (be). [2]Meteorologists (estimate) that 10,000 statistical varieties of weather (occur) at any given moment in the United States alone, and that throughout the world at least 45,000 thunderstorms (may develop) in an average period of twenty-four hours.

[3]Nevertheless, weather (compose) of four basic elements: temperature, pressure, humidity, and wind. [4]The influences that (manipulate) them (can describe), with drastic simplification, in a few sentences.

[5]The sun (fuel) the global engine that (produce) weather. [6]The earth (receive) enough energy from the sun every minute to match an entire

year's output of all of man's power plants. [7]Nearly half this solar energy (disappear) in space, however, because the sun's heat (reflect) by cloud tops, ice fields, and snow. [8]The rest (absorb) by the land and water, and then it (reradiate) as heat by oceans—covering almost three-quarters of the planet—and by land.

[9]Water vapor (absorb) this heat, (condense) to clouds, and (churn) the atmosphere with the energy born of heat transfer. [10]The clouds (put) in motion by this energy, and their circulation (manipulate) by high-altitude, high-speed winds caused by the earth's rotation.

Exercise 5

Fill in the blanks with the verb, tense, and voice given in parentheses.

[1]Glass _____ (*invent*, past passive) in the Middle East approximately 3500 years ago. [2]Probably, the Mesopotamians _____ (*invent*, past active) it after they _____ (*discover*, past perfect active) that nature's own glass, obsidian, _____ (*can find*, past passive) at volcanic fires or earth fissures.

[3]Glass _____ (*be*, present active) a combination of sand, lime, and ash that _____ (*heat*, present passive) to extremely high tem-

peratures. [4]At approximately 1500° Centigrade, the powder mixture

_____ (*liquify*, present active) into a bright red "lava."

[5]Magic _____ (*occur*, present active) when the mass

_____ (*cool*, present active). [6]It _____ (*harden*, present active) to a consistency not solid, liquid, or gas, but what _____ (*know*, present passive) as the "vitreous state." [7]*Vitreous* _____ (*mean*, present active) "active," which, in a way, is accurate, since the life and light around it _____ (*reflect*, present passive) from its heart.

[8]Color _____ (*add*, past passive) almost from the beginning as craftsmen _____ (*learn*, past active) that the addition of metallic oxides would dye the product in dazzling ways. [9]For example, they _____ (*discover*, past active) that copper or gold _____ (*make*, present active) red, cobalt _____ (*make*, present active) royal blue, and a pinch of iron ferrite _____ (*make*, present active) yellow-orange glass. [10]Then, apparently sometime in the late thirteenth century, in northern France, when someone accidentally _____ (*drag*, past active) his sleeve wet with silver salts across a plate of cooling glass, it _____ (*discover*, past passive) that such chemicals _____ (*create*, present active) special, magnetic yellows, from lemon to deep amber.

USES OF THE PASSIVE VOICE

The passive voice is used when the performer of the action is unknown or unimportant.

who performs action is unknown or unimportant

This house <u>was built</u> in 1981.

John and Mary <u>were married</u> last year.

The paintings <u>were donated</u> by a wealthy art collector.

Note: Most professional writers avoid the passive voice as much as possible, because active sentences are usually more direct and effective.

Passive: According to Greek mythology, ~~it <u>was believed</u> that~~ the phoenix was a symbol of rebirth and immortality.

Active: According to Greek mythology, the phoenix <u>was</u> a symbol of rebirth and immortality.

Exercise 6

Rewrite the following passive sentences as active ones. Make all the necessary subject and verb changes, and make sure you keep the original tense. The part that needs to become the subject has been set off with brackets. The first one has been done for you.

1. The tarot is used by [fortune-tellers].

   Fortune-tellers use the tarot.

2. These cards were introduced by [gypsies] during the fourteenth century in Europe.

   _____

   _____

3. A certain philosophy embracing the true nature of the human being, the universe, and God is represented by [the pack].

   _____

   _____

4. Insight into these mysteries can be gained with these cards by [people who believe in the tarot].

_____

_____

5. Most often, however, the cards are used by [people] for fortune-telling.

_____

6. These cards are shuffled and set out by [fortune-tellers] in the Tree of Life pattern.

_____

_____

7. The cards are placed in piles of seven by [the dealer].

_____

8. The rest of the cards are set aside by [this individual].

_____

9. A certain aspect of life—intelligence, creativity, virtue, strength, love, imagination, and so on—is represented by [each pile].

_____

_____

10. A person's fortune is unfolded by [each turned over and interpreted card].

_____

_____

Exercise 7

After underlining each complete verb, change all passive sentences to active ones to make them more direct and effective. The first one has been done for you.

¹According to Greek mythology, ~~it was believed that the Phoenix was~~ *the Phoenix was* the symbol of rebirth and immortality. ²This beautiful, ancient creature had feathers of green and gold. ³Its voice was so sad that other creatures often dropped dead after its voice was heard by them. ⁴This bird lived many times longer than other birds or humans. ⁵It was said by some that its lifespan was 97,200 years. ⁶When it felt death approaching, a funeral pyre was built by it, and it died in the flames. ⁷A phoenix reborn would arise from the ashes, and the ashes were carried by him to the altar of the sun god. ⁸It was believed by the Greeks that the ashes held the power of immortality.

SUMMARY

Fill in the blanks with the appropriate response, to show your understanding of the principles in this chapter.

1. There are two voices: the active voice and the _____ voice. In the _____ voice the subject performs the action of the verb. In the _____ voice the subject receives the action.

2. The passive voice is made with a form of the _____ helping verb followed by the _____ form of the main verb.

3. Change each of the following sentences to the active voice.

   a. Many patients *are examined* by the doctor.

   _____

   b. Many patients *were examined* by the doctor.

   _____

   c. Many patients *will be examined* by the doctor.

   _____

   d. Many patients *have been examined* by her.

   _____

   e. Many patients *had been examined* by her.

   _____

   f. Many patients *will have been examined* by her.

   _____

4. In your own words explain why the passive voice is used in each of the following sentences.

   a. The movie was produced in 1967 at the Walt Disney Studios.

   _____

   _____

   b. Arabic numerals were first used in India, not in Arabia.

   _____

   _____

5. In your own words explain why the passive voice should *not* be used in each of the following sentences.

a. The first time the Dutch painter Pieter Breughel's famous painting was seen by me will never be forgotten.

_____

_____

b. A cold winter day in a typical Dutch village was depicted by the painting.

_____

_____

Summary Exercise

Change the unnecessary passive voice verbs to the active voice. Keep passive verbs only in sentences where the doer is unknown or unimportant.

[1]The famous Hope Diamond <u>is</u> now <u>housed</u> in the Smithsonian Institute in Washington, D.C. [2]This brilliant ice-blue gem has a bloody history that <u>can be traced</u> back over three centuries. [3]Almost all the jewel's owners have had horrible things happen to them when the stone <u>was owned</u> by them. [4]The diamond <u>was stolen</u> from an Indian temple by its first owner, a Hindu priest. [5]He <u>was caught</u> and <u>tortured</u> to death for his greed. [6]In the 1600s, the diamond wound up in the hands of King Louis XIV. [7]He died and three members of his family <u>were killed</u> before the jewel <u>was passed</u> into the hands of another owner. [8]The jewel <u>was lost</u> for several decades and later appeared in the possession of a French jeweler. [9]The diamond <u>was hoarded</u> by him for its great beauty, and later he

went insane. [10]The diamond <u>was received</u> by the mistress of a Russian prince—just before she <u>was killed</u> by him. [11]Later the prince <u>was murdered</u>. [12]The stone continued to move around Europe, leaving death as its calling card.

[13]In the nineteenth century, Henry Hope, a wealthy banker, purchased the diamond, and it <u>was given</u> his name. [14]His family later lost all of their fortune. [15]In 1908 the diamond <u>was given</u> by a Turkish sultan to his wife; she <u>was</u> then <u>stabbed</u> to death by him. [16]He later <u>was removed</u> from his throne. [17]In 1914 the jewel <u>was brought</u> to America. [18]It <u>was purchased</u> by Ned McLean. [19]From that point on his family suffered horrible tragedies, from traffic accidents to drug-related deaths to insanity. [20]The diamond <u>was bought</u> from the McLean estate by jeweler Harry Winston. [21]He alone <u>has been spared</u> the tragedy of the other owners of the stone—he gave it away to the Smithsonian.

WRITING PRACTICE

Write ten sentences or a short passage about one or more of the following topics, using the guidelines of your teacher. Make sure you avoid using the passive voice unnecessarily.

1. the importance of glass

2. a specific, accurate (or inaccurate) weather prediction

3. a myth about an unusual animal

4. how the weather affects your emotions

5. why you would or would not like to know your future

REVIEW
Avoiding Verb Errors

In Chapters 5 and 6 you learned to form and use the three basic tenses (present, past, and future), the perfect tenses, the progressive tenses, and the active voice and the passive voice. This review will show you some common verb errors.

COMMON ERRORS

Using the Past Form Instead of the Past Participle

Remember that after helping verbs the past form is *not* used.

Incorrect: The doctor told him his arm was broke.
Correct: The doctor told him his arm was broken.

Incorrect: Jesse has swam all afternoon.
Correct: Jesse has swum all afternoon.

Using *of* As a Helping Verb

The preposition *of* is never a helping verb. It should not be used in place of *have* when forming the present perfect tense preceded by a helping verb of mood (*will/would, may/might, can/could,* etc.). Do not be tricked by the pronunciation of *have* after these helping verbs.

Incorrect: Susan could of helped me.
Correct: Susan could have helped me.
Correct: Susan could've helped me.

Incorrect: Steven might of been here.
Correct: Steven might have been here.
Correct: Steven might've been here.

Using the Base After the *be* Helping Verb

Remember that after the *be* helping verb, often a past participle is used, not the base form. Don't forget to write the *-d* ending, even though it is silent next to the *t* of the following infinitive.

Incorrect:	Sarah is suppose to come over tonight.
Correct:	Sarah is supposed to come over tonight.

Incorrect:	Catherine use to help me.
Correct:	Catherine used to help me.

Using *better* Without a Helping Verb

A sentence must have a complete verb. The word *better* is not a verb but an adverb. It is usually preceded by *had*, which is often contracted to *d*. Don't forget to write the verb, even though it is contracted.

Incorrect:	You better go now.
Correct:	You'd better go now.
Correct:	You had better go now.

Using Unacceptable Forms from Spoken English

In spoken English, certain forms are used that are not yet accepted in formal, written English.

Incorrect:	Andrew snuck out of the room.
Correct:	Andrew sneaked out of the room.

Incorrect:	Brian busted into my room.
Correct:	Brian burst into my room.
Correct:	Brian broke into my room.

Incorrect:	The lecture drug on.
Correct:	The lecture dragged on.

Incorrect:	The child swang so high that he fell off his swing.
Correct:	The child swung so high that he fell off his swing.

Misusing Closely Related Verbs

Closely related verbs such as *lie/lay, sit/set, rise/raise* are often confused. Understanding the exact meaning of these verbs should help you use them correctly.

lie, lay, lain (lying) sit, sat, sat rise, rose, risen	to be (or put oneself) in a lying, sitting, or standing position (not followed by a *what* word)
lay, laid, laid (laying) set, set, set raise, raised, raised	to put something down or lift something up (followed by a *what* word)

Incorrect: He ~~rose~~ the flag.
Correct: He raised the flag.

Incorrect: He ~~set~~ down.
Correct: He sat down.

Incorrect: He has been ~~laying~~ on the sofa all day.
Correct: He has been lying on the sofa all day.

Mixing Tenses or Voices Incorrectly

When you write, you may need to use a different tense or voice in the same passage to show the different times of events or make the passage coherent. However, you should be careful not to shift tense or voice unnecessarily.

Incorrect: After I took the test, I ~~go~~ home.
Correct: After I took the test, I went home.

Incorrect: Dogs could ~~be~~ heard barking when we approached the farm.
Correct: We could hear the dogs barking when we approached the farm.

Incorrect: Add an egg and then ~~you should~~ stir vigorously.
Correct: Add an egg and then stir vigorously.

EDITING EXERCISE

In the following passage many sentences contain *one* error. Besides the verb errors discussed in this review, you may find subject–verb agreement errors. Correct all the errors.

A Place for Birds of Prey

¹Since the Carolina Raptor Center opened a few years ago, hundreds of raptors, or birds of prey, has been treated and released. ²Those who are restored to health are returned to the wild, usually to the place where they use to live. ³Others, permanently maimed, remain.

⁴Every weekend, visitors watch the birds fly around in roped-off enclosures. ⁵In one aviary, a few of the hawks and falcons is staring with dark, unblinking eyes at the visitors.

⁶During one visit, we observed the unsuccessful release of one bird. ⁷The vulture's wounds had healed and it was suppose to leave. ⁸However, flying hesitantly, the large black bird swang around the chain link pen again and again. ⁹Finally it lands nearby. ¹⁰Inside the pen, the rest of the flock set watching the newly freed bird, one of nearly two hundred at the Carolina Raptor Center.

¹¹Sylvia Larson, a center volunteer, explained, "That has sometimes gave us a problem. ¹²A bird don't always want to leave the rest of the flock even though it has gotten well."

¹³Some of the falcons has no physical ailments; instead the birds suffer from an identity problem known as "imprinting." ¹⁴According to Lar-

son, a raptor that is risen by humans will often have this special problem.

[15]If a raptor is took too soon from its parents, it will imprint on the humans around it and not know it's a bird. [16]These birds better not be released because the process is considered to be irreversible. [17]"We have saw some severely emaciated falcons who had been released in the wild and nearly starved because they didn't know how to hunt," she added. [18]"If we had released them again, they would of died."

WRITING ASSIGNMENTS

Write at least two pages about one or both of the following topics, using the guidelines of your teacher. Check your paper for any of the errors listed under items 1 and 2 on the proofreading checklist at the end of Unit 4 (p. 322).

1. Describe an aviary, reptile house, or lion's cage at a local zoo.

2. Write about something specific an animal could be trained to do for you.

The Writing Process
Selecting and Adding Detail

Let's return to the story given at the end of Unit 1 about the party you attended. When you tell that story, you select details according to your audience. Writers do the same. But as you become a writer you will need to learn to select details that are interesting and relevant to your subject. We do this by writing logically, omitting details that don't belong, adding details that help tell the story, and using language that is lively.

In your essay on friendship, the first anecdote concerned Henry coming to rescue you at 3:00 A.M. At this stage in writing the essay you will sit down and rewrite that story, keeping in mind the subject of the essay (the definition of friendship) and filling in as many details as you can remember.

Suppose the first section starts as follows:

Once my friend Henry woke up because I called him. He wasn't happy to hear from me. He was tired. My car was deader than a doornail and it was three o'clock in the morning. I was at a Shell station in Shreveport. They had closed up years ago. I had called him collect because I had no money. It was dark and the moon was behind the clouds. But he was there for me.

Let's look at this. In logical order, what are the important details?

1. You had car trouble.

2. You had no money.

3. You called Henry collect.

4. He rescued you.

Now let's put the paragraph in proper order and add a summary sentence at the end (or the beginning) of the paragraph.

Once on my way home, my car broke down in Shreveport at three o'clock in the morning. It was deader than a doornail. I was at a Shell station that had been closed for years. Because I had no money, I called my friend Henry collect. The night was dark and the moon was hidden behind the clouds. Henry was tired and he wasn't happy to hear from me, but when he heard my problem, he was there for me. Friendship means being willing to help even when it's inconvenient.

Next you might want to see what details you don't need. Is the Shell station important to this story? Is the hidden moon helpful to show what friendship is? When you have details that do not help you to say what you want, you cross them out and find others that will help. You might want to mention that it was raining, or that it was your father's car—not yours. You might also mention that Henry was actually angry with you until you explained what had happened. Maybe Henry had to be at work at 6:00 A.M. and had gone to bed at midnight. All these details help to show how much an act of friendship was his rescue of you.

Now check for details that could make the anecdote more interesting. Look at the sentence beginning with "Henry was tired . . . " Is there a way you can show this to be true without telling the reader? What if you say that you knew he had worked a double shift that day but that no one else was home? Or maybe you can say that, when Henry arrived, you felt embarrassed at having called him: He was wearing his pajamas under his raincoat and he had to be at work at 6:00 A.M. We begin to feel very sorry for Henry. More important, we begin to understand friendship.

Next look for overused phrases, which we will call *clichés*. A cliché is really a group of words that no longer mean very much. When we say "as white as snow," we no longer see snow. When it rains "cats and dogs," we no longer really picture cats and dogs tumbling out of the clouds.

In this essay, you say that your car was "deader than a doornail." When was the last time you noticed a doornail? Or saw how dead it was? Perhaps you could say that the car was so dead it had no motor reflexes left. Or perhaps when you cranked the motor all you could hear were the crickets outside the car or the sound of your own breathing.

Now look at the phrase "He was there for me." Although in this case he really was there, does the phrase help you see Henry standing in his pajamas in the rain, trying to help you get your car started? Telling us what Henry looked like and what he actually did—the way his pajamas looked, all crumpled by the overcoat, as he helped you jump the battery—is more interesting than simply saying "he was there" for you.

Such details give the reader pictures and let the reader experience what you felt when you saw Henry with his bedroom slippers on, oil stains on his hands, soaking wet hair falling into his eyes. We feel your appreciation of Henry, and we recognize his friendship. We understand before you even say it that friendship means being willing to help even when it's inconvenient.

Exercise 1

Make a logically ordered list of the important events in the following passages, and then reorder the sentences to follow that list. Add a summary sentence at the beginning or end of the new passage.

> Mark told me Susan was bad. She left town a month later and no one knew it. I was very angry when he bad-mouthed her. I was trying to do her a favor. She needed money to fix her car. I was falling for her, but Mark told me I shouldn't lend her any money. She owed my friends a thousand dollars when she left town. Mark was a good friend.

> Jeannie was a good friend. Sometimes holidays are hard. She saved me a bunch of turkey from her mom's dinner. She even heated it up. I had always loved holidays because our family was always together. My father had been real sick. I didn't tell anyone how sad I was. But Jeannie saved me that turkey. I ate at her house that night.

Exercise 2

Cross out all the unnecessary detail in the following passage. Be prepared to explain why you think each phrase you deleted isn't necessary.

[1]I remember my mom's hands. [2]She always washed dishes without wearing rubber gloves. [3]Her favorite dish soap was Joy. [4]She thought it made her happier. [5]Her fingers were long like icicles, white and almost clear. [6]She kept them stretched out straight in front on her lap when we were in church. [7]We always went to that old church on the corner with the fake red velvet seats. [8]They were hands that flew before her face when she talked. [9]They resembled wild birds when I was a child. [10]But

they were quiet birds, and gentle. [11]In the hospital there were steel bars on her bed, and her hands were at her sides, now with age spots, and so white against the pale blue sheets. [12]When I saw them quiet, half curled even though she was talking, I knew she was dying. [13]Now, five years later, I barely remember her face in that old, fading photograph over our new Wurlitzer, but I remember those hands folded and quiet for the first time ever at her funeral.

Exercise 3

Imagine a story or anecdote based on the following. Make a list of details that could be important. See if you can summarize in one sentence the point of your imagined anecdote.

1. an argument in a restaurant

2. a father's pride in his son

3. your grandfather's kindness

4. a description of the last house you lived in

5. the importance of truth

6. the best way to meet someone in a bar or restaurant

7. good teaching

8. the worst night of your life

Exercise 4

Divide your class into groups of four. Have one person in each foursome describe what happened in a restaurant. Two people play detectives, one making sure that all important details are told, the other making sure no unnecessary details are kept. Appoint the fourth person as secretary to keep notes. After one story is told, trade roles.

Exercise 5

Discuss the following two passages in groups, and on a separate sheet of paper rewrite the passages by substituting better, more interesting details.

My father is a hard-working man, a real patriot. He grew up in the good old days, when men were men and women stayed in the kitchen. He was as poor as a church mouse as a child, but later was able to keep up with the Joneses when he became the head of a household. He was also a real ladies' man and a snazzy dresser.

My sister is really classy. She always wears up-to-date clothes and high-fashion jewelry. She wasn't born yesterday. Everyone thinks she's a real princess, and she's kind to a fault. Of course, she does have her breaking point. Everything has to be just so, and she don't take kindly to dirt.

UNIT 3 Writing Complete Sentences

In the preceding chapters you probably noticed that many sentences contain more than one clause (more than one subject—circled here—and complete verb—underlined). For instance:

One (cup) of rice <u>becomes</u> three cups when (it) <u>is cooked</u>.

Good writing usually combines several clauses into one sentence. For example, compare the following two passages and you will probably agree that Paul Theroux's original (the one on the left) is more effective, with its combined clauses, than the one on the right, which is how it *might* have been written.

From Paul Theroux's *The Mosquito Coast* (Boston: Houghton Mifflin, 1982), p. 11	How Another Author Might Have Written It
That night I opened my eyes in the dark and knew that my father was not in the house. The sense of something missing is stronger than the sense of someone there. It was not only that I didn't hear his whistling snore (usually he sounded like one of his own original expansion valves), or even that all the lights were out. It was a feeling of lonesome emptiness, as if there was a mummy-shaped hole of air in the house where my father's body should have been. And my fear was	That night I opened my eyes in the dark. I knew that my father was not in the house. The sense of something missing is strong. It is stronger than the sense of someone there. It wasn't that I didn't hear his whistling snore. Usually he sounded like one of his own original expansion valves. It wasn't even that all the lights were out. It was a feeling of lonesome emptiness. I sensed a mummy-shaped hole of air in the house. My father's body should have been in that hole. My fear was that this

that this unpredictable man was dead, or worse than dead—hollowed out and haunting the property. I knew he was gone, and in a worried guilty way—I was thirteen years old—I felt responsible for him.

unpredictable man was dead. Perhaps he was worse than dead—hollowed out and haunting the property. I knew he was gone. I was only thirteen years old. In a worried, guilty way I felt responsible for him.

The purpose of this unit is to help you recognize the types of structures that may be combined and to give you practice in combining them.

CHAPTER 7
Recognizing Sentences, Clauses, and Phrases

In this chapter you will learn to recognize the clauses and phrases within sentences and how to use them correctly in your own writing.

RECOGNIZING CLAUSES AND PHRASES

A **clause** is a structure with its own subject (circled here) and complete verb (underlined) with a first verb (also circled here) in a present or past form.

(superstitions) (can) explain mysterious things

(many) of these explanations (have) been with us for centuries

our (lives) (are) still affected by some

A **phrase** is a group of words without a complete verb. As you know, an infinitive, an *-ing* form, or a past participle by itself (without a helping verb) is not a complete verb. Therefore, a group of words with only an infinitive, *-ing*, or past participle form is *never* a clause.

superstitions *to explain* mysterious things

many of these explanations *having been* with us for centuries

our lives still *affected* by some

Exercise 1

In the following sentences, underline the complete verb, if there is one. Then put a *C* in front of each structure that contains a complete verb and a *P* in front of each structure that does not.

_____ 1. do you ever open an umbrella indoors

_____ 2. opening an umbrella indoors to bring bad luck

_____ 3. earlier cultures believed opening an umbrella indoors was a

violation of natural order

_____ 4. this violation insulting the gods and inviting their revenge

_____ 5. black cats, cracks in sidewalks, or the number thirteen also felt

to bring bad luck

_____ 6. in France there being no house or apartment numbered thirteen

_____ 7. many tall buildings not to have a thirteenth floor

_____ 8. have you ever looked for the thirteenth row on an airplane

Exercise 2

Go back to Exercise 1 and change the phrases (the structures without a complete verb) into clauses by either adding a helping verb or changing an infinitive, *-ing* form, or past participle to a first verb. Here is an example:

_____ 2. ~~O~~pening an umbrella indoors ~~to~~ br~~ing~~ *brings* bad luck.

Exercise 3

Put a *C* in front of each structure that contains a complete verb and a *P* in front of each structure that does not.

_____ 1. computers have a long history

_____ 2. as early as 3000 B.C., the Babylonians known to use the abacus

for mathematical calculations

_____ 3. in 1833, Charles Babbage, an Englishman, to invent the first automatic calculating machine

_____ 4. during World War II, two researchers at the University of Pennsylvania built the first modern computers

_____ 5. these machines designed to help the military calculate the trajectory of shells

_____ 6. today, computers helping compose music, create art, play games, create recipes, and organize the workplace

Exercise 4

Go back to Exercise 3 and change the phrases into clauses by either adding a helping verb or changing an infinitive, *-ing* form, or past participle to a present or past form.

TYPES OF SENTENCES

Many sentences contain only one clause (one subject–complete verb combination). Such sentences are called **simple sentences**.

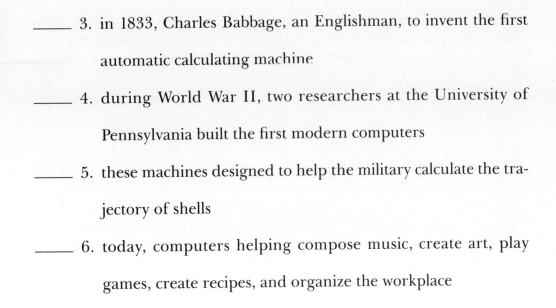

Penicillin does not kill germs.

Note: Two complete verbs for the same subject or two subjects for the same complete verb count as one combination (a simple sentence).

It merely stops their growth and prevents their reproduction.

Scientists and survey teams have found no reliable way to measure mountains.

When a sentence consists of more than one subject–complete verb combination, it is either a compound sentence or a complex sentence. For right now, we will call both types **comp sentences**.

The (inside) of a refrigerator <u>is</u> cold, for the (heat) <u>has been pumped</u> out of it.

(Dr. John Mudd), ((who) <u>was</u> the physician) ((who) <u>treated</u> John Wilkes Booth) (after (he) <u>had assassinated</u> Abraham Lincoln,) <u>was</u> <u>resented</u> by many people.

(It) <u>is</u> not a proven theory (that (fish) <u>bite</u> more readily in certain kinds of weather.)

Exercise 5

Put an *S* in front of each simple sentence and *Comp* in front of each sentence containing more than one clause.

_____ 1. There are some strange ideas associated with our modern eating habits.

_____ 2. Some items on our menus have interesting beginnings.

_____ 3. Sundaes, for example, were once thought to be made from the leftover ice cream from the other days of the week.

_____ 4. Sundaes really were the invention of an American drugstore owner.

_____ 5. Because Puritan traditions had created "blue laws" outlawing many things on Sunday—even ice cream sodas, the inventive drugstore owner began to sell ice cream with syrup on Sunday and called this creation a "Sunday."

_____ 6. Although people could not object to such a thing, they did object to his use of the Sabbath day as a name for a food.

_____ 7. For this reason the proprietor changed the spelling of his creation to "sundae."

Exercise 6

Put an *S* in front of each simple sentence and *Comp* in front of each sentence containing more than one clause.

_____ 1. Thomas A. Edison did not make the first electric light bulb as it is popularly believed.

_____ 2. The wettest place on earth is Cherrapunji, India, for it has an average annual rainfall of 427 inches.

_____ 3. Intoxication is a condition with recognizable disturbance of intellect, movement, and coordination.

_____ 4. Only 5 percent of the people in the United States say that they dream in color.

_____ 5. If marshmallows were packed in tin cans and taken to a height above 7000 feet, the lessened air pressure would cause the cans to explode.

_____ 6. The largest fish ever caught was a 2176-pound white shark.

_____ 7. Naturalists are inclined to believe that no animals are voiceless.

_____ 8. Thomas Jefferson was 35 years old when he drafted the Declaration of Independence.

MAIN CLAUSES AND DEPENDENT CLAUSES

There are two types of clauses: main clauses (in capital letters here) and dependent clauses (in parentheses).

dependent clause   *main clause*

(Although it is called a worm,) THE SILKWORM IS A CATERPILLAR.

A **dependent clause** (in parentheses here) is one that starts with a **subordinator**, which is a connecting word such as *who, which, because,* or *if* (set off here by angle brackets).

No animal or bird bleeds well(⟨*if*⟩ it is killed in an excited or overheated condition.)

A **main clause** (in capital letters here) does *not* start with a subordinator and can usually stand by itself as a simple sentence.

THE ARMISTICE(⟨which⟩ ended the Korean war) WAS SIGNED ON JULY 27, 1953.

Main clause: THE ARMISTICE WAS SIGNED ON JULY 27, 1953.

Dependent clause: (which ended the Korean War)

   Note: As you can see from these examples, a dependent clause can come before, after, or in the middle of a main clause. However, when a dependent clause answers a *who* or a *what* question, we cannot really remove it from the sentence to discover the main clause because what remains would not make any sense. In such a case, we mentally substitute *it, he/she,* or *him/her* for the dependent clause to come up with the complete main clause of that sentence.

It

(⟨That⟩ the common housefly spreads diseases)IS A KNOWN FACT.

Main clause: *IT* IS A KNOWN FACT.

it

SCIENTISTS ESTIMATE (⟨that⟩ the world's average rainfall is sixteen million tons per second).

Main clause: SCIENTISTS ESTIMATE *IT*.

He/She

(⟨Whoever⟩ discovered the law of gravitation) WAS ABLE TO

it

EXPLAIN (⟨why⟩ people did not float into the sky).

Main clause: *HE/SHE* WAS ABLE TO EXPLAIN *IT*.

Note: When a sentence consists of a main clause and one or more dependent clauses, it is called a **complex sentence**.

Exercise 7

As in the preceding examples, each subordinator in the following sentences has been set off with ⟨angle brackets⟩. Set off each dependent clause, including the subordinator, with (parentheses). Then write down the main clause. Use the word *it* where necessary.

1. Did you know ⟨that⟩ Thomas Jefferson was the first president of the

    United States to wear long trousers?

    Main clause: _____

2. Water does not actually boil ⟨when⟩ dry ice is dropped into it.

    Main clause: _____

3. The most common poisonous snake in the United States, ⟨whose⟩ bite

    is not always fatal, is the copperhead.

    Main clause: _____

4. ⟨That⟩ a single pail of water could produce enough fog to cover over 105 square miles to a depth of fifty feet is amazing.

    Main clause: _____

5. ⟨Although⟩ frost does not cause the chemical process ⟨that⟩ produces the brilliant colors in autumn leaves, it often hastens the coloring process.

    Main clause: _____

TYPES OF DEPENDENT CLAUSES

A dependent clause, one that starts with a subordinator, is not a complete sentence by itself. In order to make sense, it depends on a main clause. Thus:

> **A group of words is only a sentence if it has a *main* clause.**

A dependent clause may take the place of a noun, an adjective, or an adverb in the sentence.

   A **noun clause** (in brackets here) answers the *who* or the *what* question. (You can usually substitute the word *it* for this dependent clause.)

tells what (It)

[⟨That⟩ no animals are voiceless] is an interesting theory.

An **adjective clause** modifies a noun.

modifies fish

THE LARGEST FISH (⟨that⟩ anyone has ever caught) WAS A

modifies shark

WHITE SHARK (⟨that⟩ weighed 2176 pounds).

   An **adverb clause** tells *where, when, why, how, in spite of what*, or *under what condition* something takes place.

tells why

THE INSIDE OF A REFRIGERATOR IS COLD (⟨because⟩ the

heat has been pumped out of it).

Common Subordinators for Noun, Adjective, and Adverb Clauses

Noun	Adjective	Adverb
that	who	because
if	whom	if
whether	whose	although
what	which	since
which	that	until
how		after
why		where
who		when
whom		while
whose		as
whoever		so that
whomever		

Note: These words may have other functions. They are subordinators only when they introduce a subject–complete verb combination.

Exercise 8

As in the preceding examples, set off each subordinator in the following sentences with 〈angle brackets〉 and set off with (parentheses) the dependent clause it introduces. Then write down the main clause. Use the word *it* where necessary.

1. Twins who are not identical are fraternal.

   Main clause: _____

2. Scientists estimate that the world's average rainfall is sixteen million tons per second.

   Main clause: _____

3. Napoleon Bonaparte was the man who originated the idea of placing odd and even numbers on houses on different sides of the street.

   Main clause: _____

4. The armistice that ended the Korean War was signed on July 27, 1953.

   Main clause: _____

5. The silkworm, although it is called a worm, is really a caterpillar.

   Main clause: _____

6. In 1687, when the law of gravitation was first discovered, man was able to explain why he did not float into the sky.

   Main clause: _____

7. Studies reveal that at least ten different species of salmon exist.

   Main clause: _____

8. Fish bones are softened by heat, not by oil as it is popularly believed.

   Main clause: _____

9. That the common housefly is probably the most dangerous insect in America is a known fact.

   Main clause: _____

10. The greatest depth in the ocean that has been measured is 6.7 miles.

    Main clause: _____

Exercise 9

The following structures are dependent clauses. Add a main clause to make them complete sentences.

1. What you want to do _____.

2. _____ where you go.

3. _____ who is my friend _____.

4. _____ that I heard _____.

5. _____ because he passed the test.

6. If it rains, _____.

Understood *that*

The subordinator *that*, which can introduce either noun or adjective clauses, is often not stated but understood.

> *Alma mater*, a Latin term meaning "bounteous mother," is applied to the college or university ⟨*that*⟩ a student graduated from.
>
> Did you know ⟨*that*⟩ one jelly bean contains seven calories?

Exercise 10

Set off each subordinator with ⟨angle brackets⟩. Add ⟨*that*⟩ where it is understood.

[1]Superstitions are common in the world of athletics. [2]Athletes often believe certain jerseys, special meals, or mascots will bring them good luck. [3]Golfers, who are especially known for their belief in charms and amulets, seem to be some of the most superstitious athletes. [4]Tony Jacklin, who won the 1969 Open, carried a tiny wishing well in his pocket. [5]When Bert Yancey won the Bing Crosby tournament, he gave credit to the copper "voodoo bracelet" he was wearing. [6]The colors

players wear are important, too. ⁷Some players will avoid wearing certain colors; others always wear the same color. ⁸Some golfers believe the numbers on the golf balls carry special meaning. ⁹High numbers, which might bring high scores, are thought unlucky. ¹⁰The athlete, who needs a mixture of fine skill and a little luck, will probably always remain a superstitious being.

Exercise 11

Use complex sentences (containing a *main* clause and a *dependent* clause) to answer the following questions based on the information in Exercise 10.

1. What do athletes often believe? _____

    _____

2. Why do golfers seem to be some of the most superstitious athletes?

    _____

3. Who carried a tiny wishing well in his pocket? _____

    _____

4. What did Bert Yancey credit for winning the Bing Crosby tournament?

    _____

    _____

5. What do some golfers believe about numbers? _____

    _____

Punctuating Adverb Clauses

The punctuation rules for noun and adjective clauses are somewhat complicated and will be discussed in detail in Chapters 13 and 14.

Punctuation rules for adverb clauses, on the other hand, are easy to apply. An adverbial clause at the beginning or in the middle of a sentence is set off with commas, but one at the end of a sentence is usually not.

Position of Adverbial Clause	
At the beginning:	*Comma* ⟨When⟩ he drafted the Declaration of Independence, Thomas Jefferson was 35 years old.
In the middle:	*a pair of commas* Thomas Jefferson, ⟨when⟩ he drafted the Declaration of Independence, was 35 years old.
At the end:	*no comma* Thomas Jefferson was 35 years old ⟨when⟩ he drafted the Declaration of Independence.

Exercise 12

After setting off each subordinator in the following sentences with ⟨angle brackets⟩, as in the preceding examples, add commas where necessary.

1. When people in earlier civilizations wanted justice they determined

    guilt or innocence quite simply.

2. Often, when a person had been accused of a crime he was tried by

    ordeal.

3. The accused was considered guilty until he could pass a severe test of character or endurance.

4. For example, when a man accused was tried by battle he was forced to fight with his accuser.

5. Because people assumed that the gods awarded victory to the righteous person the winner was proven innocent.

6. If the accused was of high rank he or she was forced to hold his or her hands or feet over hot fire.

7. The accused were assumed innocent if they did not burn.

8. Whenever the accused was tried by water he or she was tied up and thrown into a pond.

9. Ironically, the accused were believed to be guilty unless they sank and drowned.

Exercise 13

Each of the following sentences contains an underlined adverb clause at the end. Rewrite the sentence by placing the adverb clause (a) first at the beginning of the main clause and (b) then in the middle of the main clause. Remember to punctuate correctly.

1. Jury trials have replaced trials by ordeal <u>because the earlier trials were very cruel</u>.

    a. _____

    _____

    _____

b. _____

_____

_____

2. A person may or may not ask for a jury to decide his guilt or inno-

cence <u>if he is accused of a crime</u>.

a. _____

_____

_____

_____

b. _____

_____

_____

_____

3. The accused is considered innocent <u>until evidence proves his or her</u>

<u>guilt</u>.

a. _____

_____

_____

b. _____

_____

_____

USING MAIN CLAUSES, DEPENDENT CLAUSES, AND PHRASES CORRECTLY

Here we will briefly summarize the differences between main clauses, dependent clauses, and phrases.

Main clauses have complete verbs and do not start with a subordinator. Remember that a sentence *must* have a main clause to be complete.

> *Main clause:*   Dr. John Mudd <u>treated</u> John Wilkes Booth.

Dependent clauses have complete verbs and start with a subordinator (unless the word *that* is understood). Remember, dependent clauses by themselves are not sentences; they must be connected to a main clause to form a complete sentence.

> *Dependent clause*   ⟨because⟩ Dr. John Mudd <u>treated</u> John Wilkes Booth

Phrases are structures that do not contain a complete verb. They may have a verb form such as an infinitive, *-ing*, or a past participle, or they may be a group of words containing a preposition, a noun, or an adjective. Remember that phrases by themselves are not sentences; they must be connected to a main clause to form a complete sentence.

> *Phrase:*   Dr. John Mudd <u>having treated</u> John Wilkes Booth

Exercise 14

Identify the following structures as main clause (*M*), dependent clause (*D*), or phrase (*P*).

_____ 1. John Wilkes Booth had assassinated Abraham Lincoln

_____ 2. who had assassinated Abraham Lincoln

_____ 3. Abraham Lincoln's assassinator

_____ 4. why Dr. John Mudd was resented by many people

_____ 5. resented by many people

_____ 6. Dr. John Mudd was resented by many people

Exercise 15

Combine the following simple sentences into more complicated ones containing a main clause and a dependent clause and/or a phrase.

1. Dr. John Mudd had treated John Wilkes Booth.
    John Wilkes Booth had assassinated Abraham Lincoln.
    Dr. John Mudd was resented by many people.

    _____

    _____

2. The silkworm is called a worm.
    The silkworm is really a caterpillar.

    _____

    _____

3. Fishbones are softened by heat.
    Fishbones are not softened by oil.

    _____

    _____

4. Napoleon Bonaparte was the emperor of France.
    He originated an idea.
    This idea was to place odd and even numbers on houses on different sides of the street.

    _____

    _____

5. The wettest place on earth is Cherrapunji, India.
    It has an average rainfall of 427 inches.

    _____

    _____

Exercise 16

Identify each underlined structure as main clause (*M*), dependent clause (*D*), or phrase (*P*).

_____ 1. The symbol of the staff and serpent <u>that represents the medical profession</u> goes back to Aesculapius, the god of healing, and to Greek mythology.

_____
_____ 2. Aesculapius, <u>also called the father of physicians</u>, was depicted in one statue <u>with his hand holding a staff</u> that has a serpent wrapped around it.

_____ 3. <u>The staff was believed to be a divine rod</u> that could heal.

_____
_____ 4. <u>Although the serpent is often seen as a symbol of evil</u>, its position on the staff is seen as a sign <u>that the magic of the staff could overcome the evil of illness.</u>

_____ 5. Also, the Greeks believed that the serpent was <u>a symbol of renewal and regeneration</u> and gave the physician the same powers over the sick.

_____ 6. The Bible also has references to the "rod and the snake" as a tool <u>that heals and protects.</u>

_____ 7. When the Israelites were journeying through the desert, Moses instructed them to construct snakes of copper and <u>to hoist them on poles to ward off desert snakes.</u>

_____ 8. <u>These copper snakes and poles appeared to have protected them from the poisonous snakes</u> that had long plagued them on their journey.

Exercise 17

To help yourself understand differences between main clauses, dependent clauses, and phrases, change the following excerpts from Exercise 16 to *simple sentences*. Reread the corresponding sentences in Exercise 16; then make any necessary changes. The first one has been done for you.

1. that represents the medical profession

   The symbol of the staff and serpent represents the medical profession.

2. also called the father of physicians

   _____

3. with his hand holding a staff

   _____

4. although the serpent is often seen as a symbol of evil

   _____

   _____

5. a symbol of renewal and regeneration

   _____

6. which heals and protects

   _____

7. to hoist them on poles to ward off desert snakes

   _____

   _____

8. these copper snakes to protect them from the poisonous snakes

   _____

   _____

SUMMARY

Fill in the blanks with the appropriate response, to show your under-standing of the principles in this chapter. Where indicated, write a sentence of your own to illustrate those principles.

1. Explain why "opening an umbrella indoors" is *not* a clause and "he

   opened an umbrella indoors" is a clause. _____

   _____

   _____

2. Explain why "he opened an umbrella indoors" is a simple sentence and "he believed that opening an umbrella indoors would bring bad luck" is *not* a simple sentence.

   _____

   _____

   _____

3. How many clauses does a simple sentence have? _____

4. There are two types of clauses: main and dependent ones.

   a. Which is the most important one in the sentence? Why? _____

      _____

      _____

   b. Why is a dependent clause by itself not a sentence? _____

      _____

      _____

5. How can you easily recognize a dependent clause? _____

   _____

6. a. _____, _____, _____, _____, and

_____ are common noun clause connectors.

b. _____, _____, _____, _____, and

_____ are common adjective clause connectors.

c. _____, _____, _____, _____, and

_____ are common adverb clause connectors.

7. Which subordinator is often not stated but understood? _____

Illustrate with your own example.

_____

_____

_____

8. Adverbial clauses may appear at the beginning, in the middle, or at

the end of a sentence. Which one is *not* usually set off with a comma?

_____ Illustrate with your own example.

_____

_____

_____

9. Explain why "he opened the umbrella" is a main clause, "because he

opened the umbrella" is a dependent clause, and "having opened the

umbrella" is a phrase. _____

_____

_____

Summary Exercise

The following passage is divided into segments. First read the passage to understand its contents. Then put a *D* in front of each dependent clause (structure that starts with a subordinator) and a *P* in front of each phrase (structure without a complete verb). After that, punctuate and capitalize where necessary. Make sure dependent clauses and phrases are attached to a main clause.

[1]Styles in clothing have changed drastically over the centuries / [2]originally people wore clothes / [3]for protection from the elements / [4]later modesty became another reason for wearing clothes / [5]later on clothes became decorations / [6]designed to impress others and designate class levels / [7]traditions from centuries ago are often reflected in the styles / [8]that we follow today / [9]cuffs on pants, for example, evolved from the Englishman's desire / [10]to protect his pants / [11]during rainy weather / [12]tradition also advocates / [13]that a man should never button the last button on his sports jacket / [14]the English are also responsible for this / [15]a member of the Royal Family appeared at a function / [16]without the last button on his jacket buttoned / [17]not wanting to be rude or unfashionable / [18]Englishmen in the room quickly did the same / [19]a trend was set at that moment / [20]whatever the century or country may be / [21]it seems / [22]that a man is often judged by the clothes / [23]that he wears / [24]today as much as ever / [25]clothes make the man

WRITING PRACTICE

Write ten sentences or a short passage about one or more of the following topics, using the guidelines of your teacher. Use different types of sentences.

1. your opinion of a specific editorial in your newspaper

2. the fairness of jury trials

3. how you imagine a particular food name came about

4. a symbol (such as a flag) and what it means to you

5. how you imagine a clothing fad came about

CHAPTER 8
Joining Equal Elements

In Chapter 7 you saw how a dependent clause is attached to a main clause with a subordinator. As the word implies, a *subordinator* connects a clause that is lower in rank to a main clause. In this chapter you will see how a different kind of connector, a coordinator, is used. As the word implies, a *coordinator* can only join elements that are equal in rank.

COORDINATORS

We use **coordinators** (in double angle brackets here) (**coordinating conjunctions** and **correlative conjunctions**) to connect two or more elements that are of equal rank in structure. They may connect sentences, main clauses, dependent clauses, phrases, or words (all in capital letters here).

sentence   *sentence*
JOHN WENT TO CLASS EVERY DAY. ⟨⟨Yet⟩⟩ HIS FRIENDS ATTENDED ONLY HALF THE TIME.

main clause   *main clause*
JOHN WENT TO CLASS EVERY DAY, ⟨⟨and⟩⟩ HE STUDIED HARD.

dependent clause   *dependent clause*
WHAT YOU DO ⟨⟨or⟩⟩ WHERE YOU GO is your own business.

predicate   *predicate*
John WENT TO CLASS EVERY DAY ⟨⟨and⟩⟩ STUDIED HARD.

prepositional phrase   *prepositional phrase*
He works ⟨⟨either⟩⟩ AT SEARS ⟨⟨or⟩⟩ AT SELBERS.

word   *word*
⟨⟨Not only⟩⟩ JOHN ⟨⟨but also⟩⟩ MARY went to class every day.

There is only a very small group of coordinators. To distinguish them from other types of connecting words, you may want to memorize the following list.

Coordinators	
Coordinating Conjunctions	Correlative Conjunctions
and for	both . . . and
but so	not only . . . but (also)
or yet	either . . . or
nor	neither . . . nor

Note: Be careful not to confuse the conjunction *for*, which means "because," with the preposition *for*.

Exercise 1

Read the following passage and set off coordinating and correlative conjunctions with ⟨⟨double angle brackets⟩⟩.

¹Baboons live on the ground during the day, but at night they sleep high up in the trees. ²They have not only strong arms and legs but also sharp teeth, so they can easily fight off enemies. ³Baboons live in troops, and they hunt together for food. ⁴The babies cling either to the chest or to the back of their parents. ⁵Both the parents and unrelated adults in a troop look after the young ones.

USING LOGICAL CONNECTORS

When using a coordinator, you must carefully consider its meaning.

Adding ideas

John missed three classes *and* an important test.
John missed *not only* three classes *but also* an important test.

Contrasting ideas

John was sick, *but* he went to school.
John was sick, *yet* he went to school.

Showing result

John was sick, *so* he stayed home.

Showing reason

John stayed home, *for* he was sick.

Showing choice

John didn't like being sick *or* missing three classes.
John liked *neither* being sick *nor* missing three classes.

Exercise 2

First read the following sentences for meaning. Then insert the most meaningful connector: *and, so, for,* or *or.* Don't overuse *and.*

[1]The tiniest of all birds is the hummingbird. [2]Princess Helena's hummingbird is the smallest, _____ it is less than three inches long. [3]The hummingbird's eggs are no bigger than peas, _____ its nest is no bigger than half a walnut shell.

[4]These beautiful little creatures feed on insects _____ on the nectar from flowers. [5]These birds can go deep inside of a flower, _____ they are very small. [6]They have very long beaks _____ coiled tongues. [7]Hummingbirds move their wings very fast, _____ the wings make a humming sound. [8]These tiny creatures are like helicopters, _____ they can stay still in the air, move backward, move forward, _____ move sideways.

[9]Their feathers are very beautiful, _____ people compare them to jewels. [10]They may also have long tails, crests, _____ ruffs. [11]What a wonder nature is!

JOINING ELEMENTS WITH COORDINATORS

When we combine sentences that have certain words that are the same, the coordinating and correlative conjunctions are especially useful because they allow us to eliminate repeated words.

What you do ~~is your own business.~~
Where you go is your own business.

Both what you do *and* where you go are your own business.

John went to class every day.
~~John~~ studied hard.

John went to class every day *and* studied hard.

He works at Sears.
~~He works at~~ Selbers.

He works *either* at Sears *or* at Selbers.

John went to class every day.
~~Mary went to class every day.~~

John *and* Mary went to class every day.

Exercise 3

As in the foregoing examples, combine the following short, choppy sentences into one longer, logical, and meaningful sentence containing coordinators. Try not to repeat the same words in one sentence. You may want to look at Exercise 1 for ideas, but try to connect these sentences differently.

1. Baboons have strong arms.
   Baboons have strong legs.

   _____

2. Baboons have sharp teeth.
   Baboons can easily fight off enemies.

   _____

3. Baboons live in troops.
   Baboons hunt together for food.

---

4. The babies cling to the chest of their parents.
   The babies cling to the back of their parents.

---

5. The parents look after the young ones.
   Unrelated adults in a troop look after the young ones.

PARALLEL STRUCTURE

The parts joined by coordinators must be **parallel**, which means that they have to be alike in structure: subjects, predicates, gerund phrases, *to*-infinitive phrases, prepositional phrases, dependent clauses, main clauses, sentences, and so on.

subject   *subject*
JOHN ⟨⟨and⟩⟩ MARY are students.
       predicate   *predicate*
Both STUDY WELL ⟨⟨and⟩⟩ WORK HARD.
          prepositional phrase   *prepositional phrase*
Mary works FOR A LARGE COMPANY ⟨⟨or⟩⟩ FOR A SMALL
RETAIL BUSINESS.
          dependent clause   *dependent clause*
John doesn't know WHAT HE WANTS TO DO ⟨⟨or⟩⟩ WHERE HE
WANTS TO WORK.
          main clause   *main clause*
Now, ⟨⟨not only⟩⟩ DO THEY STUDY, ⟨⟨but⟩⟩ THEY ⟨⟨also⟩⟩ WORK
PART-TIME.
     gerund   *gerund*
STUDYING ⟨⟨and⟩⟩ WORKING leave them little free time.
               infinitive phrase   *infinitive phrase*
When they can, they love TO STAY HOME ⟨⟨and⟩⟩ TO RELAX IN
FRONT OF THE TELEVISION.

Exercise 4

Set off the coordinating and correlative conjunctions with ⟨⟨double angle brackets⟩⟩ and underline the parallel structures they join.

1. All sports are subject to controversy about cheating, but baseball has gone crazy on the subject recently.

2. Nowadays both athletes and managers in baseball seem to be more concerned with playing detective and finding out whodunit with what than with who scored what when.

3. Hitters find new ways to hit the ball farther, so pitchers find new ways to strike batters out.

4. First there were lively balls, and now there are scuffed balls and lively bats.

5. Cheating controversies in the major leagues may seem like news, but fifteen years ago Jim Bouton told us in *Ball Four* all about cheating.

6. Here you can read that Whitey Ford wore a diamond ring to scuff up baseballs and that Yogi Berra supposedly sharpened a buckle on his shin guards to scuff up the balls for Ford after he had been caught.

7. Subtly cheating or violating regulations happens in football, too.

8. Offensive linemen wear hand pads matching the color of their opponents' jerseys to make holding more difficult to spot, and footballs are slightly deflated to make it tough on opposing kickers.

9. Even a gentleman's game like golf has outlaws always experimenting with "hot" balls and with specially grooved clubs.

Exercise 5

In your own words, complete the following sentences adapted from Exercise 4. Notice that the sentences have been changed somewhat; so even though you will need the information from Exercise 4, you may need to change the wording to keep the structures parallel.

1. All sports, but especially _____, are subject to controversy about cheating.

2. Nowadays both athletes and _____ in baseball like to play detective and _____ out whodunit with what.

3. Hitters invent new ways to hit the ball farther, so pitchers _____ _____.

4. First we had lively balls, and now _____ _____.

5. Cheating controversies in the major leagues are not really new, for _____.

6. Supposedly, Whitey Ford wore a diamond ring to scuff up baseballs, and _____.

7. In football, too, players cheat subtly or _____ _____.

8. a. Offensive linemen wear hand pads to match the color of their opponents' jerseys, so it _____ _____.

    b. Footballs are slightly deflated, so opposing kickers _____ _____.

9. Even in golf, supposedly a gentleman's game, outlaws experiment

with "hot" balls and _____.

Exercise 6

Write five sentences about a problem in a sport you know about. Use a coordinator in each sentence and be sure to keep items parallel.

_____

_____

_____

_____

_____

_____

_____

_____

PUNCTUATION RULES FOR COORDINATORS

As you have probably noticed in the examples and exercises, we don't always use a comma with coordinators. We use commas only when main clauses or more than two items are joined.

Joining *Two* Clauses, Phrases, or Words

When coordinators join two main clauses (each with its own subject and complete verb), we usually use a comma before the coordinator.

Comma

JOHN WENT TO SCHOOL, ⟨⟨but⟩⟩ MARY STAYED HOME.

⟨⟨Either⟩⟩ JOHN WENT TO SCHOOL, ⟨⟨or⟩⟩ HE WENT TO THE LIBRARY.

⟨⟨Not only⟩⟩ DID I READ THE MATERIAL, ⟨⟨but also⟩⟩ I MEMORIZED IT.

When coordinators join two dependent clauses, phrases, or words, we usually do not use a comma.

no comma

John stayed home BECAUSE HE WANTED TO STUDY ⟨⟨and⟩⟩ BECAUSE HE HAD A LOT OF READING TO DO.

Mary STUDIED HARD ⟨⟨yet⟩⟩ FAILED THE TEST.

⟨⟨Both⟩⟩ JOHN ⟨⟨and⟩⟩ MARY are at school.

⟨⟨Neither⟩⟩ JOHN ⟨⟨nor⟩⟩ MARY was at home.

However, we do use a comma before *but* or *yet* when expressing a strong contrast, even if no main clause follows.

comma

The dress was EXPENSIVE, ⟨⟨but⟩⟩ NOT WELL MADE.

Exercise 7

Set off coordinators with ⟨⟨double angle brackets⟩⟩. Place a comma before these conjunctions if they join main clauses.

1. Free education wasn't available in ancient times but military service was a possible yet lengthy alternative.

2. One could attain an education but there were no "official" schools.

3. Neither were there academic administrators nor were there certified teachers.

4. When a scholarly minded person had established himself in a private house and enrolled a handful of pupil-boarders, he would be considered a schoolmaster.

5. The school was usually a one-person operation for the schoolmaster taught all subjects to the students, all of whom were boys.

6. Not only was an education rare for girls but it was also given in a different manner.

7. Girls could be educated but they were taught at home by live-in tutors.

8. Boys also left home for military service yet their term of service was hardly an incentive to join.

9. A full hitch in the Roman army or navy meant twenty to twenty-six years so a young man made a lifetime commitment.

10. Either the respect associated with this profession attracted the young men or the fair pay was an incentive to enlist; certainly, the length of service couldn't have been the incentive.

Joining Three or More Clauses, Phrases, or Words

If more than two main or dependent clauses, phrases, or words are joined, there is a comma between each item and usually a comma and a coordinating conjunction between the last two items. This is known as **items in a series**.

JOHN, PETER, ⟨⟨and⟩⟩ MARY went to the movies.

Please explain WHAT YOUR PLANS ARE, WHERE YOU ARE GOING, ⟨⟨and⟩⟩ HOW YOU ARE GOING TO TRAVEL.

JOHN WENT TO THE MOVIES, MARY WENT SHOPPING, PETER STUDIED, ⟨⟨but⟩⟩ I SLEPT.

X, Y, ⟨⟨and⟩⟩ Z are letters frequently used in algebra.

Note: Even though some writers omit the conjunction or comma before the last item of the series, most English teachers prefer to put the comma and the conjunction there.

Exercise 8

Put commas where necessary in the following sentences. Remember all punctuation rules covered in this chapter.

1. In the fantasy world of television, technology rebuilds human bodies with wires computers and bionic powers.

2. In the modern world of medical science, the line between fiction and fact becomes thinner every day for technology teamed with medicine has given us miracles.

3. Bone grafts can repair broken or crushed bones artificial joints can relieve the pain of arthritis metal rods can straighten out the curvature of spines and tiny metal plates add strength to ruptured discs.

4. Artificial parts can replace nearly every human appendage including shoulders arms hands or toes; electrodes inside the artificial part respond to nerve signals remaining in the patient's muscles.

5. Using a plasticized rubber, doctors can sculpt facial features—such as noses eye sockets ears or cheeks—for patients who have been disfigured by cancer or accidents.

6. They are also able to fashion upper and lower jaws eyelids parts of the skull and palates.

7. Medical researchers are already striving to develop artificial blood (known as *flusol*) now that they have had successes with artificial hearts synthetic eye lenses ear implants and most recently knee ligaments.

8. Surgeons rely more and more heavily on synthetic, bio-acceptable metals to replace or to rebuild vital parts of the human body so the possibility of a real bionic man or woman is getting closer every day.

Exercise 9

Combine the following short, choppy sentences into a logical and meaningful sentence containing coordinators and/or subordinators. Try to avoid repeating the same words, keep items parallel, and punctuate correctly.

1. The roly-poly giant panda is not a bear.
   The roly-poly giant panda is not a raccoon.
   The roly-poly giant panda has traits of both.

   _____

   _____

   _____

2. Pandas are designed to be meat eaters.
   Pandas have to survive on a diet of bamboo.

   _____

   _____

3. The panda's native habitat is a bamboo forest in China.
   In the panda's native habitat, wildlife is scarce.
   Wildlife is difficult for the relatively slow panda to catch.

   _____

   _____

   _____

   _____

4. Only bamboo can provide an easy food source, especially in winter.
   Bamboo leaves remain fresh throughout the year.
   Bamboo leaves remain green throughout the year.

   _____

   _____

   _____

5. The panda's stomach is designed to digest meat.
   The panda is unable to digest bamboo efficiently.
   The panda obtains only a few nutrients from bamboo.

   _____

   _____

   _____

6. The panda has to eat 650 shoots of bamboo daily.
   The panda has to eat 85 pounds of bamboo daily.

   _____

   _____

   _____

7. The panda swallows the leaves to obtain protein, digestible carbohydrates, and minerals.
   The panda swallows the stalks to obtain protein, digestible carbohydrates, and minerals.

   _____

   _____

   _____

Summary of Punctuation Rules with Coordinators	
If the Conjunction Joins:	**We Use:**
1. Two main clauses	Comma before the coordinator
2. Two dependent clauses, phrases, or words	No comma (unless a strong contrast is expressed)
3. Three or more items	Comma after each item except the last one

Exercise 10

Illustrate each of the preceding punctuation rules with your own examples.

1. _____

_____

2. _____

_____

3. _____

_____

Exercise 11

Punctuate the following passage correctly. Capitalize when beginning a new sentence. Do not change the punctuation already present.

The idea that numbers not only are a means of enumeration but are also sacred perfect friendly lucky or evil goes back to antiquity in the sixth century B.C., Pythagoras (who first realized the square of the hypotenuse of a right triangle always equals the sum of the squares of its sides) made a religion out of numbers this religion is known as numerology.

In numerology the number twelve has always represented completeness for there are twelve months of the year twelve signs of the zodiac twelve hours of light and darkness in a day twelve gods of Olympus in Greek mythology twelve tribes of Israel twelve apostles of Jesus and so on the number thirteen exceeds twelve by only one so the number lies beyond completeness and is restless to the point of being evil.

USING SUBORDINATORS AND COORDINATORS CORRECTLY

As you may have noticed, some subordinators and coordinators have similar meanings. Be aware that they may have different word order and punctuation patterns.

John was sick, *but* he went to school.
Although John was sick, he went to school.
John went to school *although* he was sick.
Because John was sick, he stayed home.
John stayed home, *for* he was sick.
John was sick, *so* he stayed home.

Exercise 12

To practice using logical coordinators and subordinators, fill in the blanks with one of the following words: *and, but, or, for, nor, although,* or *because.* Make sure your sentences are meaningful. You may want to look back at Exercise 7.

1. _____ free education wasn't available in ancient times, military service was a possible _____ lengthy alternative.

2. _____ there were no "official" schools, one could attain an education.

3. There were neither academic administrators _____ certified teachers.

4. To be considered a teacher, a scholarly minded person simply established himself in a private house _____ enrolled a handful of pupil-boarders.

5. _____ the schoolmaster taught all subjects to the students, the school was usually a one-person operation.

6. For girls an education was rare _____ given in a different manner, _____ they were taught at home by live-in tutors.

7. Boys also left home for military service, _____ their term of service was hardly an incentive to join.

8. _____ a full hitch in the Roman army or navy meant twenty to twenty-six years, a young man made a lifetime commitment when he joined.

9. The young men must have been attracted by either the respect associated with this profession _____ the fair pay; certainly, the length of service couldn't have been the incentive.

Exercise 13

After setting off ⟨subordinators⟩ and ⟨⟨coordinators⟩⟩ with single and double angle brackets, respectively, punctuate the passage. Capitalize when beginning a new sentence. (Some commas have already been added for you.)

The roly-poly giant panda, which looks like a black-and-white walking toy, is neither a bear nor raccoon but has traits of both although pandas are designed to be meat eaters they have to survive on a diet of bamboo in their native habitat, a bamboo forest in China, wildlife is scarce and difficult for the relatively slow panda to catch only bamboo can provide an easy food source, especially in winter for its leaves remain fresh and green throughout the year since the panda's stomach is designed to digest meat the panda is unable to digest bamboo efficiently and obtains only a few nutrients from it yet the panda has either to eat 650 shoots or 85 pounds of bamboo daily or to starve the panda swallows both the leaves and the stalks to obtain protein, digestible carbohydrates, and minerals.

Exercise 14

Using the connectors given in parentheses, combine the following sentences into one longer, meaningful, and logical sentence. Remember to avoid repeating words, to keep items parallel, and to punctuate correctly.

1.   Friday the thirteenth is doubly potent.
   (because)   Friday the thirteenth draws on the evil power of the number thirteen.
   (and)   Friday the thirteenth draws on Friday's reputation as a day of bad luck.

   _____

   _____

   _____

2.   The superstitious believe the day to be a time for endings, not beginnings.
   (for)   Christ was crucified on a Friday.

   _____

   _____

   _____

3.   Perhaps because of this association, Friday was reserved
            for executions until the end of the nineteenth century.
(and)   Perhaps because of this association, Friday was known
            as Hangman's Day.

_____

_____

_____

4.   It has been claimed that Friday is no day to get
            married.
            It has been claimed that Friday is no day to embark on
            a journey.
            It has been claimed that Friday is no day to move into a
            new house.
(or)   It has been claimed that Friday is no day to start a new
            job.

_____

_____

_____

5. (neither)   Cutting your nails on Friday is not advised.
   (nor)   Turning over a mattress on Friday is not advised.

_____

_____

_____

6.   Some of these activities seem to have about as much to
            do with beginnings as with endings.
(yet)   These superstitions persist.

_____

_____

_____

SUBJECT–VERB AGREEMENT WITH COMPOUND SUBJECTS

Remember that you must examine the meaning of the conjunction to see whether a compound subject (circled here) is singular or plural. When the conjunction expresses addition of persons or things, the subject is, of course, plural.

Both (John) *and* (Mary) attend a university.

When the conjunction expresses a choice, the first verb agrees with the nearer subject.

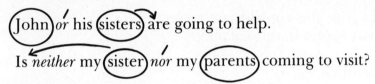

(John) *or* his (sisters) are going to help.

Is *neither* my (sister) *nor* my (parents) coming to visit?

Exercise 15

Find the subject in each sentence and fill in the blank with the correct present tense form of the verb given in parentheses.

[1]Soundproofing _____ (be) often a necessary type of insulation. [2]Either sound-absorbing or sound-deadening materials _____ (be) placed in or on walls, ceilings, and furniture to reduce echoes. [3]Reducing objectionable echoes _____ (help) to improve sound quality. [4]For example, the quality of a speaker's voice and the clarity of music _____ (be) improved by reducing these echoes. [5]Hair felt covered with burlap, perforated fiberboard, corkboard, or a special type of acoustical plaster and tile _____ (be) often used. [6]Heavy cloth curtains and upholstered furniture _____ (be) also effective. [7]Each of these materials _____ (work) to reduce echoes

because each _____ (contain) a large number of small air passages. [8]As sound waves _____ (penetrate) these passages, a part of their energy _____ (be) converted by friction into heat energy, and the volume of sound and echoes _____ (be) reduced.

SUMMARY

Fill in the blanks with the appropriate response, to show your understanding of the principles in this chapter.

1. Know the coordinators:

    a. List the seven coordinating conjunctions: _____

    _____

    b. List the four sets of correlative conjunctions: _____

    _____

2. Explain "parallel structure" in your own words: _____

    _____

    _____

3. Give examples of parallel structures by creating "partners" for the

    ones given.

    Neither <u>this</u>   nor   _____

    <u>swimming</u>   or   _____

    <u>at the bank</u>   and   _____

    <u>what you say</u>   but   _____

4. Put commas wherever they belong in the following.

MAIN CLAUSE **and** MAIN CLAUSE.

PHRASE **but** PHRASE

WORD **or** WORD

DEPENDENT CLAUSE **and** DEPENDENT CLAUSE

MAIN CLAUSE MAIN CLAUSE **but** MAIN CLAUSE.

DEPENDENT CLAUSE DEPENDENT CLAUSE **and**
DEPENDENT CLAUSE

PHRASE PHRASE **or** PHRASE

WORD WORD **and** WORD

Summary Exercise

Capitalize and punctuate the following passage. (Some periods and commas have already been added for you.)

Some names trigger a positive response when we hear them but others we tend to associate with negative qualities we may find such bits of knowledge in Christopher P. Andersen's 1987 book entitled *The Baby Boomer's Name Game* (New York: Perigee Books) the book contains everything anyone has ever wanted to know about names: history etymology (origin and derivation) trends effectiveness steps to change a name legally names of famous people who have changed their names bizarre names and the "real" meanings of names.

Andersen claims a person's name can make the difference between being successful or unsuccessful criminal or law-abiding social or unsocial popular or unpopular and even intelligent or unintelligent studies and polls indicating the characteristics most commonly associated with a particular name were the source for his "real" meanings of 1000 listed names although the name Michael etymologically means "godlike" the "real" meaning, according to Andersen, is "very popular and extremely manly but surprisingly not too dynamic" the name Albert means "noble and bright" etymologically but the "real" definition is "not terribly well-liked and lazy."

Andersen claims parents should carefully choose the names they give their offspring for names can affect every aspect of life from his data, he concludes that women with "sexy" sounding names like Michelle and Jacqueline are less likely to get hired or promoted in his book he also asserts that behavior problems occur more frequently among people with "peculiar" names and that people with such names are much more likely to commit crimes or suffer from serious mental disorders.

People sometimes attain fame and fortune by exchanging an unusual name for one more ordinary yet others achieve the same by doing the opposite did you know Lee Iaccoca's first name was Lido how many of you realize Arnold Dorsey is known worldwide as Engelbert Humperdinck.

WRITING PRACTICE

Write ten sentences or a short passage about one or more of the following topics, using the guidelines of your teacher. Make sure you use coordinators correctly.

1. an unusual animal

2. a problem in professional sports

3. your own experiences in the military, at boarding school, at summer camp, or with tutors

4. your lucky number and why you consider it to be so lucky

5. what parents should consider in choosing a name for their child

CHAPTER 9
Main Clauses Joined with Semicolons

In Chapter 8 you saw that equal elements such as sentences, clauses, phrases, and words may be joined with coordinators. In this chapter you will see that one of these equal elements—main clauses—may also be joined with semicolons.

SEMICOLONS

As you saw in Chapter 8, you may use a coordinator to join main clauses. Another way to show that two main clauses are closely related in meaning is to join them with a semicolon.

A **semicolon** has the force of a coordinator and indicates that two main clauses are logically related in meaning.

The washing machine broke; she called the repair man.
The washing machine broke, ⟨⟨so⟩⟩ she called the repair man.

Tom was drunk; his friend realized it too late.
Tom was drunk, ⟨⟨but⟩⟩ his friend realized it too late.

Note: The main clause following the semicolon does not start with a capital letter.

Exercise 1

In the following, if the sentences are logically related, replace the period with a semicolon and the capital letter with a lowercase letter.

1. Babies are born with the sense of touch. The sense of smell develops

   immediately after birth.

2. A fly is not a fly, nor is a glowworm a worm. They are both beetles.

3. Unidentical twins are called fraternal twins. Quadruplets occur only once in every million births.

4. Halloween is a popular holiday in the United States. Children especially enjoy it.

5. School chalk is not chalk. It is plaster of Paris.

6. Water literally runs off a duck's back. It takes seven billion fog particles to make a teaspoon of water.

7. The weasel, a small reddish-brown animal, turns white in frigid, cold climates. The cheetah is the world's speediest four-legged animal.

8. Celluloid was the first plastic. It was used to make billiard balls.

Exercise 2

Add periods, semicolons, and commas where necessary.

Most scientists think that our earth and the moon were formed at the same time, about 4500 million years ago because the moon is much closer to us than the sun its size is deceptive its surface area is actually only about the size of Australia the moon is a dry and lifeless world there is no air to breathe no rain or snow no wind nor clouds at midday the temperature is scorching the sun blasts heat from a black sky night temperatures on the moon drop quickly to a terrifying −220° Fahrenheit the lowest temperature on earth is −126°

Exercise 3

Join the following groups of sentences into one sentence with semicolons, or a comma and a coordinator. Do *not* use more than one semicolon per sentence.

1. Animals have specific characteristics that help them gather the food they need. Monkeys have nimble fingers for plucking fruit. The giraffe's long neck enables it to reach the leaves atop trees.

   _____

   _____

   _____

   _____

   _____

2. Some animals, like bears, are *omnivores*. They eat both meat and plants.

   _____

   _____

3. Animals that eat only meat are called *carnivores*. These species have special teeth for chewing up muscle. These species have stomachs designed to digest meat.

   _____

   _____

   _____

   _____

   _____

4. Zoo animals and tame housepets must eat on a daily basis. Wild carnivores, however, eat whatever they kill one day. They rest for a day or two before looking for more.

_____

_____

_____

_____

5. Carnivores are often specially equipped to be night hunters. They usually have large eyes and a keen sense of smell.

_____

_____

_____

6. People forget that birds like the eagle and the owl are carnivorous. In one year an owl can consume 200 mice, 450 other small rodents, 400 birds, 100 frogs, 250 worms, and 150 snails.

_____

_____

_____

_____

7. *Herbivores* are animals that eat plants. Most herbivores need daylight to seek their food.

_____

_____

8. A big plant-eating animal has to spend a lot of time eating. It must eat as much in food every day as it weighs. Smaller herbivores, like rabbits, hunt for food only at dawn and dusk to avoid their enemies.

_____

_____

_____

Exercise 4

Write five sentences of your own about animals, using a semicolon correctly in each sentence.

1. _____

_____

_____

2. _____

_____

_____

3. _____

_____

_____

4. _____

_____

_____

5. _____

_____

_____

CONJUNCTIVE ADVERBS

Sometimes the semicolon by itself does not make clear how the ideas in two main clauses or sentences are related.

Tom was drunk; his friend realized it too late.

The washing machine broke; she called the repair man.

To make the logical relationship between the main clauses clearer, you may add a special kind of adverb along with the semicolon (or after a period).

Tom was drunk; *however*, his friend realized it too late.

The washing machine broke. *Therefore*, she called the repair man.

These special kinds of adverbs that join ideas are called **conjunctive adverbs**. Just like coordinators and subordinators they indicate that you add ideas, contrast ideas, show result, or show time relationship.

Add ideas
John had to study hard for his test.
Furthermore, he had to finish his term paper.

Show result
John was at school. *Therefore*, he was not at home yesterday.

Show contrast
John went to school; Mary, *however*, stayed at home.

Show time relationship
Mary studied for her physics test; *then* she took a break.

Exercise 5

Complete the following sentences in your own words. You may look at Exercise 3 for ideas. Keep in mind the meaning that the conjunctive adverb expresses.

1. The giraffe has a long neck; therefore, _____

   _____.

2. Carnivores have special teeth for chewing up muscle. Furthermore,

   _____.

3. Wild carnivores eat whatever they kill one day; then _____

_____.

4. Carnivores usually have large eyes and a keen sense of smell. There-

fore, _____.

5. People forget that birds like the eagle and the owl are carnivorous.

However, _____

_____.

Meanings of Conjunctive Adverbs

There are many more conjunctive adverbs besides *furthermore, however, then,* and *therefore.* Many of them are similar in meaning, but some have very specific, special meanings. In the following listing, conjunctive adverbs are grouped according to meaning.

Addition: *moreover, besides, in addition, furthermore, also*

I write my parents every week; *moreover,* I call them once a month.

Similarity: *similarly, likewise*

Sam didn't do well in math; *similarly,* he did very poorly in chemistry.

Fact to Support Statement: *in fact, indeed*

Emily is a superior student. *In fact,* she has a 4.00 average.

Fact to Contradict Statement: *actually*

He looks honest; *actually,* he is a thief.

Concession (something different from what one normally expects): *however, on the other hand, nevertheless, still*

This car is old; *however*, it runs well.

Contrast: *on the contrary, in contrast*

I thought he had no money; *on the contrary*, he has enough to buy a new stereo.

Result: *consequently, therefore, as a result, thus*

Some ethnic food is very spicy. *Consequently*, I find it irritates my ulcers.

Negative Result: *otherwise*

You must put on a warm coat; *otherwise*, you will catch a cold.

Time: *next, then, later, meanwhile, first, secondly, finally, at last*

Boil the water. *Next* add the rice.

Example: *for example, for instance*

There are many ways to avoid wasting time; *for example*, you could establish a schedule.

Paraphrase: *in other words*

Attending class is mandatory; *in other words*, a student is penalized for absences.

Summary: *in summary, in conclusion*

In German, "kinder" is the word for children and "garten" for garden; *in summary*, kindergarten means "children's garden."

Exercise 6

Carefully consider the logical relationship between the main clauses or sentences in each of the following pairs. Then circle the more logical conjunctive adverb.

1. Amber becomes magnetic through friction; (therefore/moreover) after it has been rubbed, it draws feathers and other light objects to it.

2. People in ancient cultures were aware of these magnetic properties; (however/in fact) they made amber love amulets to attract a lover.

3. Friction can also make amber give off sparks. (Moreover/Therefore) the Greeks named it *elektron* from the word *elektor*, "the beaming sun."

4. This word passed into Latin as *electrum* and turned into the adjective *electricus*; (in summary/later) it evolved into our words *electric* and *electricity*.

5. In the first century Pliny the Elder noted that some fish gave off quite a charge. (In other words/In fact) the electric ray or torpedo fish could give a spear fisherman a nasty shock.

6. Many people through the ages commented on "electric" animals; (therefore/however) little was known about electricity until comparatively modern times. (Therefore/However) the origins of most other words used in reference to electricity are much more recent.

7. Many recent terms are names of scientists; (similarly/for instance) James Watt (1736–1819), the inventor of the steam engine, gave us the term *watt*.

8. The term *volt* derived from the famous Italian physicist Alessandro Volta (1745–1827); (then/likewise) the word *ohm* came from G. S. Ohm, a German physicist (1781–1854).

9. In 1881, *ampere* became the term referring to the current sent through one ohm by one volt; (however/in other words) again the name of a scientist, Andre Marie Ampere, was used for a term referring to electricity.

Exercise 7

Write five sentences of your own about electricity, using one of the following conjunctive adverbs correctly in each sentence.

1. therefore: _____

   _____

2. moreover: _____

   _____

3. in fact: _____

   _____

4. for example: _____

   _____

5. however: _____

   _____

Punctuating with Conjunctive Adverbs

Remember that two main clauses may be joined with a semicolon. We must place the semicolon *between* the two main clauses, no matter where the conjunctive adverb (between braces here) is.

John went to school; {*however*}, Mary stayed home.

John went to school; Mary, {*however*}, stayed home.

John went to school; Mary stayed home, {*however*}.

As you can see, a conjunctive adverb may occur at the beginning, in the middle, or at the end of a main clause or sentence. Notice that a comma is placed before and/or after the conjunctive adverb.

Exercise 8

Put a semicolon *between* the main clauses. Then add commas where necessary.

1. Alabaster is a stone that looks like marble however it is much softer and is used for both statues and vases.

2. There are two kinds of alabaster. There is a white or delicately shaded variety moreover there is a semitransparent variety with a pearly luster.

3. The first variety, a kind of gypsum, is chiefly found in Italy furthermore it can be found in Spain and England.

4. The other variety is called *Oriental alabaster* or *onyx marble* it is in fact a calcium carbonate deposited as stalagmites in caves along the Mediterranean Sea.

5. This variety is much harder than the other it was therefore often used in sculpture by the ancient Greeks and Romans.

USING DIFFERENT SENTENCE PATTERNS

As you already know, different types of connectors may have similar meanings. For example, the following groups of sentences express similar meanings but give different kinds of emphasis.

John was sick. He went to school.

Although John was sick, he went to school.
John was sick, *but* he went to school.
John was sick; *however*, he went to school.

John was sick. He stayed home.

Because John was sick, he stayed home.
John stayed home, *for* he was sick.

John was sick, *so* he stayed home.
John was sick; *therefore*, he stayed home.

Remember that each type of connector has its own punctuation conventions. Here we will briefly review them.

Subordinator:　　　　⟨Because⟩ John was sick, *comma* he stayed home.

John stayed home ⟨because⟩ *no comma* he was sick.

Coordinator:　　　　John stayed home, ⟨⟨for⟩⟩ *comma* he was sick.

John was sick ⟨⟨but⟩⟩ *no comma* went to school anyway.

Conjunctive adverb:　John was sick; {therefore}, *semicolon comma* he stayed home.

John was sick. He decided, therefore, to stay *period comma comma* home.

John was sick; he went to school, {however}. *semicolon comma*

Exercise 9

To practice your sentence-combining skills with different connectors, rewrite the following sentences with the connectors indicated in ⟨angle brackets⟩ and {braces}. Be sure to punctuate and capitalize correctly.

1. ⟨when⟩ She marries for the first time. An American bride usually wears a white gown.

_____

_____

2. Popular tradition is that white suggests the purity of the bride. {however} The original symbolism of wedding white had to do not with purity but with joy.

_____

_____

_____

_____

3. In Japan white is a color not for joy. ⟨⟨but⟩⟩ White is a color for mourning. ⟨because⟩ The Japanese bride's white gown symbolizes that a girl is "dead to her parents." ⟨when⟩ She marries into her husband's family.

_____

_____

_____

_____

_____

4. Not all cultures favor white for wedding gowns. {for example} Norwegians favor green. ⟨⟨and⟩⟩ Spanish peasants often wear black to their weddings.

_____

_____

_____

_____

5. The eighteenth century colonists associated red with rebellion. ⟨⟨so⟩⟩ Red became a popular color for bridal gowns during the American Revolution.

_____

_____

_____

_____

6. Weddings certainly are celebrations that follow traditions rigidly. {however} Most of us don't realize how much these traditions owe to past beliefs and practices.

_____

_____

_____

_____

7. ⟨just as⟩ Early cultures scattered wheat at a wedding to symbolize fruitfulness. We often throw rice over newlyweds.

_____

_____

_____

_____

8. Moroccan Jews may throw raw eggs at the bride. {of course} The fact that hens lay many eggs makes this too a symbol of fertility.

_____

_____

_____

_____

9. The earliest wedding cake probably was a loaf of barley bread in Roman times. ⟨⟨but⟩⟩ The groom did not feed it to his bride. {instead} He broke some of it over his bride's head to symbolize that the wife must submit to her spouse.

_____

_____

_____

_____

10. Today the bridal couple kisses. ⟨when⟩ They cut their wedding cake. ⟨⟨but⟩⟩ The bride and groom in early Anglo-Saxon times tried to kiss over a mound or stack of small, hard biscuits in the belief that this would ensure a prosperous life.

_____

_____

_____

_____

_____

_____

Exercise 10

To practice using different sentence patterns, combine the same sets of sentences with the connectors indicated. The first one has been done for you.

1. Academy Awards are given each year by the Academy of Motion Picture Arts and Sciences for the best performances. They are given for other work involved in making motion pictures.

   a. (and)

   Academy Awards are given each year by the Academy of Motion Picture Arts and Sciences for the best performance and for other work involved in making motion pictures.

b. (also)

_____

_____

_____

_____

2. The Academy has numerous branches (actors, art directors, cine-matographers, directors, film editors, musicians, producers, public relations, short subjects, sound, writers, and so on). Each branch is represented on its Board of Directors.

a. (because)

_____

_____

_____

_____

b. (so)

_____

_____

_____

_____

3. Over twenty-five awards are made each year, for best motion picture, best actor and actress in leading and supporting roles, best direction, and so on. Awards are made for technical advances.

a. (and)

_____

_____

_____

_____

b. (moreover)

_____

_____

_____

4. Special awards are sometimes given for contributions that do not fit any particular classification. The Irving Thalberg Award may be given for outstanding contributions to movie-making over a period of years.

a. (so)

_____

_____

_____

_____

b. (for example)

_____

_____

_____

_____

_____

5. Academy members in each branch nominate their colleagues for awards. All Academy members vote to select the prizewinners.

   a. (after)

   _____

   _____

   _____

   b. (then)

   _____

   _____

   _____

6. Every year the public is curious to see who won the awards. A television broadcast of the Academy Awards is eagerly awaited.

   a. (because)

   _____

   _____

   _____

   b. (therefore)

   _____

   _____

   _____

7. Each prize is a little statue of a man called an "Oscar." These statues have not always been called Oscars.

a. (although)

_____

_____

_____

b. (but)

_____

_____

_____

8. Some people believe that Margaret Herrick, an early executive director of the Academy, was the first to nickname the little man "Oscar." The statue reminded her of her uncle.

a. (for)

_____

_____

_____

_____

b. (because)

_____

_____

_____

_____

9. Other people say that Bette Davis, one of the first actresses to win one of these statues, said that the statue looked like her husband, Oscar. She gave it that nickname.

a. (so)

_____

_____

_____

_____

b. (therefore)

_____

_____

_____

10. No matter who gave the name, it has stuck. Winning an Academy Award has been known as "winning an Oscar" ever since.

a. (in other words)

_____

_____

_____

b. (so)

_____

_____

_____

SUMMARY

Fill in the blanks with the appropriate response, to show your understanding of the principles in this chapter. Where indicated, write a sentence of your own to illustrate those principles.

1. What does a semicolon between two main clauses indicate? _____

   _____

   Illustrate with an example: _____

   _____

   _____

2. Why do we sometimes use conjunctive adverbs to join two main

   clauses or sentences? _____

   _____

   Illustrate with an example: _____

   _____

   _____

3. Where can conjunctive adverbs occur? _____

   _____

   _____

4. Punctuate the following correctly. (Note the capital and lowercase letters.)

   John was sick however he went to school.
   John was sick However he went to school.
   John was sick he went to school however.
   John was sick He went to school however.
   John went to school his brother however stayed home.
   John went to school His brother however stayed home.

5. Name *two* other conjunctive adverbs that are synonyms for each of the following.

therefore: _____   _____

in addition: _____   _____

however: _____   _____

Summary Exercise

Using information from the passage, complete the sentences that follow. Your answers should be both true according to the information and grammatically correct.

Radar uses pulses of radio waves in an echo system for locating objects and measuring how far away they are. If you shout toward a cliff, the sound of your voice moves to the cliff, strikes it, and then bounces back as an echo. A radar transmitter sends out a pulse of radio waves instead of a sound. If the pulse strikes an object in its path, it bounces back as an echo, which can be picked up by a radio receiver.

A radar transmitter sends out pulses in a narrow beam. The beam reaches out like a probing finger in one direction at a time, so that if an echo comes back we can tell which direction it came from. To change the direction in which a beam travels, the radar antenna keeps turning. In this way, it scans the space surrounding it.

It takes time for a radar pulse to travel. It travels with the speed of light, which is 186,000 miles per second. When a pulse strikes an object and comes back as an echo, there is an interval between the time that the pulse leaves the antenna and the time that it comes back. The length of this interval is the amount of time it takes for the pulse to make a round trip from the antenna to the object and back again. By measuring this interval, we can calculate how far away the object is.

1. Radar uses pulses of radio waves in an echo system not only for

   _____ but also _____

   _____.

2. An echo is a sound that has bounced back. For example, _____

   _____.

3. Similarly, a radar transmitter _____

_____ .

4. A pulse of radio waves strikes an object in its path. Then _____

_____ .

5. A radar transmitter sends out pulses in a narrow beam in one direction at a time; therefore, _____ .

6. The radar antenna keeps turning to change the direction in which a beam travels; in other words, _____

_____ .

7. _____ , for it travels with the speed of light; therefore, _____

_____ .

8. The length of this interval is the amount of time it takes for the pulse to make a round trip from the antenna to the object and back again; in other words, _____ .

WRITING PRACTICE

Write ten sentences or a short passage about one or more of the following topics, using the guidelines of your teacher. Make sure you use semicolons and conjunctive adverbs correctly.

1. what you imagine the first city in space will look like

2. life without electricity

3. an unusual wedding

4. the person that you feel should win an Academy Award this year (pick a category)

5. the qualities you look for in a movie

REVIEW
Avoiding Fragments, Comma Splices, Fused Sentences, and Other Problems

In Chapters 7 and 8 you learned to recognize main clauses, dependent clauses, and phrases. You also saw how these different structures may be joined. Here we will first review the materials from Chapter 7, then review Chapters 8 and 9.

Remember that a structure lacking a main clause is *not* a sentence. In writing, a sentence starts with a capital letter and ends with a period, exclamation mark, or question mark.

A dependent clause or phrase is only a *part* of a sentence and must be attached to a main clause. Therefore, you should not start a dependent clause or phrase with a capital letter and end it with a period.

A dependent clause or a phrase that is punctuated as if it were a sentence is called a **fragment**. The next five "incorrect" examples are fragments.

COMMON ERRORS

Writing a Sentence Without a Complete Verb

A structure must have a complete verb to be a sentence.

Incorrect: The boy working here.
Correct: The boy is working here.

Writing a Sentence Without a Subject

A sentence must have a subject. The subject is *never* found inside a prepositional phrase.

Incorrect: By working hard helped him to pass the course.
Correct: Working hard helped him to pass the course.

Writing a Sentence Without a Main Clause

A sentence must have a main clause (one that does not start with a subordinator).

Incorrect: When I came to work.
Correct: When I came to work, I started writing a report.
Correct: I came to work.

Incorrect: The girl who works where I work.
Correct: The girl works where I work.
Correct: The girl who works where I work won a trip to the Bahamas.

Using a Semicolon Other Than to Separate Two Main Clauses

Semicolons function very much like periods. Therefore, it is incorrect to set off a dependent clause or a phrase with a semicolon. Make sure a semicolon goes between two main clauses.

Incorrect: Although I was tired; I went to work.
Correct: Although I was tired, I went to work.
Correct: I was tired; I went to work anyway.

Incorrect: I hate to do housework; especially mopping the floors.
Correct: I hate to do housework, especially mopping the floors.
Correct: I hate to do housework; I especially hate mopping the floors.

Incorrect: She sings beautifully; although, she can't dance.
Correct: She sings beautifully, although she can't dance.

Confusing the Use of Introductory Words

Remember that words may have different functions. *That, where, when, what, how,* and so on often act as subordinators to introduce a dependent clause, but not always. Other times they may function as a pronoun or question word in an independent clause.

Incorrect:	T̶h̶at he has a good idea.
Correct:	That is a good idea.

Incorrect:	W̶h̶en you are leaving.
Correct:	When are you leaving?

EDITING EXERCISE 1

Set off each fragment in the following essay with (parentheses). Then rewrite the passage correcting the fragments. To correct a fragment, you can:

a. Hook the phrase or dependent clause to a main clause.

b. Delete, add, or change words to make a phrase a sentence.

c. Take the subordinator off the dependent clause to make it a main clause.

Choose the method that is the most meaningful in each situation.

¹To a greater or lesser degree, everyone lies. ²Lies range from complimenting a friend's new—but ugly—dress to misstating facts before congressional committees. ³Such as at the recent Iran/Contra-arms-sale hearings. ⁴Most of the lies we tell are small ones. ⁵On the level of "I'm feeling fine, thanks." ⁶But for some people, lying becomes a way of life. ⁷Lying at high levels of business and government is often risky. ⁸And,

once revealed, can have serious consequences. [9]According to Dr. Beverly Palmer, a professor of psychology at California State University.

[10]Sometimes liars—especially pathological ones—can be convincing, but their deceptions can be detected. [11]Palmer asserts there are ways to tell when someone is lying. [12]For instance, we can look for these clues. [13]First, absence of typical gestures during speech. [14]For example, someone who uses a lot of spontaneous gestures will sometimes keep his hands still or behind his back when lying. [15]Second, a discrepancy between facial expression and body posture. [16]If you try to hide anger while being Mr. Nice-Guy, the anger may be exposed because your fists are clenched while you have a calm look, Palmer notes. [17]Third, a discrepancy in the facial expression alone, such as smiling through tightly closed lips. [18]"Or perhaps the liar has a wide smile plastered on his face while he is looking away from you," Palmer says.

[19]No one can really recognize all the specific clues. [20]"You may just have a feeling that something isn't quite right," she says. [21]"What isn't quite right is that the verbal message doesn't quite match the nonverbal message."

[22]Lying falls into two categories. [23]The first, Palmer claims, is falsifying information, such as inventing excuses like these: "Uh, I forget." [24]"It's in the mail." [25]"Oh, it's only my dentist's office on the phone, honey." [26]Or when a child wants to know why he has to take out the trash. [27]An adult may say that it builds character, rather than telling the child

the truth. [28]Which is that the parent doesn't want to do it herself or himself. [29]The second kind of lying is known as concealment. [30]Much of what we try to conceal is our real feelings, some flaw, or information, Palmer says. [31]An example of concealment is smiling when you are actually feeling sad or angry.

[32]Remember the saying "True honesty in human relations means saying what you mean and meaning what you say"? [33]In Palmer's view, "the concealment is not saying what you mean, and the falsification is not meaning what you say."

[34]Why do people lie? [35]Palmer feels lying is predominantly a defense mechanism. [36]"We lie when we feel insecure, scared, or we're trying to escape the consequences of our actions," she says. [37]We tell ourselves lying is a justifiable defense. [38]To protect ourselves or someone else. [39]But actually we're just shielding ourselves from the other person's angry or hurt feelings.

[40]Lying can be the most destructive force relationships can encounter. [41]Because it undermines trust. [42]In fact, some people lie because they mistrust, Palmer notes. [43]But, she adds, untruths do more than just harm relationships. [44]Individuals can wind up believing their own untruths. [45]Especially those involving concealment. [46]The danger Palmer warns us about is serious: "We can spend so much time concealing and falsifying that we can't remember the truth anymore ourselves."

In Chapters 8 and 9 you learned that equal elements may be joined with coordinators (coordinating and correlative conjunctions) and that main clauses may be joined with semicolons. You also saw that conjunctive adverbs may be used to make the logical relationship between main clauses or sentences clearer. Probably most confusing are the punctuation rules. Let's briefly review them again.

Coordinators

SENTENCE . ⟨⟨So⟩⟩ SENTENCE.
MAIN CLAUSE , ⟨⟨yet⟩⟩ MAIN CLAUSE.
DEPENDENT CLAUSE ⟨⟨and⟩⟩ DEPENDENT CLAUSE
PHRASE ⟨⟨but⟩⟩ PHRASE
WORD ⟨⟨or⟩⟩ WORD

MAIN CLAUSE , MAIN CLAUSE , ⟨⟨and⟩⟩ MAIN CLAUSE.
DEPENDENT CLAUSE , DEPENDENT CLAUSE , ⟨⟨but⟩⟩
DEPENDENT CLAUSE
PHRASE , PHRASE , ⟨⟨or⟩⟩ PHRASE
WORD , WORD , ⟨⟨nor⟩⟩ WORD

Conjunctive Adverbs

SENTENCE ; {however} , SENTENCE.
SENTENCE . {However} , SENTENCE.

SENTENCE ; SEN- , {however} , -TENCE.
SENTENCE . SEN- , {however} , -TENCE.

SENTENCE ; SENTENCE , {however}.
SENTENCE . SENTENCE , {however}.

Misusing these punctuation rules can cause comma splices and fused sentences, which are serious sentence errors. The next three examples illustrate these errors.

MORE COMMON ERRORS

Fusing Sentences

Many people write two or more main clauses in a row without a connector or punctuation mark; the result is called a **fused sentence**.

Incorrect: Bats are flying mammals ✗ they are not birds.
Correct: Bats are flying mammals; they are not birds.

Correct:	Bats are flying mammals. They are not birds.
Correct:	Bats are flying mammals, so they are not birds.
Correct:	Bats are flying mammals; consequently, they are not birds.

Joining Main Clauses by Using a Comma

Another common error, a **comma splice**, is the result of joining two or more main clauses with only a comma. Remember that a comma alone cannot join main clauses, but a semicolon can. A comma must be used before a coordinator joining the two clauses.

Incorrect:	The carrier pigeon flies at fast speeds,✗it can cover four miles in a few minutes.
Correct:	The carrier pigeon flies at fast speeds, for it can cover four miles in a few minutes.
Correct:	Because the carrier pigeon flies at fast speeds, it can cover four miles in a few minutes.
Correct:	The carrier pigeon flies at fast speeds; it can cover four miles in a few minutes.
Correct:	The carrier pigeon flies at fast speeds; therefore, it can cover four miles in a few minutes.
Correct:	The carrier piegeon flies at fast speeds. It can cover four miles in a few minutes.

Confusing Short Adverbs with Coordinators

A comma splice also results when short adverbs such as *then, thus, next, also,* and *even* are confused with coordinators.

Incorrect:	He left town,✗then his house burned down.
Correct:	He left town; then his house burned down.
Correct:	He left town, and then his house burned down.

Incorrect:	The test was very difficult,✗even Michael failed it.
Correct:	The test was very difficult; even Michael failed it.
Correct:	The test was very difficult, so even Michael failed it.

Using Coordinators to Join Nonparallel Elements

Elements that are joined with coordinators must have the same form to show parallel structure.

Incorrect: I don't like jogging or ~~to swim~~.
Correct: I don't like jogging or swimming.

Incorrect: We saw Mr. Johnson, my advisor and the man ~~who teaches math~~.
Correct: We saw Mr. Johnson, my advisor and math teacher.

Incorrect: Not only did he discover the leak but fixed it.
Correct: Not only did he discover the leak, but he ~~fixed~~ it.
Correct: He not only discovered the leak but fixed it.

Overusing *and* and the Semicolon

While trying to avoid short, choppy sentences, inexperienced writers tend to "string" sentences together with *and*s and semicolons. One way to avoid "stringy sentences" is to use the connector *and* and the semicolon sparingly.

Awkward: In the early 1900s many aviators wanted to fly nonstop across the Atlantic Ocean, and in 1919 a prize of $25,000 was offered by a New York hotel owner, and the first aviator who could fly nonstop across the Atlantic Ocean from New York to France would receive it; many fliers tried to claim the prize; in fact, a few even lost their lives in the attempt.

Better: In the early 1900s many aviators wanted to fly nonstop across the Atlantic Ocean. In 1919 a prize of $25,000 was offered by a New York hotel owner to the first aviator who could fly nonstop across the Atlantic Ocean from New York to France. Many fliers tried to claim the prize; in fact, a few even lost their lives in the attempt.

Using the Wrong Conjunctive Adverb

When inexperienced writers first start experimenting with conjunctive adverbs, they often pick one without really considering the exact meaning. Writers must understand the logical relation between the main clauses or sentences and the exact meaning of the conjunctive adverb.

Incorrect:	He asked me to help him; consequently, I did not have time.
Correct:	He asked me to help him; however, I did not have time.
Incorrect:	He is a superior student; in fact, he is a good athlete.
Correct:	He is a superior student; besides, he is a good athlete.
Correct:	He is a superior student; in fact, he has a 3.8 average.
Incorrect:	I write my parents every week; likewise, I call them once a month.
Correct:	I write my parents every week; moreover, I call them once a month.

EDITING EXERCISE 2

In the following passage, check each sentence for the errors covered in this review (including conjunctive adverbs that don't fit in meaning). Identify each error; then correct it. There is only *one* error per sentence, but *all* sentences are incorrect.

[1]In the early 1900s many aviators wanted to fly nonstop across the Atlantic Ocean; however, in 1919 a prize of $25,000 was offered by a New York hotel owner to the first aviator who could fly nonstop across the Atlantic Ocean from New York to France. [2]Many fliers tried to claim the prize a few even lost their lives in the attempt. [3]Not only was Charles Lindbergh a pilot with a dream but also with great skill. [4]Likewise, he climbed aboard *The Spirit of Saint Louis* early in the morning on May 20. [5]All he brought with him to eat and drink during the flight were five

chicken sandwiches, and a canteen of water. ⁶However, the specially built plane was heavily loaded with a huge supply of fuel for the long journey, thus the wheels just barely managed to clear the telephone wires at the end of the runway.

⁷His biggest problems were feeling drowsy and to find himself dozing off. ⁸As he reached the halfway point. ⁹After twenty-five hours in the air, he passed over a fishing boat, then he saw the coastline of Ireland on the horizon. ¹⁰Lindbergh was neither surprised nor was he terribly excited, for he was exactly where he had planned to be at that hour.

¹¹After thirty-three hours alone in the air, he had conquered the Atlantic yet he was worried that he would be in trouble with the French immigration officials. ¹²Because he had forgotten to apply for an entry visa. ¹³For example, he was surprised, relieved and excited when a cheering crowd greeted him as he landed.

WRITING ASSIGNMENTS

Write at least two pages about one or both of the following topics, using the guidelines of your teacher. Check your paper for any of the errors listed under items 1–3 on the proofreading checklist at the end of Unit 4 (p. 322).

1. Illustrate with examples or anecdotes the difference between a so-called "little white lie" and a LIE.

2. Create an imaginative account of a trip across the ocean or to another galaxy.

The Writing Process
Polishing

Suppose you start telling your story by saying simply that you were at a party last night. You may find that you have to wait a while before someone is interested enough to ask, "Well, how was it?" If you begin by saying, "You'll never believe what happened at the party I went to last night," your listeners will probably be more eager to find out. But if you say that you were outside at 4:00 A.M. last night talking to a policeman, few people will be able to resist asking why. Telling a good story means beginning the story in a way that gets your listeners' attention. The same principle applies to writing. You want the opening of your essay to interest your readers, and you do that the same way you interest your listeners when you talk: You say something or show something that is intriguing.

Let's return to that essay on friendship. In high school you probably learned to begin your essays with a thesis sentence that stated three major points. In your essay on friendship, that thesis sentence might be: Friendship means being willing to tell each other the truth, to help each other even when it's inconvenient, and to be aware of each other's problems. Such a sentence would work as a beginning, but probably few people besides your teacher will want to read more than the opening line.

So how do you make the opening interesting? In the conversation about the party, we created a picture of someone talking to the police at 4:00 A.M.—a picture that is interesting. For your essay, suppose you begin with a picture of your running into a childhood friend at O'Hare airport, or sitting alone at the funeral of a friend you used to be close to. Immediately the essay seems more interesting. As before, you will sit down and write a rough draft, then add and select details. In the end you may have something similar to the following:

> Once five years ago I was walking around O'Hare airport, stranded by a snowstorm. I was standing in line at the ticket counter when I suddenly heard my nickname from junior high. I turned to see Henry, my next-door neighbor when I was a child and once my best friend. We talked about an hour, and when we parted, I realized we had been

very good friends—friends because we had always helped each other, always listened to each other, always told each other the truth.

Helping each other even when it's inconvenient is an important part of friendship. Once I was on my way home from Shreveport. . . .

The story about running into this old friend is far more interesting than the original thesis sentence, yet it contains the major elements of that thesis sentence and eases the reader into the essay.

Every good essay, like every good story, also needs an ending. In high school you were probably taught that the ending of an essay is the re-statement of the thesis sentence or perhaps a simple summary of what you have already said. Either of these two methods will work as an ending, but that's rather like telling your friend, "In conclusion, Joe got drunk, Madge lost her keys, and I got lost," or simply saying, "Boy, that was some party." Your listener knows you're through talking and knows what happened at the party, but still has no real idea how you now feel or what you have learned. You might instead say, "I was so tired, I was thinking about getting crutches for my eyelids," or "Believe me, I will never invite Joe to a party again," or even, "The next time I go to a party, I'll make sure one of the drivers stays sober."

In ending an essay you want to do something similar. Writers try to finish an essay by stating something they have learned in writing the piece or in living through the anecdotes. If you have used a beginning like the one presented earlier, you may find the easiest and most effective way to end it is to refer back to the opening and continue that story here at the end of your essay. In this essay on friendship you might refer to that childhood friend and realize sadly that continued friendship requires not just shared history, but also active interdependence—a willingness to really be there in oil-stained pajamas, to tell unpleasant truths, and to pay close enough attention to each other to notice when something goes wrong.

Such an ending not only summarizes the essay and restates the thesis sentence, but it also adds insight into the definition of friendship. The reader has now seen what you have seen, experienced what you have experienced, and is now ready and perhaps even eager to discover what you have learned.

Exercise

Discuss in groups possible beginnings and endings for the following subjects.

1. a comparison of two classrooms

2. a comparison of two grandparents

3. a definition of love

4. a definition of truth

5. how to change a light bulb

6. how to kill a fly

7. a paper in favor of men using makeup

8. a paper against men using makeup

9. an imagined explanation of why leaves fall

10. a personal explanation of how you learn

UNIT 4 Using Words Correctly

In this unit you will learn to use and spell adjectives, adverbs, and pronouns correctly. Although misusing "good" for "well," "me" for "I," and "who" for "whom" is not considered serious, too many of these little errors make your writing look sloppy and uneducated. Learning to use these words correctly is not difficult once you understand the underlying principles.

CHAPTER 10
Adjectives and Adverbs

In speaking, many people use an adjective when an adverb is needed or an adverb when an adjective is needed. For example, many people now say, "He ran *real* fast" instead of "He ran *really* fast." In other words, the adjective *real* is misused as an adverb. In this chapter you will see when you should use an adjective and when an adverb.

ADJECTIVES VS. ADVERBS

An **adjective** modifies a noun or a pronoun; an **adverb** modifies any other kind of word or group of words.

adjective
The *loud* music scared the child.

adjective
The music sounded *loud*.

adverb
The child screamed *loudly*.

Using adjectives correctly in front of a noun is not very difficult. But when a modifier comes after a complete verb, it is sometimes difficult to decide whether to use an adjective or an adverb. Remember, adjectives modify only nouns and pronouns; other modifiers are therefore adverbs. After certain verbs, however, an adjective modifies the noun or pronoun in the subject. We will examine such verbs more closely here.

Adjectives After Linking Verbs

Adjectives, not adverbs, must often be used after a linking verb. A **linking verb** is a verb that indicates a state of being rather than an action. It must be followed by a "complement" to "complete" its meaning. The **complement**—a noun, a pronoun, or an adjective—either renames or modifies the subject of the linking verb.

> *renames subject*
> This older man <u>is</u> a student.
> *renames subject*
> The right person <u>was</u> he.
> *modifies subject*
> He <u>has remained</u> silent.

A linking verb functions to "link" the subject and complement. The linking verb, which itself does not have much meaning, could be likened to an equals sign.

> The older man = student.
>
> The right person = he.
>
> He = silent.

The most common linking verb is *be* (in any of its forms), but there are also a few other common linking verbs.

> ## Common Linking Verbs
>
> | | | | |
> |---|---|---|---|
> | be | appear | look | taste |
> | become | seem | smell | feel |
> | remain | act | sound | grow |
>
> *Note*: Like so many words we have seen so far, the common linking verbs may have different functions: Most of them may be used either as linking verbs or as action verbs. You must look at how the verb is used in the sentence to decide which it is.

One easy way to tell whether a verb is a linking verb or not is to substitute the *be* verb for it. If the sentence still makes sense and says about the same thing, the original verb is a linking verb. A single modifier following the linking verb must be an adjective describing or completing the subject.

The soup ~~tastes~~ *is* delicious.

My brother ~~tasted~~ *is* the soup.

She ~~looks~~ *is* angry.

She ~~looked~~ *was* angrily in my direction.

He ~~appeared~~ *was* suddenly.

He ~~appeared~~ *was* sad.

Exercise 1

In the following passage put an *L* over each underlined linking verb and an *A* over each underlined action verb (active or passive voice).

¹Fiction sometimes <u>becomes</u> reality. ²In her novel *Futility* (1898), Morgan Robertson <u>wrote</u> of a great "unsinkable" luxury liner named the *Titan* that <u>sank</u> on its maiden voyage after hitting an iceberg. ³Almost all passengers <u>were lost</u> because not enough lifeboats <u>were</u> available. ⁴Fourteen years later, the *Titanic* sank. ⁵The fictitious *Titan* and the real *Titanic* <u>had</u> many more things in common. ⁶Both vessels <u>were</u> huge liners driven by three propellers. ⁷The length of each ship <u>was</u> at least 800 feet, and their speed <u>remained</u> between twenty-three and twenty-five knots until impact. ⁸Two to three thousand people <u>were</u> passengers on each. ⁹Both liners <u>carried</u> about twenty lifeboats, and both ships <u>sank</u> in the month of April. ¹⁰Such extreme similarities <u>seem</u> uncanny, but I <u>feel</u> certain that coincidences like this <u>happen</u> seldom.

Exercise 2

Write sentences of your own, using each of the following verbs as linking verbs.

1. appear

2. act

3. sound

4. look

5. feel

Exercise 3

In the following, to make sure you use an adjective (not an adverb) to modify the subject, first mark each underlined verb as action (*A*) or linking (*L*). Then choose the appropriate form of the word in parentheses. (The first word in parentheses is an adjective, the second an adverb.)

1. Leonardo da Vinci (1452–1519), the son of a servant girl and a law-

   yer, <u>was</u> (illegitimate, illegitimately).

2. When the young boy's talent <u>seemed</u> (extraordinary, extraordinar-

   ily), his father <u>took</u> him (quick, quickly) from his village of Vinci to

   the city of Florence to study, and no one <u>feels</u> (certain, certainly) that

   he ever saw his mother again.

3. Leonardo probably <u>became</u> most (famous, famously) for the *Mona*

   Lisa, a painting that took him four years to finish.

4. Because Leonardo <u>appeared</u> (slow, slowly) in finishing *The Last Supper*, the prior of the Dominican monastery where the painting was commissioned <u>became</u> (angry, angrily).

5. Leonardo's reaction to the complaints <u>remains</u> (apparent, apparently): He painted the prior's face on the figure of Judas.

6. Unfortunately, *The Last Supper*, which many consider to be the greatest painting in the world, <u>looked</u> very (faint, faintly) after a few years because it was done in tempera, a painting mixture that <u>is</u> (water soluble, water solubly).

7. Because the city of Milan and particularly the Refectory—the room where he <u>worked</u> (continual, continually) on this great painting—<u>is</u> always very (damp, damply), only a shadow of the original <u>remained</u> (visible, visibly), but now restoration has begun.

8. At the end of his life, da Vinci left only twenty beautiful paintings and 5000 pages of notes, which <u>remained</u> (mysterious, mysteriously) for many years.

9. Not until 300 years after his death did these notebooks <u>become</u> (decipherable, decipherably).

10. Now considered some of the most outstanding of all times, these documents <u>had seemed</u> (illegible, illegibly) because Leonardo <u>had written</u> them (intentional, intentionally) in mirror writing.

ADVERBS

Whereas adjectives can modify only nouns and pronouns, **adverbs** (in italics here) modify different words or groups of words.

Adverbs Modify Action Verbs:

Penicillin was first produced *synthetically* in a laboratory in 1946.

In politics, a "dark horse" is a little-known person who gets a nomination *unexpectedly.*

Adverbs Modify Adjectives:

The ocean is never *perfectly* calm.

Some sugar is found in *almost* every food, including meat.

Very few people are rude.

Adverbs Modify Adverbs:

A hummingbird's wings move *too quickly* for the eye.

A person with talent displays his skill *quite naturally.*

Adverbs Modify Clauses or Sentences (in parentheses here):

Surely, (elephants can swim).

Botanically, (the tomato is a fruit).

Exercise 4

After marking each italicized word as adverb (adv) or adjective (adj), draw a line to the word(s) it modifies.

1. Thomas Alva Edison may have been a genius at invention, but *his*

   personal habits were *quite* unusual.

2. Rats lived *freely* in *his* laboratory.

3. He lived on *only five* hours of sleep a night.

4. He didn't believe in exercising and *frequently* told *his* friends that he *mainly* used *his* body to carry *his* brain around.

5. He is also *famous* for saying that genius "is *one percent* inspiration and ninety-nine percent perspiration."

6. Edison put his trust in *hard* work.

7. But *apparently* it was not *only scientific* curiosity that drove Edison.

8. He *once* said: "Anything that won't sell, I do*n't* want to invent."

9. But although he perspired, he *seldom* changed *his* clothes, and his employees nicknamed him "Dungyard."

10. He *firmly* believed that changing clothes caused insomnia and that food poisoned *the* intestines.

Placing Adverbs Correctly

To make your intended meaning clear, you should put modifiers—especially adverbs such as *only, just, simply, almost, even,* and *nearly*—immediately before (or as near as possible to) the words they modify.

He did nothing but order
He only ordered two bowls of chili.

only two (not more)
He ordered only two bowls of chili.

only chili (not rice)
He ordered two bowls of only chili.

Exercise 5

Indicate with a caret (∧) where the modifier in parentheses should be placed to be most effective.

1. Bowling has an odd history, although the derivation of the word itself is simple. (very)

2. The Latin term *bulla* meant "bubble" but came to mean "bowl," in the sense of the active cast or delivery of the ball. (originally)

3. According to British archaeologist Sir Flinders Petrie, bowling dates back to 5200 B.C., for he discovered all necessary equipment for this ancient game in an Egyptian tomb. (extremely)

4. Bowling was forbidden in England by three monarchs: Edward III, Richard II, and Henry VIII. (actually)

5. The sport wasn't banned because of its danger, but because it was harmless. (too)

6. Kings approved of sports that provided training for war, such as archery and horseback riding. (only)

7. Although Henry VIII forbade bowling, he played it himself, for he had a fine bowling alley in his palace at Whitehall. (officially, surely)

8. The Dutch brought a version of this game over to their colony in New York and played at Bowling Green, now an area of New York's financial district. (apparently)

Exercise 6

Indicate with a caret (∧) where the modifier (in parentheses) would be most effective.

1. Although now definitely against the rules, the spitball was an accepted element in baseball. (once)

2. At the first professional league game, the Fort Wayne Kekiongas defeated the Cleveland Forest Citys 2–0. (clearly)

3. At that game, the winning pitcher, Bobby Mathews, spat on his fingers before he threw the ball. (openly)

4. The spitball was outlawed in 1920. (finally)

5. But the technique is in use. (still)

6. When a player makes the ball soggy or scuffed, he causes a sudden, late break before the throw arrives at home plate. (intentionally or unintentionally)

7. According to Gaylord Perry, who retired as a 300-game winner, the scuffed area must be held opposite to the direction of the desired break. (exactly)

8. "If you want it to go down, hold it scuff up and it will sink," Perry said. (merely)

9. Tampering with the ball, though, is the tricky part. (in the first place)

10. Nevertheless, about all that prevents a player from cheating is his own conscience. (only)

Exercise 7

Using each of the following adverbs, write a sentence of your own. Be sure to place the adverb where it is most effective.

1. only: _____

   _____

2. almost: _____

   _____

3. just: _____

   _____

4. nearly: _____

_____

5. even: _____

_____

FORMS OF ADJECTIVES AND ADVERBS

You have probably learned that adverbs usually end in *-ly*, but many adjectives also end in *-ly*. Thus, the *-ly* marker is not a very reliable indicator.

See if you can tell which of the following words are adjectives: *lovely, slowly, friendly, sure, quickly*. To tell whether a word is an adjective or not, put it in front of a noun, as follows:

the __(adjective)__ person

the _____ thing

Slowly and *quickly* do not sound right in front of the noun: They are adverbs.

Sometimes there is no difference between the adjective form and the adverb form.

Adjective and Adverb Forms That Are the Same	
Adjective	**Adverb**
fast	fast
hard	hard
wrong	wrong
well (healthy)	well

Most adverbs, though, are different from their adjective counterparts (*terrible, terribly; extreme, extremely*).

Although in spoken or informal written English the *-ly* ending is often left off ("He runs *slow*" instead of "He runs *slowly*"), in formal or academic writing the *-ly* spelling is preferred. The following lists show which commonly confused words are adjectives and which ones are adverbs.

Commonly Confused Adjectives and Adverbs

Adjective	Adverb
awful	awfully
bad	badly
easy	easily
good	well
most	almost
near	nearly
quick	quickly
real	really
slow	slowly
some	somewhat
sure	surely
terrible	terribly

Exercise 8

Circle the appropriate form of the word and draw a line to the word(s) it modifies. Remember, adjectives modify only nouns or pronouns.

1. (Most, Almost) all cultures have stories about (real, really) amazing heroes or godlike beings.

2. It was (awful, awfully) difficult to defeat or destroy these beings, even if they acted (terrible, terribly).

3. Many legends concern those who behaved (good, well) but were betrayed or destroyed, although their betrayal did not happen (easy, easily).

4. One legendary hero of the Trojan War, Achilles, was (some, somewhat) vulnerable, but killing him was (hard, hardly) because only a wound to his heel would kill him.

5. Antaeus, a giant in Greek myth whom Hercules fought, was (near, nearly) impossible to defeat until Hercules discovered that Antaeus lost his strength (quick, quickly) when not touching mother earth.

6. In old Norse myth, it was a (real, really) horrible day when the evil Loki discovered what he wanted to know so (bad, badly): the secret that mistletoe was the only thing in existence capable of piercing the skin of the "shining one," the favorite god, Balder.

7. Other Germanic legends tell of the mighty warrior Siegfried whose skin likewise could not be penetrated to harm him except for one spot (direct, directly) between his shoulder blades, yet (slow but sure, slowly but surely), that information too fell into the hands of his enemies.

8. The Old Testament strong man Samson was defeated (bad, badly) when Delilah betrayed him and cut his hair, the secret behind his mighty strength.

9. Even today's comic book hero, Superman, weakens (quick, quickly) when Kryptonite is (close, closely).

10. Obviously, (most, almost) every time there is a legend about an (apparent, apparently) invincible figure, whether he is (good or bad, well or badly), there is also a part of the legend that tells of his (weak, weakly) spot.

Positive, Comparative, and Superlative Forms of Adjectives and Adverbs

Positive Form: When comparing *two* items that are the *same*, we use the **positive** (unchanged) form of an adjective or adverb, usually with the connectors *as . . . as*.

Adjective: John is as *fast* as Peter.
Adverb: John runs as *fast* as Peter.

Comparative Form: When comparing *two unequal* items, we use the **comparative** (*-er/more*) form of adjectives or adverbs, usually with the connector *than*. Short adjectives and adverbs usually make their comparative forms by adding *-er* to the end of the word, but longer words do so by adding *more* in front of the word.

Adjective: John is *faster* than Peter.
Adverb: John runs *faster* than Peter.

Adjective: Peter is *slower* than John.
Adverb: Peter runs *more slowly* than John.

Adjective: Derrick seems the *more cautious* one of the twins.
Adverb: Derrick drives *more cautiously* than his twin brother.

Superlative Form: When comparing *three* or more *unequal* items, we use the **superlative** (*-est/most*) form of adjectives or adverbs without a connector. Short adjectives and adverbs make their superlative form by adding *-est* to the end of the word, but longer words do so by adding *most* in front of the word.

Adjective: John is the *fastest* runner in the class.
Adverb: John runs *fastest*.

Adjective: Peter is the *slowest* runner in the class.
Adverb: Peter runs *most slowly*.

Adjective: Derrick is the *most cautious* one of the three brothers.
Adverb: Derrick drives the *most cautiously*.

Irregular Comparative and Superlative Forms: Some adjectives and adverbs have irregular comparative and superlative forms. Note that adjectives or adverbs (such as *good/well*) may have different positive forms but the same comparative and superlative forms.

Irregular Comparatives and Superlatives

Positive	Comparative	Superlative
good (adjective)	better	best
well (adverb)	better	best
many	more	most
much	more	most
bad	worse	worst
ill	worse	worst
little	less	least
(*But:* few	fewer	fewest)

Note: Either the *-er/-est* endings or the words *more/most* should be used, but never both together. Thus, it is incorrect to say or write "the more better" or "the most loveliest."

Exercise 9

Examine the following statistics. Then compose sentences using the correct positive, comparative, or superlative form of the modifier to describe what is true in each situation.

1. tiny, tinier, tiniest   _____

   house mouse weighs   .60 oz   _____

   pygmy shrew weighs   .14 oz   _____

   harvest mouse weighs   .28 oz   _____

   Savi's shrew weighs   .07 oz   _____

   _____

   _____

2. large, larger, largest

    rhinoceros weighs   3¼ ton

    African elephant weighs   7½ ton

3. long, longer, longest

    giant anteater's tongue   24 in.

    giraffe's tongue   20 in.

    okapi's tongue   14 in.
    (kind of antelope)

4. big, bigger, biggest

    human eye   1 in. diam.

    blue whale's eye   6 in. across

    giant squid's eye   16 in. across

    horse's eye   2 in. across

5. heavy, heavier, heaviest

    newborn blue whale   4400 lb

    newborn sperm whale   2200 lb

_____

_____

_____

_____

_____

6. high, higher, highest

    leap of a thoroughbred horse   8 ft

    leap of a Desert Jerboa   8 ft
       (jumping mouse)

_____

_____

_____

_____

_____

7. deep, deeper, deepest

    bathyscaphe,   3300 ft below
       2-man crew (1934)   sea level

    bathyscaphe,   13,100 ft below
       3-man crew (1964)   sea level

    bathyscaphe,
       2-man crew (1960)   36,000 ft below
                          sea level

_____

_____

_____

_____

8. curious, more curious, most curious

_____

The tail feathers of a Japanese breed

_____

of rooster, the Onagadori, grow 35

_____

feet long, so someone must carry its

_____

tail if it walks.

_____

_____

_____

9. fast, faster, fastest

_____

peregrine falcon   81 mph

_____

cheetah   71 mph

_____

_____

_____

_____

_____

10. Slowly, more slowly, most slowly

_____

Sloth travels 1 mile   42 days

_____

Red slug travels 1 mile   36 days

_____

Gray carnivorous shelled   73 days
slug travels 1 mile

_____

_____

_____

11. old, older, oldest   _____

    Madagascar radiated tortoise   200 yr _____

    Marion's tortoise   152 yr _____

    human being   117 yr _____

                                      _____

                                      _____

                                      _____

12. many, more, most   _____

    tusks on an African elephant   2–9 ft _____

    tusks on a Babirusa (a wild hog) 4 ft _____

                                        _____

                                      _____

                                      _____

SUMMARY

Fill in the blanks with the appropriate response, to show your understanding of the principles in this chapter.

1. Adjectives modify _____ and _____.

2. Adjectives usually precede the noun or pronun, but after a _____

   verb, the adjective is separated from the noun or pronoun it modifies

   in the subject.

3. The most common linking verb is the verb _____.

4. Some other commonly used linking verbs are <u>become</u>, _____,

_____, _____, _____, and _____.

5. Adverbs modify <u>action verbs</u>, _____, _____, and

_____ or _____.

6. What is the difference in meaning among the following sentences?

Only I saw him.   _____

_____

I only saw him.   _____

_____

I saw only him.   _____

_____

7. In formal or academic writing, if you wish to modify an action verb,

you use _____ instead of *slow*, _____ instead of *sure*,

and _____ instead of *good*.

8. If you wish to modify an adjective, you use _____ instead of

near, _____ instead of *terrible*, _____ instead of *most*,

and _____ instead of *some*.

9. When comparing two unequal items, either add _____ to the

end of the word or put _____ in front of the word.

10. When comparing three or more unequal items, either add _____

to the end of the word or put _____ in front of the word.

Summary Exercise

For each sentence, choose the correct form and draw an arrow to the word(s) it modifies.

1. History records some (most, more) unusual deaths.

2. Legend says the Greek playwright Aeschylus died (quick, quickly) when an eagle, which mistook his bald head for a rock, dropped a tortoise on it.

3. The body of the Italian poet Petrarch was laid out for twenty-four hours, in accordance with local law, when it sat up (sudden, suddenly); he lived for another thirty years.

4. British philosopher Francis Bacon died of a cold contracted through an experiment: He stuffed snow into a fowl to see how (easy, easily) it could be preserved.

5. American author James Otis, who had prayed (real, really) seriously that he would die in a "heaven-sent" manner, was struck down by a bolt of lightning.

6. English poet Percy Bysshe Shelley drowned and was cremated on the beach where his body had washed ashore. (Most, almost) all of his body burned, but his wife carried his heart, which would not burn, with her for the rest of her life.

7. American author Nathaniel Hawthorne, who died in 1864, felt (sure, surely) that the number 64 was mystical; he had scribbled it on (almost, most) every one of his papers.

8. The English philosopher Jeremy Bentham left a large inheritance to London's University College on a (special, specially) condition: His preserved body was to be displayed annually at the board of directors meeting. This condition, despite being (some, somewhat) gruesome, was met for ninety-two years.

9. British poet Rupert Brooke died (slow, slowly) of blood poisoning from a tiny mosquito bite.

10. Perhaps the (weirdest, most weirdest) example is Mark Twain's death. He was born when Halley's comet appeared in 1835 and died, as he had predicted, when it appeared again in 1910.

WRITING PRACTICE

Write ten sentences or a short passage about one or more of the following topics, using the guidelines of your teacher. Make sure you use your adjectives and adverbs correctly.

1. an unusual coincidence

2. a modern-day hero

3. a recently added rule in a sport, in education, or on the job

4. an eccentric person

5. a profession that requires great skill and patience

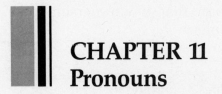

CHAPTER 11
Pronouns

Pronouns are words that may substitute for nouns or groups of words used as nouns. In fact, the word *pronoun* means literally "for a noun."

Abraham Lincoln was the tallest president of the United States.

~~Abraham Lincoln~~ *He* was six feet, four inches tall.

Rattlesnakes do not lay eggs.

~~Rattlesnakes~~ *They* give birth to their living young.

Most pronouns are rather easy to use. But some people have trouble deciding when to use *who* rather than *whom, its* instead of *it's,* or *you and I* rather than *you and me.* These common problem areas are easy to solve when you understand the underlying principle, which we will discuss in this chapter. You will first learn about the different pronoun forms and spellings, then how to identify the **antecedent** (the word that a pronoun refers back to), and finally about the uses of the different pronoun forms.

FORMS AND SPELLINGS OF PRONOUNS

We have already seen several forms of pronouns:

Singular	Plural
I	we
you	you
he/she/it	they

These pronouns have different forms for different functions.

In the table below, notice that the pronouns that show ownership (possessive pronouns) do *not* have an apostrophe.

Pronouns That Change Their Spelling According to Their Function

Subject	Object	(Possessive Adjective)	Possessive Pronoun	Reflexive
I	me	my	mine	myself
you	you	your	yours	yourself
he	him	his	his	himself
she	her	her	hers	herself
it	it	its	its	itself
we	us	our	ours	ourselves
you	you	your	yours	yourselves
they	them	their	theirs	themselves
who	whom	whose	whose	

Note: Even though possessive adjectives are not pronouns, they have been included in the table (and the following exercises) because they are related in meaning to these pronouns.

Exercise 1

Underline the antecedents; then refer to the table of pronouns that change their spelling to fill in the blanks with an appropriate form of a pronoun or a possessive adjective.

1. People have a way of picking up traditional words and phrases and

   using _____ without actually knowing _____ true

   meanings and origins.

2. We are frequently taught a word or phrase in childhood by _____

   parents. Sometimes, even _____ don't know the original meanings.

3. "Blue-blooded" has long been used to refer to those people _____

   were aristocratic or thought that _____ were better than others.

4. The term actually comes from *sangre azul*, which Spanish aristocrats used to describe _____ because _____ blood was not mixed with Moorish or Jewish blood.

5. "Blue-blooded" seemed appropriate for backgrounds such as _____ because _____ fair skin made _____ bluish veins visible.

6. If you do not want to associate with another person, _____ reaction is often to give _____ the "cold shoulder."

7. The person usually gets the message that _____ presence is not desired.

8. The term originated in medieval France. A guest _____ welcome had worn out was served cold shoulder of beef instead of hot.

9. Most of us have probably possessed a "white elephant" at one time or another. _____ think of _____ as any item that is useless or has become burdensome.

10. The idea originated with the King of Siam, _____ decree was that white (albino) elephants were sacred and that anyone _____ owned one could give _____ only the best.

11. When the king had courtiers who displeased _____, he gave _____ one of _____ white elephants.

12. Once the elephant was _____, the courtiers usually were ruined because they had to keep _____ in the style the king demanded.

REFERENCE WITH PRONOUNS AND POSSESSIVE ADJECTIVES

Every pronoun and possessive adjective has an antecedent (a word it refers to), and you must make sure to identify the true antecedent. Often this means ignoring a prepositional phrase.

antecedent   *pronoun*

A *fish* continues to grow until *it* dies.

possessive adjective

One (of the girls) lost *her* grammar book.

Each (of the boys) will receive *his* merit badge.

Exercise 2

First underline the antecedent. Then fill in the blank with the correct form of the pronoun or possessive adjective.

1. Myths about animals are numerous, and all too often we tend to believe _____ without question.

2. While each of these myths has _____ own reason for existing, most of _____ are not reliable.

3. Porcupines and hedgehogs cannot, as is believed, shoot _____ quills at enemies.

4. A mouse, along with other rodents, does not necessarily consider cheese _____ favorite meal.

5. Many believe that ostriches bury _____ heads in the sand to evade their enemies. Instead, this giant bird is actually trying to put

_____ head near or on the ground to rest _____ neck muscles.

6. Gorillas, in contradiction to how _____ are presented in the movies, are not ferocious creatures by habit. _____ are actually shy, and a gorilla will usually avoid a conflict if _____ can.

COMPOUND AND PRONOUN ANTECEDENTS

Usually it is not difficult to determine which pronoun or possessive adjective to use. But as you saw in Chapter 3, there are some antecedents that may be confusing. Here we will briefly review these nouns and pronouns and point out a few more trouble spots.

Coordinating Conjunctions Help Distinguish Singular from Plural Antecedents

Remember to look at the meaning of coordinating conjunctions to determine whether some antecedents are singular or plural. Thus, when the conjunction adds two items together, the phrase is usually plural.

Both the students **and** the instructor worked hard on *their* class project.

When the conjunction indicates a choice, the item closer to the verb or pronoun determines whether it is singular or plural.

Neither the deans **nor** the president had announced *his* decision in the matter.

Special Cases of Singular and Plural Pronoun Antecedents

Remember that some pronouns are always singular, some always plural, and some either singular or plural, depending on the context.

Anyone in *his* or *her* right mind would study for that test.

No one is allowed near the room unless *he* or *she* has a pass.

All of the boys should do *their* best.

None of the students have *their* I.D. cards.

None of the paint has lost *its* color.

Note: Often it is unclear whether a pronoun refers to males, females, or both (for example, *everybody*). In such a case you should use the phrase *he or she* or *him or her*. Because such double pronoun phrases are wordy, you might want to avoid them by rewriting the sentence in the plural.

Students in *their* right minds would study for that test.

People are not allowed near the room unless *they* have a pass.

Exercise 3

Fill in each blank with an appropriate pronoun or possessive adjective.

[1]Everyone has _____ own image of writers. [2]Poets or play-wrights are expected to be creative, but few believe that _____ can also be athletic or even remotely interested in sports. [3]A writer's involvement in athletics just doesn't fit this stereotype.

[4]The truth is that many famous authors have been known for _____ participation in athletics. [5]Boxing and wrestling are very

physical sports, so most people would be surprised to know writers have excelled at _____. [6]Yet the ancient Greek playwright Sophocles, the English poet Lord Byron, and the American author Ernest Hemingway were all quite good at _____. [7]Not only was Benjamin Franklin America's first great swimmer, but _____ also taught swimming and invented swim fins. [8]Edgar Allan Poe, however, apparently didn't need _____. [9]He once swam seven and a half miles at almost three miles per hour without _____.

[10]Although not participants, other authors have been avid sports fans. [11]Neither Shakespeare nor Walt Whitman was active in sports, but each celebrated _____ in _____ writings. [12]Herman Melville and Stephen Crane often referrred to sports in _____ writing also.

[13]While none of the athletic writers might ever win the Super Bowl or a gold medal, _____ would certainly defeat the stereotype some people associate with the writer's sedentary occupation.

TROUBLESOME ANTECEDENTS

Some nouns cause errors of pronoun reference and subject–verb agreement errors because they look plural but are really singular, or look singular but are plural. Here we will discuss five unusual kinds of nouns.

Group Nouns

Words like *jury* usually represent a group acting as one body and are replaceable with *it*.

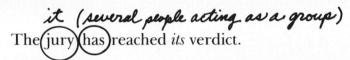

it (several people acting as a group)
The ⟨jury⟩ ⟨has⟩ reached *its* verdict.

Group Nouns				
audience	crew	family	herd	public
band	crowd	flock	jury	staff
cast	committee	folk	nation	team
class	enemy	government	orchestra	
club	faculty	group	press	

Note: A word like *jury* is almost always replaceable by *it*, but when the context clearly indicates that each member of the group acts on his or her own, such a word is replaceable by *they*. Compare the next two examples.

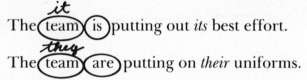

it
The ⟨team⟩ ⟨is⟩ putting out *its* best effort.

they
The ⟨team⟩ ⟨are⟩ putting on *their* uniforms.

Singular and Plural Nouns That Are Spelled the Same

Words like *fish, crawfish,* and *deer* are also unusual, because we typically use the same forms for them whether they are singular or plural. When a word like *fish* or *deer* refers to a class as a whole, it is replaceable by *they*. But when it refers to food, it is singular.

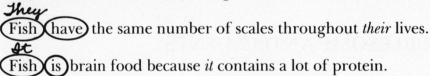

They
⟨Fish⟩ ⟨have⟩ the same number of scales throughout *their* lives.

It
⟨Fish⟩ ⟨is⟩ brain food because *it* contains a lot of protein.

Also, when the word has *a* or *an* before it or refers to one member of the species, it is singular and is replaceable by *it*.

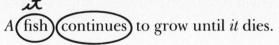

it
A ⟨fish⟩ ⟨continues⟩ to grow until *it* dies.

Certain Nouns Ending in -s

Words like *scissors*, referring to things consisting of two distinct parts, are plural and are replaceable with *they*. But words like *physics*, that name a course of studies, are replaceable with *it*, although the *-s* ending makes them look plural.

The (scissors) (are) on the table. Please hand *them* to me.

I took physics with Dr. Johnson. *It* was an interesting subject.

Plural Pronoun vs. Singular Pronoun	
They	**It**
binoculars	economics
blue jeans	mathematics
glasses	news
pants	physics
pliers	politics
scissors	
spectacles	
tweezers	

Units of Measure

Expressions with a word such as *dollars, cents, miles, hours,* or *minutes* are singular when they refer to an amount of money, a distance, or a period of time.

It (one distance)

[Thirty-six hundred miles] <u>was</u> the distance that Lindbergh flew on May 20 and 21, 1927. *It* was a world record.

It (one time period)

[Thirty-three and a half hours] <u>was</u> his flying time. *It* was a long time to stay awake.

It (one amount of money)

[Forty thousand dollars] <u>was</u> the cost of taking the first national census in 1790. *It* was a lot of money then.

Titles

Titles of books, movies, poems, shows, and so on are singular.

It (title of a book)

Leaves of Grass <u>is</u> Walt Whitman's most famous work. *It* is considered his masterpiece.

It (poem title)

"Birches" <u>is</u> a poem by Robert Frost. *It* is included in almost every literature textbook.

   Because the foregoing troublesome antecedents cause problems in both pronoun reference and subject–verb agreement, the following three exercises will give you practice using them.

Exercise 4

In each of the following, circle the correct form of the verb and/or fill in the blank with an appropriate pronoun or possessive adjective.

1. The audience (has, have) finally become quiet.

2. The graduating class (is, are) now entering the auditorium.

3. As the class march to _____ seats, the band (play, plays).

4. Each graduate's family (look, looks) on with pride.

5. The faculty (is, are) seated on stage.

6. Papier-mâché fish (is, are) used as decorations. Hanging from the ceiling, _____ sparkle in the lights.

7. The orchestra (begin, begins) to play the national anthem, and the crowd (rise, rises).

8. A faculty committee (has, have) selected those students who will win special awards.

9. The crowd (applaud, applauds) enthusiastically for each winner.

10. With such a festive atmosphere, no wonder the graduating class (is, are) so excited about this special night.

Exercise 5

In each of the following, circle the correct form of the verb and/or fill in the blank with an appropriate pronoun or possessive adjective.

1. The football team (study, studies) in the weight room behind the new stadium.

2. The team are trying to improve _____ grades before football season.

3. Faculty politics (has, have) been responsible for these new study habits.

4. John, the star quarterback, is taking Mathematics 103. _____ is a hard subject for _____.

5. His class (is, are) meeting this afternoon.

6. The class agrees that _____ last exam was difficult.

7. This group also (question, questions) if the exam was fair.

8. In the teacher's view, she is the captain, and the crew only (follow, follows) _____ orders.

9. But that afternoon her crew (was, were) deciding whether to mutiny.

10. Although John was one of those afraid that the news (was, were) not going to be good, _____ discovered that _____ was good: He had passed, as had most of the class.

Exercise 6

Circle the correct form of the verb and fill in each blank with an appropriate pronoun or possessive adjective.

[1]Twenty dollars (is, are) not a lot to pay for a weekend in New Orleans, but 500 miles (is, are) a long way to travel just to hear New Orleans jazz. [2]"When the Saints Come Marching In" (is, are) going to be the first tune the group intends to request when _____ gets to Preservation Hall. [3]Richard brought Ellen Gilchrist's collection of short stories *In the Land of Dreamy Dreams* to read while riding on the bus because _____ first story, "Rich," (take, takes) place in New Orleans.

You have learned to spell quite a few pronouns and possessive adjectives correctly and learned to identify some troublesome antecedents. Now you will learn how the different forms are used.

SUBJECT PRONOUNS

The following four situations require a subject pronoun.

Subject: When the pronoun is the subject, or a part of the subject after a coordinating conjunction, the subject form of the pronoun is used.

[Molly, Audrey, and *I*] plan to attend the concert.
[Kevin and *they*] are responsible for buying the tickets.
[Who] is in charge of the entertainment?

Renaming the Subject: When a pronoun directly follows and renames the subject, a subject form of the pronoun is used.

My friends, Robert and *she*, helped me with the planning.
George and I, *we* were responsible.

Complement: When a pronoun renames the subject after a linking verb, a subject form of the pronoun is used.

It was *we* who suggested to have the party.

The woman we talked to is *she*.

The entertainers are *they*.

Subject of a Comparison Phrase: When the pronoun is the subject of an understood verb in a phrase starting with *as* or *than*, the subject form of the pronoun is used. (To help you decide which pronoun form to use, substitute the *as* or *than* phrase with a short sentence.)

He is as tall as *I*.   *I am tall*

She is taller than *he*.   *he is tall*

Exercise 7

Fill in each blank with an appropriate pronoun or possessive adjective.

¹Mary and _____ got small cameras as gifts. ²Mary has had hers longer than _____, and _____ can do more with hers because _____ is fancier than the one _____ have. ³My grandmother calls all small cameras Kodaks, no matter _____ makes _____. ⁴We, Mary and _____, did not understand why until Gran explained that originally Kodak meant any small camera. ⁵The name was created by George Eastman, _____ was an American inventor. ⁶_____ desired to replace the large, bulky cameras of the 1880s with smaller ones. ⁷It was _____ who chose the name Kodak because _____ said that _____ was "short,

vigorous, could not be misspelt, and to satisfy trademark laws meant

nothing." ⁸Both of us, Mary and _____, wish that _____

were as creative as _____.

OBJECT PRONOUNS

Object pronouns are used when the pronoun is a *whom* or *what* word that
comes after the following:

After a verb:	I saw *him*. I gave *him* a book.
After a preposition:	I gave the book to *him*.
After an infinitive:	I want to see *him*.
After a gerund:	I enjoyed seeing *him*.
After than *or* as (*if it is not the subject of the understood clause*):	*she likes him* She likes me better than *him*. *she likes him* She likes me as much as *him*.
Or renames any of the previously mentioned objects:	I saw the children, Mary and *him*.

Rather than trying to memorize this list, it might be easier to remember the following rule of thumb: If the pronoun is not the subject or does
not rename the subject, it probably has the object form.

The (boss) ordered *him* to be released from his duties.

understood subject
(you)   Let *us, you* and *me*, find a way to help *him*.

Whom did (you) talk to on the phone?

The person *whom* (I) am talking about moved last year.

(She) likes *me* as much as (she) likes *him*.

Note: Because the correct form in subject phrases such as *you and I* is emphasized so much, many people have a tendency to "overcorrect" and use the subject form when, in fact, the object form is needed.

preposition
Between *you* and *me*, I didn't like the program anyway.

Remember also that the object form is needed after a preposition even if the preposition and pronoun are part of the complete subject (in brackets here).

preposition
[Nobody but *him*] knows the solution to this problem.

preposition
[The president, along with *us*,] has decided to cancel the program.

Exercise 8

Fill in each blank with an appropriate form of a pronoun or possessive adjective.

¹One of the oldest medical practices in the world is the Chinese art of acupuncture. ²The Chinese first used _____ more than 4000 years ago, yet no one but _____ knew its importance until recently. ³This practice involves the placement of needles into over 900 specific points on the human body. ⁴Sticking _____ in exactly the right place is the art of acupuncture. ⁵The acupuncture doctor knows exactly where on the body to insert _____ to control pain. ⁶People _____ are suffering some sort of pain claim to get almost immediate relief from this process. ⁷According to the old tradition, acupuncture works because the process is balancing forces of good and evil in the body of a person _____ is ill. ⁸These forces are out of balance

when _____ becomes ill. [9]_____ must be restored to an equilibrium by the needles, which are placed to block off or stimulate one of these forces. [10]Chinese doctors, many of _____ still follow this practice, have shared its benefits with _____ colleagues in the Western world. [11]In the West, an old medical practice has become a new one for those _____ were previously unfamiliar with _____. [12]Appreciating this ancient medical practice should give us, you and _____, a new respect for the past.

Exercise 9

To practice choosing the subject or object form of the pronoun, create a short sentence of the *as* or *than* phrase or clause. Then fill in the blank with an appropriate form of the pronoun *I*.

1. Because you are dating his sister, the boss treats you better than

    _____.

2. Everyone was more interested in the program than _____.

3. Are you as fascinated with numbers as _____?

4. Susan is shorter than _____, but she can run faster than

    _____.

5. Few people can type faster than _____.

6. My son helps his mother as much as he helps _____.

7. The coach of the men's swim team does not swim nearly as well as

_____.

Exercise 10

Fill in each blank with the correct form of an appropriate pronoun or possessive adjective.

¹Archaeologists have made some incredible finds during the last century. ²_____ have given _____ a wealth of materials that show how mankind and animals existed centuries ago. ³Howard Carter, an English archaeologist, found one of the greatest of _____ all. ⁴In 1922, after a search that had taken _____ and _____ team over twenty years, Carter unearthed the treasures of King Tut's tomb. ⁵He and those _____ had worked with _____ finally fulfilled a lifelong dream, which no one except _____ had believed possible.

⁶Once inside the tomb, the workers and _____ found riches never imagined by anyone but _____. ⁷The most fabulous of all was the jewel-shrouded body of Tutankhamen. ⁸A gold mask covered his face, and flowers were draped over his chest. ⁹After 3300 years, _____ still had a bit of color to _____. ¹⁰The tomb's contents have enabled scientists to get a glimpse of daily Egyptian life 1350 years before Christ, and much of _____ contents have toured the world.

Using *who* and *whom* Correctly

Remember, a subordinator usually comes at the beginning of the clause it introduces. To decide whether to use *who* (subject—marked with an *S* here) or *whom* (object), you must look at the remainder of the clause. If a complete verb (marked with a *V*) immediately follows the pronoun, the pronoun is almost always *who*.

The patients (*who* are in this ward) will be helped first.

Give the flowers to (*who*ever wants them).

(*Who* is going to eat lunch first)?

If there is a subject (*S*) between the *who*/*whom* pronoun and a complete verb (*V*), the pronoun is usually *whom*.

The man (*whom* you met) is my instructor.

The girl (to *whom* the book was given) lost it.

The letter began with "(To *whom*ever it may concern)."

Note: There is an exception to the rule just stated. Sometimes there is a short expression such as *she thinks* or *he said* that interrupts the *who*/*whom* clause. If the expression can be taken out without changing the meaning of the sentence, it should be ignored. To decide which pronoun to use, set off (with braces) the interrupting words and look at what follows. If a verb follows the interrupter, the pronoun is *who*; if a subject follows the interrupter, the pronoun is *whom*.

We invited only those people (*who* {he said} were interested).

Louise is a singer (*whom* {I think} many people want to hear).

(*Who* {did he say} is portraying Samuel)?

Exercise 11

Fill in each blank with the appropriate form of *who*/*whom*. Remember to read what follows each blank before making your choice.

1. Parents _____ send their children to kindergarten are probably unaware that Froebel, the German educator by _____ these classes were started, wanted them to be happy places, and so named them "children's gardens."

2. Paper money was invented in the ninth century by the Chinese, _____ it is said found copper coins scarce and needed a substitute.

3. Table knives originated in France in the seventeenth century. Cardinal Richelieu, _____ was horrified by the use of sharp daggers as toothpicks, ordered their ends to be rounded by those _____ used them at the table.

4. Painters, _____ have to keep one area of paint from mixing with another, were responsible for the invention of Scotch tape in 1925.

5. The men to _____ the invention is credited called it Scotch tape because their critics felt that anyone by _____ the adhesive was used was overeconomical.

6. The Scotch people, _____ are reputed to be thrifty, have been stereotyped as stingy by those _____ do not care about the cost.

POSSESSIVE PRONOUNS AND POSSESSIVE ADJECTIVES

Possessive pronouns may occur anywhere in the sentence, as subject or object.

> His car is green. *Mine* is blue.
>
> I can't find his book, but I found *hers*.
>
> Richard is a good friend of *ours*.

Possessive adjectives are used in front of nouns to show ownership.

> On April 17, 1903, Henry Ford gave *his* first AUTOMOBILE an initial road test.
>
> "Jasmine," by Tuvach of Egypt, is one of the most costly perfumes in the world. *Its* retail PRICE in America is about $90 per ounce.
>
> Ducks, *whose* FEATHERS are kept oily by small oil glands, do not get wet.

Note: In written English, the possessive form is also required before a gerund. However, in spoken English, the object form of the pronoun is customary.

> *Written:*   He appreciated *my* VOLUNTEERING to help.
>
> *Spoken:*   He appreciated *me* VOLUNTEERING to help.

Exercise 12

Fill in each blank with the appropriate possessive pronoun or possessive adjective form of the pronoun in parentheses.

1. In all parts of Indonesia, _____ (it) richly carved temples and

    shrines can be found. One of _____ (it) most famous shrines

    is the Boro Budur, an architectural masterpiece in central Java built

    during the ninth century A.D. and dedicated to Buddha.

2. In about A.D. 100, the Hindus, _____ (who) art the Indonesians copied or blended with _____ (they), came to Indonesia.

3. Many of _____ (they) great Hindu epics, such as the *Ramayana*
   and the *Mahabharata*, have influenced Indonesian literature.

4. For example, Indonesians today still tell many stories about "kantjil,"
   a little mouse deer who always outwits _____ (he) enemies.

5. Indonesians love the puppet plays with music called "wayang." There
   are many wandering minstrels _____ (who) wayang performances are still popular today. _____ (they) musical performances usually include a "gamelang," a kind of xylophone, as well as
   gongs and other percussion instruments.

6. Indonesian dances are very different from _____ (we). Java-
   nese and Balinese dances are known for _____ (they) formal
   gestures and movements. Some famous dances are the candle dance
   of Sumatra and the Menari dance of Celebes.

7. Indonesian woodcarvers, coppersmiths, and silversmiths are famous
   for _____ (they) graceful work and great skill.

8. Did you know that many of _____ (we) "batik" fabrics come
   from Indonesia, which is world-famous for _____ (it) ancient
   process of "batik" (wax-dyeing on cloth)?

USES OF THE APOSTROPHE

The **apostrophe** is used to form contractions. The apostrophe replaces one or more missing letters.

You're a student.
You are a student.

It's a beautiful day.
It is a beautiful day.

They're my friends.
They are my friends.

Who's here?
Who is here?

There's plenty of time left.
There is plenty of time left.

The apostrophe is also used to make nouns and certain pronouns show ownership.

Singular and Plural Nouns or Pronouns Not Ending in *s* Add *'s*:

John has a book.   It is *John's* book.

The children have a book.   It is the *children's* book.

Everyone has a book.   It is *everyone's* book.

Plural Nouns Ending in *s* Add an Apostrophe Only:

The kids have a book.   It is the *kids'* book.

The Stevensons have a book.   It is the *Stevensons'* book.

Remember, the following possessive pronouns and adjectives are spelled with *no* apostrophe.

Spelled with No Apostrophe			
Possessive Adjectives		**Possessive Pronouns**	
	my		*mine.*
	your		*yours.*
This is	*his*	message. It is	*his.*
	her		*hers.*
	its		*its.*
	our		*ours.*
	their		*theirs.*
	Whose message is this?		

Exercise 13

Circle the correct word of each of the pairs of words in parentheses in the following passage.

¹(It's/Its) always interesting to find out how certain common foods acquired their names. ²(There's/Theirs) Coca-Cola, along with doughnuts and Granny Smith apples—to name just a few.

³The drink Coca-Cola got (its/it's) start in Atlanta, Georgia, in 1886. ⁴The creator, John Pemberton, (whose/who's) fondness for unusual drink recipes caused him to experiment, became rich. ⁵(Pemberton's/Pembertons') drink is known all over the world, but (its/it's) a rare person who has heard of him by name.

⁶(There're/Their) very few people who haven't heard of doughnuts. ⁷But how many know of (there/their) origin? ⁸These famous cakes were invented by Hanson Gregory, a New England schoolboy. ⁹Bored with his (mother's/mothers') cakes, he persuaded her to remove the center from (hers/her's) before frying the dough. ¹⁰His mother, (who's/whose) name is not even recorded, is actually responsible for producing the first doughnut.

¹¹(You're/Your) supermarket probably sells a tart, green apple (who's/whose) name is "Granny Smith." ¹²(It's/Its) name comes from an Australian woman, Maria Ann Smith. ¹³(Smith's/Smiths') popular strain of apples was created by grafting two seedlings in her garden. ¹⁴This

(apple's/apples') fame spread throughout Australia, and soon profes-

sional fruit growers were producing them. [15]The (grower's/growers')

distribution spread Granny Smith apples worldwide.

REFLEXIVE PRONOUNS

As the name suggests, a **reflexive pronoun** "reflects" (refers back to) the subject.

> *She* made a promise to *herself*.
> The *teacher* did not seem *herself* that day.
> *They* entertained *themselves* with boring movies.

Reflexive pronouns are sometimes used to rename either subjects or objects, for emphasis.

> *We ourselves* are responsible for the mess we made.
> *I myself* will take care of the problem.
> We complained to the *boss himself*.

Note: The reflexive pronoun should be used only to refer back to a noun or pronoun in the *same* sentence. Therefore, it is incorrect to say or write, "John, Mary, and *myself* helped Kathleen move."

Exercise 14

To practice using reflexive pronouns, fill in each blank with an appropriate choice.

[1]One of aviation's greatest feats took place in 1927, when Charles

Lindbergh flew across the Atlantic Ocean by _____. [2]What

caught everyone's eye was not the flight route _____, but the

fact that no one had ever flown by _____ across the Atlantic.

[3]Well acquainted with air travel, he knew the long flight would best be

made in an aircraft stripped of all excess weight, including the crew

_____.

⁴His enthusiasm seemed to be catching. ⁵Knowing he could not finance such a journey _____, he talked several St. Louis businessmen into backing him. ⁶In their honor, Lindbergh named his plane the *Spirit of St. Louis*.

SUMMARY

Fill in the blanks with the appropriate response to show your understanding of the principles in this chapter.

1. The word *pronoun* means literally _____.

2. The noun or pronoun that a pronoun refers back to is called its

   _____.

3. Which pronoun substitutes for each of the following complete subjects (in brackets)?

   a. [Both his brother and his sister] went.   _____

   b. [Everybody] slept.   _____

   c. [The club] is meeting tonight.   _____

   d. [Deer] can damage trees.   _____

   e. [Thirty-three miles] is too far.   _____

   f. [*Channels*] is the name of this book.   _____

   g. [My blue jeans] are faded.   _____

4. Fill in the following table with the correct form of the pronoun or adjective.

Subject	Object	Possessive Adjective	Possessive Pronoun	Reflexive
I	_____	_____	_____	_____
you	_____	_____	_____	_____
he	_____	_____	_____	_____
she	_____	_____	_____	_____
it	_____	_____	_____	_____
we	_____	_____	_____	_____
they	_____	_____	_____	_____
who	_____	_____	_____	

5. Give the possessive forms of the following nouns and pronouns:

   a. This book belongs to Robert. It is _____ book.

   b. This book belongs to the women. It is the _____ book.

   c. This book belongs to the boys. It is the _____ book.

   d. This book belongs to someone. It is _____ book.

6. Fill in each blank with the correct form of *he*.

   a. You and _____ are going to the store.

   b. Who called? It was _____.

   c. My friends, she and _____, helped me.

   d. She is as tall as _____.

   e. We like her as much as _____.

f. Everyone but _____ went out.

g. This book is _____.

h. I appreciated _____ helping us.

i. He _____ baked the cake.

7. Fill in each blank with *who, whom,* or *whose.*

a. _____ is that girl?

b. _____ did you speak to?

c. _____ book is that?

d. Give the book to _____ needs it.

e. Give the book to _____ you want.

f. I don't like the player _____ the coach says is great.

8. Write a sentence using each of the following:

a. theirs: _____

_____

b. there's: _____

_____

c. their: _____

_____

d. they're: _____

_____

e. myself: _____

_____

f. himself: _____

_____

g. themselves: _____

_____

h. it's: _____

_____

i. its: _____

_____

j. who: _____

_____

k. whom: _____

_____

l. whose: _____

_____

m. who's: _____

_____

n. your: _____

_____

o. you're: _____

_____

p. ours: _____

_____

Summary Exercise

Fill in each blank with an appropriate pronoun or possessive adjective. Make sure the pronoun agrees with its antecedent and is spelled correctly.

¹On May 10, 1927, Lindbergh flew _____ specially designed plane to New York. ²There he met two other pilots _____ intended to fly across the Atlantic as well. ³The three planes would compete for a $25,000 prize. ⁴Richard E. Byrd, _____ everyone knew was a seasoned explorer, was the pilot of another plane.

⁵On the evening of May 19, the weather cleared enough for Lindbergh to ready _____ and _____ plane for the takeoff. ⁶Although the next morning was wet and dreary, Lindbergh, _____ instruments and gear had been checked carefully, lifted off and headed for the Atlantic. ⁷Though the weather did not improve, the flight initially went very smoothly. ⁸_____ biggest problem was the terrible fatigue that Lindbergh had to deal with. ⁹The day passed into a stormy, foggy night with only the instruments to guide _____. ¹⁰After nineteen hours, the sky began to lighten, but _____ began to slap _____ to stay awake.

¹¹Finally, after thirty-three hours in the air, Charles Lindbergh landed in Paris. ¹²He introduced _____ to the waiting crowds, totally unaware that _____ had kept _____ at the runway's edge for hours—waiting for the young American, _____ they knew was the first to fly the Atlantic Ocean alone.

WRITING PRACTICE

Write ten sentences or a short passage about one or more of the following topics, using the guidelines of your teacher. Make sure you use pronouns and possessive adjectives correctly.

1. how the old saying "Necessity is the mother of invention" has been true for you in a specific case

2. the difference between "jargon" and "slang"

3. a gadget or item you would like to invent

4. a person you know well (teacher, parent, preacher) who doesn't fit the stereotype of someone in his or her position

5. an incredible find

REVIEW
Avoiding Usage Errors

In the last two chapters we have dealt with using adjectives, adverbs, and pronouns correctly. Although misusing *good* for *well* or *who* for *whom* is not considered a serious error, too many such little errors make your language appear sloppy or uneducated. In addition to adjective/adverb and pronoun errors, this review will discuss many other "little" errors that are made in careless speaking and writing. Because we will be dealing with so many different items, there are several editing exercises instead of one.

USAGE ERRORS

Misusing *bad, real,* or *sure* as an Adverb

The words *bad, real,* and *sure* are adjectives, not adverbs.

Incorrect:	She behaved ~~bad~~ at the party last night.
Correct:	She behaved badly at the party last night.
Correct:	She felt bad about her behavior at the party last night.

Incorrect:	A bottle of good champagne is ~~real~~ expensive.
Correct:	A bottle of good champagne is really expensive.
Correct:	A real gemstone is worth more than the man-made variety.

Incorrect:	His attitude ~~sure~~ has changed.
Correct:	His attitude surely has changed.
Correct:	Betting on that race was supposed to be a sure thing.

Misusing *ever*

Incorrect:	The stallion won ~~ever~~ time he raced.
Correct:	The stallion won every time he raced.

Confusing *good* and *well*

Good is always an adjective; but *well*, usually an adverb, is sometimes an adjective meaning "healthy."

Incorrect:	Jackie did ~~good~~ on her audition.
Correct:	Jackie did well on her audition.
Correct	Jackie's audition went well.
Correct:	Jackie's audition was good.

Incorrect:	I feel really ~~well~~ about the project.
Correct:	I feel really good about the project.
Correct:	I am no longer ill; in fact, I feel well enough to go on with the project.

Confusing *most* and *almost*

Some people confuse the meanings of *most* and *almost*. *Most* suggests "the majority," whereas *almost* means "nearly."

Incorrect:	~~Most~~ all of the students made an effort to attend the play.
Correct:	Almost all of the students made an effort to attend the play.
Correct:	Most students made an effort to attend the play.

Misusing *pretty*

Pretty suggests attractiveness, not a quantity.

Incorrect:	The results from the test were ~~pretty~~ disappointing.
Correct:	The results from the test were somewhat disappointing.
Correct:	You look pretty in that red dress.

Using Double Comparisons or Double Negatives

Incorrect:	Janet has the ~~most~~ loveliest voice I have ever heard.
Correct:	Janet has the most lovely voice I have ever heard.
Correct:	Janet has the loveliest voice I have ever heard.

Incorrect:	It hardly ~~doesn't~~ make any difference what you say.
Correct:	It hardly makes any difference what you say.

Incorrect:	It doesn't make ~~no~~ difference what you say.
Correct:	It doesn't make any difference what you say.

Using the Comparative and Superlative Incorrectly

When comparing *two* things, the comparative, not the superlative degree, should be used.

Incorrect:	You have a ~~worst~~ problem than I do.
Correct:	You have a worse problem than I do.

Incorrect:	Of all his family members, John has the ~~worse~~ car.
Correct:	Of all his family members, John has the worst car.

EDITING EXERCISE 1

In the following passage, almost all sentences contain *one* of the usage errors just discussed. Correct them.

[1]Most every child between the ages of 6 and 12, who is no longer a baby but not yet a teenager, operates in two separate worlds, one of adults and one of peers. [2]Both worlds play a pretty big part in his view of himself. [3]The trouble is that these two worlds can collide quick. [4]What adults see as behaving bad, the peer group might see as good behavior. [5]Every child sure wants to be well accepted. [6]But youngsters have to earn a place in the group represented by their peers. [7]If a youngster can't be the most smartest, he or she might become a smart aleck. [8]When one of the peers don't accept this youngster, his or her self-image may be seriously affected.

MORE USAGE ERRORS

Using an Inappropriate Pronoun

A pronoun should be appropriate for its antecedent.

Incorrect: The horse broke ~~his~~ leg during the race.
Correct: The horse brokes its leg during the race.
Correct: The stallion broke his leg during the race.

Incorrect: When a person hears "sugar," ~~they~~ think of "sweet."
Correct: When a person hears "sugar," she thinks of "sweet."

Misusing an Object Pronoun as a Subject

The subject form of the pronoun is used for a subject of a complete (or understood) verb or to rename the subject.

Incorrect: ~~Me~~ and Molly have always loved horses.
Correct: Molly and I have always loved horses.

Incorrect: She runs faster than ~~me~~.
Correct: She runs faster than I.

Incorrect: My friends, Molly and ~~her~~, have always loved horses.
Correct: My friends, Molly and she, have always loved horses.

Incorrect: It was ~~us~~ who volunteered to exercise the horses.
Correct: It was we who volunteered to exercise the horses.

Misusing a Subject Pronoun as an Object

The object form of the pronoun should be used as an object or to re-name an object. Also, after *let us (let's)* an object pronoun is needed.

Incorrect: The trainers wanted us, Molly and ~~I~~, to ride again.
Correct: The trainers wanted us, Molly and me, to ride again.

Incorrect: Sue doesn't allow anyone except ~~I~~ to wear her clothes.
Correct: Sue doesn't allow anyone except me to wear her clothes.

Incorrect: Let us, Sue and ~~I~~, shop for something for both of us.
Correct: Let us, Sue and me, shop for something for both of us.

Using *them* as an Adjective

Them is an object pronoun, not an adjective.

Incorrect: Sue didn't wear t~~hem~~ earrings.
Correct: Sue didn't wear those earrings.

Confusing *who* and *whom*

To decide whether to use *who* or *whom*, look at the words that follow. If a complete verb (marked *V* here) follows, the pronoun is *who*; if a subject (*S*) and a complete verb follow, the pronoun is usually *whom*. Remember to ignore interrupting expressions (in braces here) such as *I know* or *he/she says*.

Incorrect: Give the doorprize to ~~whomever~~ arrives first.
Correct: Give the doorprize to whoever arrives first.

Incorrect: Jerry did not know ~~who~~ he wanted to vote for.
Correct: Jerry did not know whom he wanted to vote for.

Incorrect: He decided to select the man ~~whom~~ {he knew} was most qualified.
Correct: He decided to select the man who he knew was most qualified.

Misusing a Reflexive Pronoun

Although common in spoken English, a reflexive pronoun shouldn't be used in written English unless it refers back to a noun or pronoun in the sentence.

Incorrect: The results of the election were a surprise to Jerry and m~~yself~~.
Correct: The results of the election were a surprise to Jerry and me.

Incorrect: Jerry and m~~yself~~ were very pleased by the results.
Correct: Jerry and I were very pleased by the results.
Correct: I, myself, couldn't have been more pleased.

Misspelling a Reflexive Pronoun

Make sure you spell reflexive pronouns correctly.

Incorrect: ~~hisself~~, ~~theirselfs~~, ~~theirselves~~
Correct: himself, themselves

Misusing or Neglecting to Use Apostrophes

Use apostrophes to form contractions and some possessives. Remember, though, that the following possessives do *not* use apostrophes: *its, yours, hers, theirs, ours,* and *whose.*

it's	it is
its	belonging to it
there	opposite of "here"
they're	they are
their	belonging to them
he's	he is
his	belonging to him
you're	you are
your	belonging to you
John's	belonging to John
boys'	belonging to the boys
boy's	belonging to a boy
children's	belonging to children

EDITING EXERCISE 2

In the following passage, almost all sentences contain *several* of the usage errors we have discussed. Correct them.

¹The "middle-aged" youngser believes that if his to be accepted by his

peers its important to be the same as them. ²Such a youngster feels

threatened if they are different from the group. ³Them youngsters fear

that any one peculiarity (freckles, thick glasses, exceptional conscien-

tiousness, fast or slow development, different clothes, an accent, or an

unusual name) may cause theirselves to be excluded from the group.

⁴However, their is a worse fate: to be ignored. ⁵Its better, in the childs'

mind, to be called them nicknames than to be ignored. [6]Therefore, some children deliberately behave badly to gain the recognition that he or she exists.

MORE USAGE ERRORS

One-Word vs. Two-Word Combinations

Although according to many current dictionaries it is now *all right* to spell *alright* as one word, other word combinations still have to be written as two. Also, different spellings may have different meanings.

Two Words	One Word
all right	alright
a lot of (many)	allot (allocate)
all ready (all of us are ready)	already (recently)
may be (two verbs)	maybe (perhaps)
every one (every single one)	everyone (everybody)
any one (any single one)	anyone (anybody)
the other (a particular one)	another (any other)

Misspelling Words That Sound or Look Alike

Word	Meaning
here	opposite of "there"
hear	perceive with your ear
two	a number
to	a preposition; an infinitive marker
too	excessive; also
now	at this moment
know	understand
no	opposite of "yes"
weather	state of atmosphere
whether	subordinator meaning "if"
then	opposite of "now"
than	subordinator to express comparison
where	question word or subordinator
were	past tense of "are"
are	present tense of "were"
or	coordinator expressing choice
a	limiting adjective used before a consonant sound
an	limiting adjective used before a vowel sound
and	coordinator

Confusing the Functions or Meanings of Words that Sound Alike

Words That Sound Alike	Function/Meaning
I will *accept* all the packages,	verb
except the one without an address.	preposition
He will *advise* you.	verb
Listen to my *advice*.	noun
Her speech *affected* me.	verb (touch)
Her speech had no *effect*.	noun/verb (result)
I don't like the *bare* wall.	empty; without covering
I can't *bear* to hear the *bear* growl.	stand; animal
Don't *break* the vase.	make into pieces
Let's take a *break*.	a rest
Brake the car with your *brake*.	stop; devise to stop
He cannot *breathe*.	verb
He tried to catch his *breath*.	noun
Can you *cite* that poem?	quote
The red tulips are a beautiful *sight*.	something to see
He is looking for a new *site* for a house.	place
Were you *conscious* of his presence?	aware; able to sense
My *conscience* tells me not to lie.	sense of right and wrong
Did you *lose* your I.D.?	opposite of ''find''
Your shoelaces are *loose*.	not tied
She has *passed* the test.	verb
In the *past*, she drove *past* the house.	noun; adverb
I talked to the *principal* of the school.	head
He owes *principal* and interest on the loan.	amount of money
What is the *principle* behind the theory?	idea
He is always *quiet*.	not loud
He is *quite* serious.	very
He is going to *quit* his job.	stop; give up
I did *worse* than you on the test.	comparing two
But she did the *worst*.	comparing more than two

EDITING EXERCISE 3

In the following passage, almost all sentences contain *several* of the usage errors we have discussed. Correct them.

[1]The worse blistering attacks children here from their peers may effect them, of course. [2]However, a child who all ready has solid self-respect when he enters these years maybe able to bare the rough treatment other children dish out without braking his spirit. [3]So, even though it is quiet annoying to see your youngster become a pawn to group values, parents need to be conscience of the fact that there or some benefits to. [4]Playmates force an child to face the realities of his world; others teach him what is exceptable an what is not.

[5]As if "middle-aged" children now that they may loose their sense of security by distancing themselves from the family as they grow older, alot of these youngsters pad their world with rigid rituals that are past on two succeeding groups of children. [6]Weather it makes a difference or not, they strictly adhere to rules. [7]They are compulsive about an other child's refusal to follow excepted procedure, even in a game. [8]Belonging, nowing the "in" talk, and sticking to rigid principals or important to growth. [9]Experts advice parents not to be to concerned about this transition toward selfhood, unless peer influences are actually destructive.

MORE USAGE ERRORS

Confusing Words with Similar, but Different, Meanings

Word	Meaning
among	of more than two
between	of two
amount	with singular noun
number	with plural noun
learn	acquire knowledge
teach	instruct
imply	suggest without saying
infer	conclude
continual	with interruption
continuous	without interruption
illusion	false impression
allusion	indirect reference
respectively	in the order given
respectfully	full of respect
uninterested	not interested
disinterested	not prejudiced
wait on	serve
wait for	await
emigrate from	come from
immigrate to	go to
bring	carry something when you arrive
take	carry something when you leave
aggravate	worsen (a situation)
irritate	anger (a person)
calculate	work with numbers
figure	work with numbers
reckon	work with numbers
suppose	assume, think
expect	know of a probable occurrence

EDITING EXERCISE 4

In the following passage, almost all sentences contain *several* of the usage errors we have discussed. Correct them.

[1]Since the very beginning, the United States has continually been effected by the emigrants who have come here from other places. [2]These immigrants, the largest amounts of whom have come from the British Isles, Germany, and Italy, respectfully, have brought with them rich cultural heritages that have learned Americans many important things.

[3]Until the late 1800s, Americans seemed disinterested in the large numbers of immigrants arriving every day. [4]In 1882, however, after the allusion that America had endless space and jobs ended, the first immigration laws took effect. [5]In 1892, a center for emigration was established on Ellis Island in New York Harbor, where newcomers often had to wait for days on government officials to process their papers before they were allowed entrance to the United States. [6]Today, although some of the laws have eased, there are still definite rules about who can and cannot immigrate to the United States.

[7]The contributions emigrants have made in art, music, theater, medicine and science, business, and politics cannot be figured. [8]People such as Irving Berlin, Mikhail Baryshnikov, Andrew Carnegie, Alexander Graham Bell, Henry Kissinger, Cary Grant, and Rudolph Valentino are between those who have enriched their adopted nation with their culture, food, art, and talent.

MORE USAGE ERRORS

Misusing Commonly Confused Verbs

Base	Past	Past Participle	Present Participle	Meaning
raise	raised	raised	raising	lift something
rise	rose	risen	rising	move up, get up
lay	laid	laid	laying	put down something
lie	lay	lain	lying	recline; rest
lie	lied	lied	lying	tell an untruth
set	set	set	setting	put down something
sit	sat	sat	sitting	be seated; rest
feel	felt	felt	feeling	sense
fail	failed	failed	failing	not succeed
fall	fell	fallen	falling	come down
fill	filled	filled	filling	make full
hang	hanged	hanged	hanging	execute a person
hung	hung	hung	hanging	suspend a picture
lead	led	led	leading	guide; conduct

Misspelling Past Verb Forms or Using *of* as a Verb

Remember, a past participle or past tense is often spelled with a *d*, and the verb *have* after the helping verbs of mood is not spelled *of*.

Incorrect: is suppose~~d~~ to, use~~d~~ to
Correct: is supposed to, used to

Incorrect: must ~~of~~, could ~~of~~
Correct: must have, could have

EDITING EXERCISE 5

In the following passage, almost all sentences contain *several* of the usage errors we have discussed. Correct them.

[1]The Golden Gate Bridge was the answer to what use to be an insurmountable problem. [2]The bay laying between the city of San Francisco and Marin County was a mile wide and extremely deep and turbulent. [3]The dimensions of the gap sat enormous engineering obstacles. [4]Any suspension bridge risen there would of been the longest and highest in the world at that time. [5]With this task in mind, the city planners were lead to Joseph B. Strauss, an experienced bridge builder, in 1917, but construction did not begin until 1933.

[6]A model of efficient engineering, the construction is supposed to have taken less material than originally estimated by Strauss. [7]It required 83,000 tons of steel, 389,000 cubic yards of concrete, and enough cable to circle the planet three times. [8]Also, Strauss fell it was important to protect his employees. [9]Therefore, before lying any section of bridge floor and in case any of his workers fail, he hanged a huge safety net, which saved lives on at least nineteen occasions.

[10]Since it opened to the public in 1937, the Golden Gate Bridge has set as a graceful as well as practical monument to human ingenuity.

MORE USAGE ERRORS

Combining Words Incorrectly

Often, two expressions with the same meaning are mixed, resulting in a word or expression with a repeated (**redundant**) or incorrect part.

Expression		Explanation
Incorrect:	where at	"Where" means "*at* which" (don't need two "at's").
Correct:	where	
Incorrect:	hardly not	"Hardly" means "*not* often" (don't need two "not's").
Correct:	hardly	
Incorrect:	irregardless	"Ir" and "less" both mean "not" (don't need two "not's").
Correct:	regardless	
Incorrect:	off of	"Off" is a preposition (don't need two prepositions).
Correct:	off	
Incorrect:	and etc.	"Etc." means "*and* so on" (don't need two "and's").
Correct:	and	
Incorrect:	different than	"Different" is followed by a preposition, not a conjunction.
Correct:	different from	
Incorrect:	prefer than	"Prefer" is followed by a preposition, not a conjunction.
Correct:	prefer to	
Incorrect:	a half a	"Half" can be a noun or adjective, but not at the same time.
Correct:	half a	
Correct:	a half	
Incorrect:	might could	Two helping verbs of mood cannot be used together.
Correct:	might be able to	
Incorrect:	used to could	A helping verb of mood is always the first verb.
Correct:	used to be able	
Incorrect:	be sure and	"Sure" and "try" are followed by *to*-infinitives.
Correct:	be sure to	
Incorrect:	try and	
Correct:	try to	

Using Nonstandard Expressions

Some newly invented words or expressions or old words with new meanings "ain't" standard yet.

Incorrect: That ain't right.
Correct: That isn't right.

Incorrect: We ain't got no car.
Correct: We do not have a car.

Incorrect: I gotta go now.
Correct: I have got to go now.

Incorrect: I'm gonna help you.
Correct: I'm going to help you.

Incorrect: He is enthused.
Correct: He is enthusiastic.

Incorrect: I suspicion him of theft.
Correct: I suspect him of theft.

Incorrect: He became nauseous.
Correct: He became nauseated.

Incorrect: He is dark complected.
Correct: He is dark complexioned.

Incorrect: He busted into the room.
Correct: He burst/broke into the room.

Incorrect: He snuck up on me.
Correct: He sneaked towards me.

Incorrect: He bugs me.
Correct: He irritates me.

Incorrect: He is fixing to go.
Correct: He is about to go.

Incorrect: He was nowheres to be found.
Correct: He was nowhere to be found.

Incorrect: He is ✗least seven feet tall.
Correct: He is at least seven feet tall.

Incorrect: He is ~~liable~~ to shoot.
Correct: He is likely to shoot.

Incorrect: I ~~calculate/reckon/figure~~ he will help me.
Correct: I suppose he will help me.

Incorrect: This ~~type~~ person is dangerous.
Correct: This type of person is dangerous.

Incorrect: These ~~kind~~ of cars are slow.
Correct: These kinds of cars are slow.
                This kind of car is slow.

EDITING EXERCISE 6

In the following passage, almost all sentences contain *several* of the usage errors we have discussed. Correct them.

[1]The title "Mr. Typewriter, U.S.A.," goes to a man named Martin Tytell, who is liable to be the world's foremost expert on typewriters. [2]Tytell is enthused about most anything relating to typewriters.

[3]During World War II, he invented typewriters who could print in sixteen languages. [4]These machines, with parachutes attached, were thrown off of planes into occupied countries. [5]Now United Nations delegates, university professors, and Arab princes, among others, often prefer his machines than others to type in 145 languages. [6]Tytell's other creations include a special typewriter with card symbols for a bridge columnist, one with special symbols for a museum botanist, and a keyboard with nothing on it but different styles of question marks, and etc.

7The fun part, according to Tytell, is being a kind of typewriter detective. 8Any one planning on forging a document should beware. 9His family—all typewriter or handwriting experts—and himself can identify forged wills, phony checks, and counterfeit contracts. 10They can also find the author of an threatening letter.

11According to certain experts, typewriting is easier to trace then handwriting. 12Apparently, every machine wears differently and leaves their individual "fingerprints." 13These kind of "fingerprints" fit only one machine. 14Each imprint is different than any other. 15This "Sherlock Holmes of typewriters" claims he can even figure accurately the writer's level of education. 16What really bugs Tytell is people who try and ignore his findings irregardless of the evidence.

17Many authorities are into Tytell's theories, which they use to solve some important mysteries. 18He has gone from state to state as an expert witness in some important court cases. 19In a famous spy trial, Tytell actually constructed a typewriter identical to the one the accused was suppose to have had; thus he proved what no one else had suspicioned: that typewriters can be forged as well as documents. 20In another case, in 1976, Tytell showed that an electric plant in New Jersey had altered their personnel records to hide the fact that it might could have hired more women. 21Because of Tytell's expertise, the women decided they were gonna sue the company for violation of there equal rights. 22Obviously, Tytell looks upon hisself as a hard man to fool when it comes to the evidence typed on a piece of paper. [23]Who would of thought that a typed note was not necessarily anonymous. [24]Somewheres out there, a type person like Martin Tytell can identify its author.

WRITING ASSIGNMENTS

Write at least two pages about one or both of the following topics, using the guidelines of your teacher. Check your paper for any of the errors listed under items 1–4 on the proofreading checklist at the end of Unit 4 (p. 322).

1. Create specific examples to illustrate the ways peer pressure can affect a person's life.

2. Explain how a specific clue helped solve a mystery or problem.

The Writing Process
Proofreading

OK. What you have done so far in "The Writing Process" sections is write and revise. But we haven't even mentioned grammar in these sections. Why not? Because grammar is not the point—clear, interesting communication is. Not until you are comfortable with what you have written does grammar become important. Once you have finished the writing, you will proofread it: Check your verb tenses, look for agreement errors, and make sure your sentences are complete and correctly punctuated. If you have trouble spelling, you should check every word you're not sure of. When you have done all this and carefully recopied the paper, you are finished. You have worked hard and well, and, if you have done what we have suggested, you have written a passing essay. Congratulations!

Exercise 1

Proofread the following passage carefully. Each sentence contains *one* error: either a usage error discussed in this unit or a misspelled word. Correct each error.

[1]"Accept it," she sayd. [2]"Everyone here is into cooking." [3]She handed me a spoon and a apron bare of any decoration. [4]There where two pots of soup on the stove and three kettles in the oven, and every one of them was hissing, burbling, or gurgling. [5]She had earlier adviced me to breathe deeply, start slowly, and stir the food constantly. [6]But now most all I could see was steam. [7]My eyes burned, my bear hands were turning red, and worst of all, I was conscious of a growing hunger in my stomach.

[8]Your on your own, I told myself, and maybe you could stop and make a sandwich. [9]I let the thought quietly drift past my nose and loose itself in the air. [10]She had told me to allot so much time per pot, and all ready I had gotten them out of order. [11]There was no list of directions to follow, no instructions to see weather I was, in fact, following the schedule she had mentioned.[12]When I met her, the site of so many red, green, and dark blue pots had quite unnerved me. [13]You maybe grown up, I thought to myself, but starvation is still frightening. [14]Either I would have to eat, are I would faint. [15]The principal obstacle then was my fear of something burning while I tried to make a sandwich.

¹⁶I know scanned the room. ¹⁷Bread and knifes were resting uncovered on the table. ¹⁸Cheese, I was sure, was in the refridgerator by the far wall. ¹⁹I stirred three of the pots and ran quick to the refrigerator. ²⁰In side were milk, cheese, apples, and more bread. ²¹I took a deep breathe and reached for the cheese. ²²Behind me, suddenly, I heard the loud gush of liquid hiting fire. ²³I turned and looked passed the open door. ²⁴Pot after pot was boiling over, and the affect of all that sauce and milk and stew pouring over the tops and into the gas flames was breathtaking. ²⁵I stood their transfixed, cheese in one hand, door in the other. ²⁶I watched the one glass kettle break, scattering peaces of flying glass across the kitchen.

²⁷After a moment the flames had all been extinguished by the overflowing liquids, and the kitchen was to smokey to see. ²⁸I walked over to the stove, turned off the now unlit burners, than sat down and made myself the largest sandwich I had ever seen.

Exercise 2

Proofread the following passage carefully. Each sentence contains *one* error: either a usage error discussed in this unit or a misspelled word. Correct each error.

¹Susan was alone for the first time with the baby, and the effect at first was frighting. ²Even one crawling child, bare bottomed, seemed to be

one to many. [3]She was quite conscience of the fact that in the past three months she had been alone with him only once. [4]Her husband had been in the garden picking tomatoes and had run into there neighbor trying to get her cat out of a tree.

[5]"He's really gone, this time," she thaught, and held her breath, consciously calming her nerves. [6]"The worse of all," she thought briefly, "will be changing the diapers." [7]Already the child was past the doorway and wondering into the kitchen. [8]She ran to follow an found him happy, rolling on his back on the fake bear rug. [9]The sight of him quite content on the rug made her feel all right. [10]"You may be faster then I think," she told him, nuzzling his neck. [11]"But I will not let you lose. [12]Not too often, any way, and not yet."

[13]Their was the crackling of the fire in the background. [14]All around the fireplace where barricades, and a fire grate blocked the sparks that occasionally threatened to catch them all on fire.

[15]"His only at the store," she thought. [16]"I can be along with this baby. [17]Anyone could watch him, anyone of the parents at least." [18]Willie, Jr., began pawwing the cat. [19]Then he changed his mine and started past the edge of the couch. [20]When he past her feet, she gave him a small nudge. [21]The affect was minimal. [22]"Babies except physical touches of plea-

sure," she thought. [23]She wondered how she had felt as a baby eyeing her dads' shoes or the dog's nose. [24]Had she really been so calm at such a site? [25]Or was it simply that, as a child, she had not really seen the nose or the shoe, but some bare, quite edge of the world? [26]Maybe she had seen the shoe or the dog's nose as the edge of the world, an edge she could of easily rolled off. [27]Perhaps she had been greatful for the solidity of the shoe, the soft wetness of the nose.

[28]"What advise do you give a parent?" she thought. [29]"Babies most never break. [30]They no unconsciously more than we imagine. [31]But don't let them lose." [32]She stated a letter in her mind. [33]"Dear Mom, you were write. [34]They don't brake."

Proofreading Checklist

After you have finished the writing process, use the following checkpoints to help find and correct errors in your writing. Search especially for mistakes you might have made in earlier writings. If you look at each sentence carefully, you can avoid these and other errors now.

1. SUBJECT–VERB AGREEMENT
   Does each sentence have a subject and verb? Have you formed your first verbs correctly? Do your subjects and verbs agree?

2. VERB TENSES
   Have you formed and used the tenses correctly? Have you changed tenses without needing to?

3. CORRECT SENTENCES
   Are all dependent clauses connected to main clauses? Are the sentence elements punctuated correctly? Have you used commas correctly? Make sure you know why a comma is used before you use it. Remember semicolons join main clauses and therefore cannot join a main clause to a dependent one.

4. CORRECT WORD USAGE
   Have you used each word with its exact meaning, or have you used "fancy" words whose meanings you are not sure of? Have you used the correct forms for pronouns, adjectives, and adverbs? Also, check for usage errors of commonly misused words such as *there/their*. Did you write faster than you think, and therefore leave out words?

5. SENTENCE VARIETY
   Look at your sentence structure. Have you used a variety of sentences by combining ideas where possible? Are your sentence connections logical? Have you punctuated correctly?

Exercise 3

Refer to the Proofreading Checklist. Proofread this sample essay carefully for all of the errors you have studied in this book so far.

The Fraility of Life

[1]I never knew how delicate life was and how precariously it hangs in the balance, until one warm, Sunday night in August. [2]The night started out in the normal way, my sister and I decided to take a short ride. [3]We left home with no definite destination in mind, and somehow ended upon the interstate heading to Putnam. [4]After we got to Putnam, we turned around and headed home. [5]Ariel and I were having a wonderful time. [6]Laughing, singing and joking with each other. [7]The highway was dark, the only illumination being the lunation and asterisks.

[8]It was my turn to drive, so we pulled over to the side of the road. [9]As I got out of the car, I paused; my right hand resting on the posterior of the car. [10]I saw headlights heading toward the car, I stood mesmerized by them. [11]They fascinated me in some ludicres way, like the eyes of a predator preparing to strike it's prey. [12]I felt like I was standing near railroad tracks and the train was nearing me, my eardrums felt as if they were going to bust. [13]The truck pushed the car into an imbankment and kept on going. [14]I stood frozen, staring at the demolish, crushed car. [15]Suddenly I found myself running, the grass whipping around my ankles and knees. [16]My sisters car looked like a carelessly discarded accordian thrown haphazardly to the ground. [17]I couldn't see my sister until I ran

to the opposite side of the car, there I found her laying partially outside of the car. [18]She resembled an old broken doll. [19]Blood encrusted her face and arms, her brething, if there was any, appeared to be shallow.

[20]The ambulance arrived before I realized it. [21]She still had not uttered a word. [22]As the attendants put her in the ambulance she moaned and stired. [23]Finally, she was fully conscious, but she had no realization of what had happened. [24]The paramedic told me she would be alright. [25]There was a possiability of a fracture, a few lazcerations, and various minor contusions. [26]I felt my lungs expand as I gave a sigh of relief at her prognosis.

[27]Life hangs like a pendulum suspend by a fragile, thread, and one never knows how quickly and easily that the thread can snap and existence can topple into nought.

UNIT 5 Writing Effective Sentences

While the first four units in this text deal mainly with correct sentence structure, this unit deals mainly with writing more effective sentences. Strings of short, choppy, simple sentences or main clauses are not necessarily incorrect, but may be ineffective because such sentences do not show the reader which ideas are most, less, or least important. We should use main clauses to express main ideas; dependent clauses, less important ideas; and phrases or single words, the least important ideas.

Compare the following passages (a string of simple sentences on the right versus the actual passage on the left) to see how John Steinbeck in *The Grapes of Wrath* combined ideas in his sentences.

From Steinbeck's *The Grapes of Wrath* (New York: Viking, 1939), pp. 1–2	How Another Author Might Have Written It
In the roads where the teams moved, where the wheels milled the ground and the hooves of the horses beat the ground, the dirt crust broke and the dust formed. Every moving thing lifted the dust into the air: a walking man lifted a thin layer as high as his waist, and a wagon lifted the dust as high as the fence tops, and an automobile boiled a cloud behind it. The dust was long in settling back again.	In the roads the teams moved. The wheels milled the ground. The hooves of the horses beat the ground. The dirt crust broke and the dust formed. Every moving thing lifted the dust into the air. A walking man lifted a thin layer. This layer was up to his waist. A wagon lifted the dust. The dust was up to the fence tops. An automobile boiled a cloud behind it. The dust was long in settling back.

Besides avoiding short, choppy sentences, effective writing contains varied sentences. English sentences usually start with a subject and verb, but if all sentences in a passage are written with subject–verb patterns, the passage, besides being dull, may be ineffective because ideas might not be related clearly. Compare the following passages to see how Steinbeck has varied sentences. Again, the original passage from *The Grapes of Wrath* is on the left.

From Steinbeck's *The Grapes of Wrath*, p. 2	How Another Author Might Have Written It
When June was half gone, the big clouds moved up out of Texas and the Gulf, high heavy clouds, rain-heads. The men in the fields looked up at the clouds and sniffed at them and held wet fingers up to sense the wind. And the horses were nervous while the clouds were up. The rain-heads dropped a little spattering and hurried on to some other country. Behind them the sky was pale again and the sun flared. In the dust there were drop craters where the rain had fallen, and there were clean splashes on the corn, and that was all.	The big clouds—high heavy clouds, rain-heads—moved up out of Texas and the Gulf when June was half gone. The men in the fields looked up at the clouds and sniffed at them and held wet fingers up to sense the wind. The horses were nervous while the clouds were up. The rain-heads dropped a little spattering and hurried on to some other country. The sky was pale again and the sun flared behind them. Drop craters were in the dust where the rain had fallen, and clean splashes were on the corn, and that was all.

The purpose of this unit is to show you different ways to subordinate ideas and to vary your sentence structure.

CHAPTER 12
Adverbial Clauses and Adverbial Phrases

In this chapter, after reviewing pertinent material, you will practice forming adverbial clauses and adverbial phrases, to help you subordinate ideas and add variety to your sentences.

MEANINGS OF ADVERBIALS

Adverbials tell things like *why, where, how, when, in spite of what, in contrast to what*, and *under what condition* something happens or happened.

why?
We cancelled the picnic *because of the rain*.

where?
There was an accident *in the park*.

how?
He traveled *by car*.

under what condition?
If the rain stops, we will play tennis.

when?
She *often* visits us.

in spite of what?
Although he still felt weak, he went to work.

in contrast to what?
They were obnoxious, *while we were polite*.

Note: As you can see from these examples, adverbials may be single words (adverbs), phrases, or clauses.

Exercise 1

As in the preceding examples, write above each of the following italicized adverbials the question it answers (why? where? how? etc.).

1. *To make plastics*, chemicals extracted from coal and oil are combined

   and heated.

2. The molecules in these chemicals join together *in long chains* to make

   larger molecules.

3. *Because "poly" means "many" and these plastics have such long-chain molecules*, plastics often have names that start with this prefix.

4. For example, polyethylene plastic is formed *by recombining ethylene gas molecules.*

5. Plastics may be "thermosetting" or "thermoplastic"; *although these terms sound similar*, they have opposite meanings.

6. Thermosetting plastics are hard and rigid and have to be molded into shape *while being formed.*

7. Thermosetting plastics are *quite* common: melamine for dishes, liquid plastic in polyurethane paints, and epoxy resins in certain glues.

8. *Unlike thermosetting plastics*, thermoplastic plastics remain flexible.

9. Thermoplastic plastics, whose long-chain molecules can bend, soften *when warmed.*

10. *Commonly* used thermoplastic plastics include vinyl for records, polythene for film and containers, and polyfluoroethylene for nonstick pans.

PUNCTUATING ADVERBIALS

Remember, an adverbial at the end is not usually separated from the rest of the sentence by a comma.

no comma

We cancelled the picnic *because it was raining.*

no comma

Peter seems tired *today.*

When a sentence begins with an adverbial clause or long phrase, the clause or phrase is usually followed by a comma. Single words or short adverbial phrases, especially those of time, are not usually followed by a comma.

comma

If the rain stops soon , we will play tennis.

no comma

Then he arrived.

An adverbial clause or a long phrase that interrupts the sentence is usually set off with commas. However, short adverbials, especially those of time, aren't.

comma   *comma*

The man , *although he was tired* , finished the work.

no commas

He *often* visits us.

Exercise 2

Punctuate the following sentences.

1. Even in ancient times personal appearance was important to people.

2. To groom or decorate their bodies people used ordinary items in extraordinary ways.

3. Celtic women used beer foam to freshen their complexion.

4. The Celtiberians washed their clothes and cleaned their teeth with urine that had been stored for a long time in special tanks.

5. Soap made from ash or tallow according to the historian Pliny was invented by the Gauls in the second century A.D.

6. The Gauls because they loved wearing brightly colored clothes also invented checked cloth.

7. Because gold was plentiful in Gaul local tribes adorned themselves with many gold bands and necklaces around their wrists, arms, and necks.

8. The Bretons besides bedecking themselves with jewelry adorned their bodies in unusual ways.

9. Whereas they grew their hair and mustaches very long they shaved the rest of their bodies.

10. Then with their bodies dyed bright blue and stark naked the Bretons would fight their enemies.

Punctuating Adverbials: Exceptions

A final adverbial clause expressing a contrast or afterthought to the main clause is usually preceded by a comma.

Comma

I wanted to try baked catfish , *although no one else did.*

Comma

We are planning to go to the movies , *in case you need to arrange for a baby-sitter.*

   An adverbial clause at the beginning of a sentence is *not* usually followed by a comma if the adverbial clause starts with *only if, only when,* or *not until.*

no comma

ONLY WHEN I have time will I go to the movies.

no comma

NOT UNTIL you help me will I finish painting this room.

Note: The subject and verb of the main clause are inverted after adverbial clauses starting with *only if*, *only when*, or *not until*.

Exercise 3

Add punctuation where needed to the sentences in the following passage.

[1]If there is one "meat-eating" plant most people have heard of it is the Venus flytrap. [2]The apparatus to trap its prey is very complex even though we may think only intelligent life forms trap their prey. [3]Six sensitive hairs plus long, stiff spikes on the edge of each leaf interlock when the two halves of the leaf shut so that they can imprison the insect inside to digest it. [4]Although a chance wind may blow a bit of debris against a hair or a raindrop may fall on one the leaf does not snap shut. [5]Not until two hairs are touched in sequence or one hair is touched twice does the trap spring. [6]Evidently, the signal two is important because it indicates to the plant that an insect has probably landed and is moving about. [7]After the leaf closes it generally remains closed for the rest of the day. [8]If it closed whenever a hair was touched the plant would waste valuable time and effort.

FORMATION OF ADVERBIAL CLAUSES

As you saw in Chapter 7, a dependent clause is a sentencelike structure that starts with a connecting word. An adverbial clause is formed by putting an appropriate subordinator in front of a sentence.

I studied the lesson. *why?* I will have a test.
I studied the lesson *because* I will have a test.

I studied the lesson. *when?* I went to class.
I studied the lesson *before*   I went to class.

Subordinators Grouped According to Meaning		
Time	**Condition**	**Result**
when	if	so . . . that
as soon as	as long as	such . . . that
while	not until	so that
after	even if	in order that
before	only if	
since	whether or not	**Comparison**
until	in case	as . . . as
till	provided that	more/-*er* . . . than
whenever	providing that	
	unless	**Manner**
Reason		as if
because	**Concession**	as though
since		as
now that	although	
as	even though	**Exception**
	though	
		beyond that
	Contrast	except that
		save that
	whereas	but that
	while	

Exercise 4

Read each sentence first. Then fill in the blanks with one of the subordinators given in parentheses.

1. _____ you spend extra money to buy health foods or diet

products instead of ordinary ones, you should compare labels care-

fully _____ health foods are not necessarily healthier nor less

caloric. (because, if, although)

2. For example, granola has a health-food image _____ it has a high fiber content and is sweetened with honey rather than sugar, but many available "granola" bars contain more fat, sugar, and calories _____ high-calorie cereals. (than, as, because)

3. Yogurt is a good source of calcium and is often included in many low-calorie diets, but _____ it is made from skim milk, it contains more fat _____ necessary, and _____ it is flavored with sweetened fruit, it can be much higher in calories _____ people suppose. (than, because, if, unless, than)

4. Yogurt-coated candies, fruits, and nuts are delicious but contain _____ much fat and sugar _____ chocolate-coated varieties. (as . . . as, so . . . that)

5. _____ carob, a common chocolate substitute, contains a variety of vitamins and no caffeine, it is not necessarily any healthier than chocolate _____ it also has plenty of natural sugar and thus is not a perfect answer for "chocoholics" _____ they must limit their caffeine intake. (although, if, because, unless)

6. _____ the caffeine in chocolate, sodas, coffee, and regular teas bothers you, you should realize that some methods of decaffeination are considered unsafe by health experts. (unless, because)

7. _____ you substitute herb teas for caffeine-laced beverages, try to limit yourself to three cups of freshly brewed tea _____ you are familiar with the herb _____ some of nature's herbs contain powerful stimulants. (unless, although, if, because)

8. Just _____ you should be careful to compare the labels of so-called diet products or those with "Lite" labels, so should you question the term "natural" on labels. (because, as)

9. _____ quite a few additives are taken from natural sources, the label could truthfully read "All Natural," yet the product could contain a lot of additives of questionable virtue. (although, because)

10. Some states, such as California, have laws strictly defining the labels "natural," "organic," and "preservative free" _____ the public can easily be misled. (because, so that)

Exercise 5

Combine each of the following pairs of sentences into one meaningful sentence by putting the subordinator in parentheses either at the beginning of the first sentence or between the two sentences. (In some of the sentences, both positions are possible.) Make any necessary changes in word order, and punctuate correctly.

1. Standardized tests are usually given to measure intelligence. Experts say their scores may be misleading. (although)

   _____

   _____

   _____

2. For many years experts have criticized intelligence tests. They charge that such tests are culturally and racially biased. (because)

   _____

   _____

   _____

3. One wants to measure how skillful a person is at taking a test. The SAT is worthwhile according to some critics. (only if)

_____

_____

_____

4. Recent research strongly suggests that human intelligence is not mea-
   surable. It is actually an interweaving of abilities. (because)

   _____

   _____

   _____

5. One contemporary researcher believes that athletic and social skills
   are two of at least seven "intelligences." Another theorist considers
   common sense one of three different skills adding up to intelligence
   in its truest sense. (whereas)

   _____

   _____

   _____

   _____

6. These researchers divide human intelligence differently. They agree
   that different kinds of intelligence exist. (even though)

   _____

   _____

   _____

7. Experts now suggest that these abilities develop as people get older.
   The findings of past experts suggested the opposite. (while)

   _____

   _____

   _____

8. Research in the mid '70s began to indicate that a person's abilities develop throughout life. Studies were done of mental development past college. (not until)

_____

_____

9. Data accumulated at Harvard, the University of Denver, and other places are correct. Intelligence is not just knowing the right answers. (if)

_____

_____

10. They forget the correct answer. Intelligent individuals will reason their way to a possible conclusion. (even if)

_____

_____

Exercise 6

Combine each set of simple sentences into one effective statement by changing the sentences in parentheses to adverbial clauses or phrases. Be sure to eliminate repeated or unnecessary words. The first one has been done for you.

1. *If you are interested in becoming a collector,* ~~(Are you interested in becoming a collector?) If so,~~ follow the techniques of successful collectors.

2. (Successful collectors have learned about a collectible item.) Then they buy it.

3. They purchase an item. (They like it.) They do not purchase it simply as an investment.

4. They usually buy an item at first sight. (They may not get a second opportunity to buy it.)

5. (They ask for a discount.) They often get a discount.

6. They beware of items at bargain prices. (These may be either damaged items or reproductions.)

7. (They look over each item very carefully. They examine an auction item especially. They use a magnifying glass.) Otherwise, they do not bid on it.

8. Successful collectors provide plenty of room to display a collection. (Hoarders stuff their objects in closets.)

Exercise 7

Write five sentences of your own about a hobby. Use an adverbial clause in each sentence.

1. _____

   _____

2. _____

   _____

3. _____

   _____

4. _____

   _____

5. _____

   _____

TENSES IN *IF* CLAUSES

Most adverbial clauses are easy to form, but conditional clauses sometimes create problems with verb tenses. By using different tenses in the *if*
clause, a speaker or writer can indicate whether a situation is real or
unreal. Compare the following sentences.

Real situation:	*present tense* *If* you <u>do</u> not <u>study</u>, you <u>may fail</u> the course.
Unreal "now" situation:	*past tense* *If* you <u>did</u> not <u>study</u>, you <u>might fail</u> the course.
Unreal "before" situation:	*past perfect tense* *If* you <u>had</u> not <u>studied</u>, you <u>would have failed</u> the course.

Note: The *be* verb has a special form to express unreal situations for
subjects *I* and *he/she/it*.

Real situation:	*past tense* *I* <u>was</u> in New York last week.
Unreal "now" situation:	*special past tense* *If I* <u>were</u> rich, I would fly to New York today.

	Real	Unreal
I	was	were
you	were	were
he/she/it	was	were
we	were	were
you	were	were
they	were	were

Exercise 8

All of the following sentences are unreal "now" situations. Fill in each
blank with an appropriate form of the verb given in parentheses.

1. A man whose normal weight is 150 pounds would weigh only 50

   pounds if all the water in his system _____ (be) evaporated.

2. If the sun _____ (stop) shining suddenly, it would take eight

   minutes for the people on earth to notice.

3. If a child _____ (eat) as much, comparatively, as a growing

   bird, he would eat three lambs and one calf in a single day.

4. If you _____ (spend) at the rate of $1.00 per minute, you

   would need approximately 2000 years to spend a billion dollars.

5. If you _____ (drop) a pint of oil in a lake or sea, it would cover

   the surface of an acre of water.

ADVERBIAL PHRASES

To add sentence variety and avoid wordiness, you can use phrases instead of complete clauses. In the next sections you will see that looking at such phrases in terms of "shortened" clauses may help you form them correctly.

Prepositional Phrases

We sometimes use prepositional phrases instead of full adverbial clauses to express similar meanings. In fact, some words, like *after*, *before*, and *since*, can be used as either a preposition or a subordinator.

After his discussion with Mary,
AFTER he had discussed it with Mary, he decided to have a party for the whole class.

Because of his diligence,
BECAUSE he is diligent, he makes good grades.

In spite of bad weather,
ALTHOUGH the weather was bad, they went swimming.

during his lifetime
He became famous WHILE he was living.

Exercise 9

To practice forming prepositional phrases, change the adverbial clauses enclosed in parentheses to prepositional phrases, as is done for you in the first sentence.

During the Spanish - American War,
[1](While the Spanish-American War was being fought), more American soldiers died of yellow fever than from Spanish bullets. [2]Generally,

50% of those who became ill died. ³But (while there was a serious epidemic), as many as eighty-five out of a hundred would die.

⁴In 1898, (after the Spanish-American War had ended), a treaty of peace was signed on December 10 which gave Cuba her complete independence. ⁵Yet (because conditions were getting worse), American troops had to remain in Cuba. ⁶Many Cubans were without homes, thousands were starving, and disease, especially yellow fever, was widespread.

⁷Many of the American troops remaining in Cuba (after the Spanish-American War had ended) became ill. ⁸Particularly in the year 1900, the whole island of Cuba seemed affected: Thousands of Cubans lay dead in the streets, completely unattended.

⁹Then on June 25, 1900, Major Walter Reed of the United States Army Medical Service arrived in Havana. ¹⁰(After he had been named head of the Yellow Fever Board), he was sent to Cuba to study yellow fever and find its cause. ¹¹(Although serious risks were involved), Reed and his companions set to work.

¹²Soon (after they established a rough laboratory outside Havana), they began experiments to test the theory that the disease was caused by mosquitoes, and mosquito-control programs were begun. ¹³(Because they had success), the whole world regarded these men as great heroes.

Comparison Phrases

As you saw in Chapter 10, comparisons are formed with *as . . . as, -er/more . . . than,* or *-est/most* constructions. When forming such phrases, you may find it helpful to keep a complete sentence or phrase in mind in order to keep the comparison parallel. Nonparallel structures often create illogical sentences.

To keep structures parallel, repeat a preposition, an article, an adjective, the *to* of an infinitive, or the introductory word of a phrase or clause.

Nonparallel: It is easier to carve meat across the grain than carving with the grain.

Parallel: It is easier TO CARVE meat across the grain than TO CARVE it with the grain.

Parallel: It is easier TO CARVE meat across the grain than TO CARVE it with the grain.

not logical because London is a city, not a land

Nonparallel: The most expensive land in the world is London.

Parallel: The most expensive land IN the world is IN London.

not logical because it compares a certain type of woman to all men

Nonparallel: Recent studies show that a divorced woman has a better chance in a second marriage than a man.

Parallel: Recent studies show that a DIVORCED woman has a better chance in a second marriage than a DIVORCED man.

Exercise 10

With information from the following table, create at least ten sentences comparing high school football, college football, and professional football. Be sure your comparisons are parallel and logical.

Football Info.	High School	College	Professional
In-bound lines on playing field	20′	20′	25′
Goal posts	23′4″ wide, 20′ high	23′4″ wide, 20′ high	18′6″ wide, 30′ high
Length of a quarter	12 min	15 min	15 min
Halftime	15 min	20 min	15 min
Time to put ball in play	25 sec	25 sec	30 sec
Kickoff line	40-yd line	40-yd line	35-yd line
Scoring	1- or 2-pt extra point conversion One foot must be in bounds	1- or 2-pt extra point conversion One foot must be in bounds	1-pt conversion only Both feet must be in bounds
Tied game	A tie if time runs out in 4th quarter (except in playoffs)	A tie if time runs out in 4th quarter (except in playoffs)	No tie—overtime of repeated quarters 'til one team scores
Fumbled ball	Recovered fumble starts new play automatically	Recovered fumble starts new play automatically	Player can immediately run with recovered fumble
Pass interference penalty	Automatic 15 yd	Automatic 15 yd	Completed pass awarded at point of infraction
Officials	4	6	7 or 8
Instant replay judgments	Unavailable	Unavailable	Available on request

Phrases Starting with Subordinators

For sentence variety, some dependent clauses can be shortened to phrases by taking out the subjects and changing or taking out the complete verbs but leaving the subordinators. Only a dependent clause with the same subject as the main clause can be shortened in this way.

Once swallowed,

Once honey is swallowed, honey enters the bloodstream within twenty minutes.

sleeping

A duck often swims while it sleeps.

Exercise 11

Shorten each dependent clause in parentheses to either a phrase starting with a subordinator (as in the previous examples) or a prepositional phrase. The first one has been done for you.

When not relying on wind to be pollinated,

1. (When blossoms do not rely on wind to be pollinated), blossoms have either distinctive coloring, smell, or nectar to attract specific insects or birds to help in the pollinating process.

2. For instance, (if blossoms are yellow, white, blue, or purple and specially scented), the blossoms usually attract bees.

3. (If a blossom attracts a bird as its pollinator), the blossom is orange or red in color, but the scent is not important to a bird (because birds have little sense of smell).

4. (When strongly scented night bloomers are white or pastel yellow), strongly scented night bloomers are usually pollinated by moths, who are active at night.

5. Moths, (because they have long tongues), are also handy pollinators if the nectar is deep inside a long, thin flower.

6. (If a flower is large enough for a bat's head to fit into it), a flower may

be pollinated by bats.

7. (Because bats have poor vision), bats are mainly attracted to blooms

with a distinctive odor.

8. And (while we are speaking of odor), we should mention tropical

plants that produce putrid odors to attract beetles and flies.

Introductory Phrases of Reason or Time

A dependent clause with a *because, while,* or *after* meaning can often be
shortened by taking out the subordinator, subject, and first verb. Sometimes the first verb must be changed to an *-ing* form instead. In such
phrases, the understood subject is also the same as the subject in the
main clause.

Because Chuck was ~~u~~nable to attend the wedding, Chuck sent a
card.

Because he was ~~d~~epressed, Ron did not speak to anyone.

While she was ~~w~~alking home, Sandra found a dollar.

Because John was sick, *Being* John did not go to school.

After Mary had *Having* had an accident, Mary drove more carefully.

There is another phrase (called a **nominative absolute**) that is also
related to a *because* clause. This phrase results from shortening the clause
by taking out the subordinator, taking out or changing the complete
verb, but keeping the subject—which is *not* the same as the subject of the
main clause.

Because the train *being* was late, we missed the plane.

Because his test was over, he felt relieved.

Exercise 12

Combine the following pairs of sentences in two ways:

a. Change the sentence in parentheses to an adverbial clause starting with *because*. Use pronouns in the dependent clause to avoid repeating the subjects.

b. Change the sentence in parentheses to a phrase, as in the previous examples of reason or time. The first one has been done for you.

1. (Many insect species have special adaptations.) Many insect species are able to avoid their enemies.

   a. *Because they have special adaptations, many insect species are able to avoid their enemies.*

   b. *Having special adaptations, many insect species are able to avoid their enemies.*

2. (Many insects are well camouflaged.) Many insects can easily hide from their enemies, as a result.

   a. _____

     _____

   b. _____

     _____

3. (Katydids, or walking sticks, look very similar to their background of leaves and twigs.) The katydids, or walking sticks, often go undetected.

   a. _____

     _____

   b. _____

     _____

4. (A seashore grasshopper has coloring to match its environment.) A seashore grasshopper is invisible in the sand.

    a. _____

    _____

    b. _____

    _____

5. (Some insects may resemble other insects very closely.) Some insects are protected in a special way.

    a. _____

    _____

    b. _____

    _____

6. For example, (the viceroy is often mistaken for a monarch.) The viceroy leads a safer life.

    a. _____

    _____

    b. _____

    _____

7. (The monarch butterfly tastes bad.) The monarch butterfly is not a choice birds would select for dinner.

    a. _____

    _____

    b. _____

    _____

8. (The viceroy butterfly looks like a monarch.) The viceroy butterfly avoids being dinner for the birds.

a. _____

_____

b. _____

_____

9. (The robber fly is very similar in size and coloring to a bumblebee.) A robber fly is avoided by insect predators.

a. _____

_____

b. _____

_____

10. (They use camouflage or mimicry.) Some insects have found protection.

a. _____

_____

b. _____

_____

To-Infinitives to Express Purpose

Instead of wordy *so that* or *in order that* clauses, *to*-infinitives or *to*-infinitive phrases may be used to express purpose (*why*). This structure should be used only if the subjects of the main clause and the dependent clause are the same.

~~In order that they might~~ *To* place their weight on the horse's withers instead of its back, jockeys ride with short stirrups.

Alligators sometimes attack human beings ~~so that they might~~ *To* defend their nests.

Exercise 13

To practice varying sentences and subordinating ideas, combine each of the following sets of sentences into one sentence, using the subordinator or structure indicated in parentheses.

1. *Ultrasound* is a term designating a sound that is very high in pitch. No one can hear it. (so . . . that)

_____

_____

2. Basically ultrasound works in a certain manner. Sonar works in the same manner. (as . . .)

_____

_____

3. Pulses of ultrasound are sent from a machine. Pulses of ultrasound are reflected from an object. (after being . . .)

_____

_____

4. The machine measures the echoes. The machine calculates the distance from the object. (to . . .)

_____

_____

5. Ultrasound can scan an unborn baby inside a mother's womb. Ultrasound is useful in the field of medicine. (because)

_____

_____

6. Echoes bounce off the baby. Echoes go into a machine. The machine projects a picture on a screen. (after bouncing . . . ; to . . .)

_____

_____

_____

7. This picture is heavily obscured by "snow." This picture is not very clear. (heavily obscured . . .)

_____

_____

8. Therefore, a trained operator is needed. This operator must interpret medical data from the screen. (to . . .)

_____

_____

9. Ultrasound devices are also built into mechanisms. These mechanisms aid the handicapped. (to . . .)

_____

_____

10. Ultrasound may detect obstacles ahead. It warns a blind person and helps her find her way. (because)

_____

_____

11. Ultrasound is useful in the field of photography. Ultrasound is useful in the field of medicine. (as . . . as)

_____

_____

12. Some cameras send out ultrasound signals. Some cameras automatically measure the distance to objects. These cameras focus automatically. (to . . . ; and)

_____

_____

_____

SUMMARY

Fill in the blanks with the appropriate response, to show your understanding of the principles in this chapter. Where indicated, write a sentence of your own to illustrate those principles.

1. Adverbials tell _why_, _____, _____, _____,

   _____, _____, and so on something happens.

   Example sentence: _____

   _____

2. Adverbials may be _words_, _____, or _____.

   Example sentence: _____

   _____

3. An adverbial is usually _not_ set off with commas if it occurs _____

   _____ of a sentence.

   Example sentence: _____

   _____

4. Adverbial clauses and long adverbial phrases are usually set off with commas when they appear _____ or _____ of a sentence.

Example sentence: _____

_____

5. An adverbial at the end of a sentence, however, is preceded by a comma if it expresses a _____ or a _____ to the main clause.

Example sentence: _____

_____

6. Introductory adverbial clauses beginning with _____,

_____, or _____ are not usually set off with commas.

Example sentence: _____

_____

7. What is the main difference between a sentence and an adverbial clause? _____

_____

8. List fifteen subordinators that introduce adverbial clauses.

(1) _____   (6) _____   (11) _____

(2) _____   (7) _____   (12) _____

(3) _____   (8) _____   (13) _____

(4) _____   (9) _____   (14) _____

(5) _____   (10) _____   (15) _____

9. With different tenses, *if* clauses may express real or unreal situations. Complete the following sentences in your own words.

Real situation: If _____, he
                             will make a lot of money.

Unreal "now" situation: If _____, he
                             would make a lot of money.

Unreal "before" situation: If _____, he
                             would have made a lot of money.

10. To avoid wordiness, phrases are often used instead of full clauses. In the following sentences, shorten each italicized adverbial clause to a phrase that begins with the word handwritten above it.

a. Hummingbirds lay only two eggs *while they are living*. [handwritten above: *during*]

   _____

   _____

b. No fibers feel as good next to the skin *as cotton and silk feel next to the skin*. [handwritten above: *as*]

   _____

   _____

c. John Keats and Robert Louis Stevenson wrote their greatest books *while they were weakened by tuberculosis*. [handwritten above: *while*]

   _____

   _____

d. *Because they have lungs instead of gills*, whales cannot breathe under water. [handwritten above: *Having*]

   _____

   _____

e. A hospital uses 70 percent of its budget *to* ~~*so that it can*~~ pay its employees.

_____

_____

Summary Exercise

Combine each set of short, choppy sentences into one effective sentence.

1. Most people suppose *cement* and *concrete* have the same meaning. These words are not interchangeable. Cement is actually only one of the four basic ingredients of concrete.

_____

_____

_____

2. A huge machine forms cement. A huge machine combines several minerals. A huge machine crushes several minerals. A huge machine mixes several minerals (lime, silica, alumina, and iron ore).

_____

_____

_____

3. Then a rotating kiln (oven) heats this mixture to about 2730° Centigrade. This cooking takes several hours.

_____

_____

_____

4. The cooked mixture in the kiln is cooled and ground up. Gypsum is added. Gypsum is needed to regulate the time the cement mix takes to harden.

_____

_____

_____

5. Water is added to the powdery cement mix. Water is needed to help the minerals recombine. Water is needed to make the mix harden.

_____

_____

_____

6. We want to form concrete from the cement mix. We need more water and two new ingredients, gravel and sand.

_____

_____

_____

7. We want to make concrete. We must thoroughly blend the cement mix, gravel, sand, and water.

_____

_____

8. We may use a cement mixer to blend them thoroughly. We may also use a shovel to blend them thoroughly.

_____

_____

9. We have done all this. We have created a thick paste that will set to form the hard material we call "concrete."

_____

_____

10. Concrete is actually not very strong. We can add steel or iron bars. We do this to strengthen it.

_____

_____

WRITING PRACTICE

Write ten sentences or a short passage on one or more of the following topics, using the guidelines of your teacher. Make sure you have combined ideas effectively.

1. an unusual way people decorate themselves today

2. how a standardized test has affected you

3. how a recent health announcement has or has not changed your eating habits

4. what "intelligence" means to you

5. a pet owner's responsibilities

REVIEW
Avoiding Ineffective Sentences

Remember that effective writing, besides containing varied sentence structure to relate ideas clearly, shows the reader which ideas are most, less, or least important by giving them proper emphasis: main clauses for main ideas, dependent clauses for less important ideas, and phrases or single words for the least important ideas. In this and the next two review sections, you will learn to recognize and improve ineffective sentences.

GUIDELINES

1. Avoid Strings of Brief, Simple Sentences or Main Clauses

Use dependent structures to give subordinate ideas less emphasis.

Stringy sentences: Horseradish is a plant. This plant is native to Europe. It persists around old house sites, and it naturalizes in rich ground, but it is usually found in gardens.

Better: Although horseradish, a plant native to Europe, persists around old house sites and sometimes naturalizes in rich ground, it is usually found in gardens.

2. Avoid Faulty Subordination

Make sure the main idea is in the main clause and the less important one is in the dependent clause.

Faulty dependent clause:	In midsummer, flowers appear on high branched stalks, when the deep, white, very pungent roots are edible.
Better:	In midsummer, when flowers appear on high branched stalks, the deep, white, very pungent roots are edible.

3. Avoid Too Much Subordination

Do not put too much loosely related detail into one sentence.

Excessive dependent clauses:	Colonists considered horseradish an excellent spring tonic because, when it was made into a tea by putting one teaspoon of ground roots in one cup of boiling water, they drank it to clear the nasal passages, reduce fluid in the system, act as a digestive aid, and cleanse the system of infection.
Better:	Colonists considered horseradish an excellent spring tonic. They put one teaspoon of ground roots in one cup of boiling water and drank this tea to clear the nasal passages, reduce fluid in the system, act as a digestive aid, and cleanse the system of infection.

4. Avoid Faulty *if* Clauses

In the *if* clause a present, past, or past perfect tense is used. The helping verbs of mood usually occur only in the main clause.

Incorrect:	If a person would have dyspepsia, rheumatism, scurvy, or hoarseness, she would eat horseradish roots.
Correct:	If a person had dyspepsia, rheumatism, scurvy, or hoarseness, she would eat horseradish roots.

5. Avoid Ambiguous Connectors

Avoid connectors with several meanings, such as *while* (which can express time, concession, or contrast) and *as* (which can express time, cause, or comparison). Instead, use connectors such as *when, because, although*, and *whereas*.

Ambiguous:	~~As~~ horseradish root is a potent stimulant for the body, it may also help to expel kidney stones.
Better:	Because horseradish root is a potent stimulant for the body, it may also help to expel kidney stones.
Ambiguous:	~~While~~ some people say the young leaves are edible, others say that they are not good to eat.
Better:	Although some people say the young leaves are edible, others say that they are not good to eat.

6. Avoid Using Connectors Illogically

Illogical:	~~Although~~ they are extremely pungent, leaves should be used only when they are very young and tender.
Better:	Because they are extremely pungent, leaves should be used only when they are very young and tender.

7. Avoid Unclear Comparisons

Keep understood clauses in mind to construct logical, parallel, and complete comparisons.

Unclear comparison:	The horseradish plant, like dock, has large, crinkled roots, but they are more pungently flavored and odorous than ~~dock~~.
Better:	The horseradish plant, like dock, has large, crinkled roots, but they are more pungently flavored and odorous than those of dock.

8. Don't Confuse Connectors

Like is a preposition and *as* is a subordinator. (*As* may, however, introduce understood clauses of comparison.)

Incorrect: The horseradish plant, ~~as~~ dock, has large, crinkled roots.

Better: The horseradish plant, like dock, has large, crinkled roots.

9. Avoid Dangling Modifiers

Remember that in a structure such as "When tired, John takes a nap," the omitted subject must be the same as the subject of the main clause; otherwise the understood clause is not properly connected (and "dangles").

Dangling: *(air is?)* When breathing in, air goes through passages in your nose, down your windpipe, and into your lungs.

Correct: When you breathe in, air goes through passages in your nose, down your windpipe, and into your lungs.

Correct: *(you are)* When breathing in, you cause air to go through passages in your nose, down your windpipe, and into your lungs.

Dangling: *Oxygen is taking itself from the air?* ~~Having taken~~ oxygen from the air, it is carried to all of your cells.

Correct: Having taken oxygen from the air, your bloodstream carries it to all of your cells.

10. Avoid Mixed Constructions

Adverbial clauses and adverbial phrases (including prepositional phrases) cannot function as subjects of sentences or as complements after linking verbs.

Mixed: ~~With~~ your blood carries oxygen to all parts of your body.

Correct: Your blood carries oxygen to all parts of your body.

Mixed: While your blood is carrying the oxygen around your body ~~is when~~ it picks up carbon dioxide gas.

Correct: While carrying the oxygen around your body, your blood picks up carbon dioxide gas.

Correct: Carrying the oxygen around your body, your blood picks up carbon dioxide gas.

11. Avoid Illogical Constructions

Remember that many introductory phrases have a *because, while,* or *after* meaning.

Is it a waste gas just because it's being expelled? No.

Illogical: Being expelled from your cells, carbon dioxide is a poisonous waste gas.

Better: Being a waste gas, carbon dioxide must be expelled from your cells.

Is the location what causes them to move? No.

Illogical: Between your ribs and under your lungs, your muscles tighten and relax continuously.

Better: Your muscles between your ribs and under your lungs tighten and relax continuously.

Do muscles cause carbon dioxide to exit your body? No.

Illogical: Your muscles pumping blood continuously, carbon dioxide waste exits your body.

Better: Your muscles working continuously, your blood is pumped back to your heart and then lungs, where the carbon dioxide exits the body along with the leftover air.

Summary of Guidelines from the Review

Here is a quick list of things to avoid if you wish to write more effective sentences. The list summarizes all of the points just covered in the review and is a handy reference for the editing exercise that follows.

1. Avoid strings of brief, simple sentences or main clauses.

2. Avoid putting main ideas in dependent clauses.

3. Avoid too many dependent clauses.

4. Avoid using helping verbs of mood in *if* clauses.

5. Avoid using a connector (such as *while* or *as*) in situations where it can have several meanings and might confuse your reader.

6. Avoid using connectors with a meaning not appropriate to the sentence.

7. Avoid unparallel structures, especially when comparing.

8. Don't confuse subordinators with prepositions.

9. Avoid dangling modifiers wherein the understood subject isn't the same as the subject of the main clause.

10. Avoid mixed constructions wherein an adverbial structure is used as a subject, an object, or a complement after a linking verb.

11. Avoid using an introductory phrase from the *because* group when it doesn't have a "because" meaning in that sentence.

EDITING EXERCISE

The following paragraphs contain many incorrect and ineffective sentences. The number enclosed in parentheses in front of a sentence or passage, keyed to the numbered rules just presented, identifies the problem to be corrected. On a separate sheet of paper rewrite the passage correctly and more effectively, using your sentence-combining skills.

The Barnstorming Era

(**1**—entire first paragraph) Early aviators were real daredevils. Planes of the early 1900s did not have enclosed cockpits. The pilot sat out in the open. He was thousands of feet above the earth. He sat on the edge of the lower wing. The plane was made of cloth, thin wooden struts, and wires. The engine of the plane was not very strong. The engine was also very unreliable.

(**2**) Nevertheless, in 1911, when Lincoln Beachey turned flying into show business, he started to do stunts with his airplane at fairgrounds and racetracks. (**3**) Flying "no hands" a few feet above the ground right in front of the grandstand was one of his usual tricks that wasn't as dangerous as it looked, while other stunts were extremely difficult. (**2**) He was at the Beachey exhibition when he became probably the first American to "loop the loop." (**4**) If people would want to see this stunt, they had to pay $500 for the first loop and $200 for others—in cash in advance.

(**3**) His favorite stunt occurred in June of 1911, when he dove from 2000 feet to skim the edge of Niagara Falls, swooped into the gorge below, flew under a bridge 400 yards downstream while buffeted by gusts of wind and spray, threaded a space 100 feet wide and 168 feet high, and then zoomed up to narrowly clear the cliffs. (**3**) Because his ascent forced his plane to climb at an angle it wasn't designed to handle, although he succeeded, he never tried it again, nor has anyone else in aeronautical history.

(**4**) After World War I, if a demobilized pilot would want to, he could buy a war surplus training plane, the so-called flying "jenny" (Curtiss JN4D), for just a few hundred dollars and enter the business of barnstorming.

One such a flyer was Clyde E. Pangborn, a former Army Air Corps pilot. (**5**) Pangborn flew up and down the West Coast as he was selling rides in his Jenny to small town Americans. (**5**) As he was buzzing the town and doing a few fancy loops and turns, people ran out of their homes and businesses to watch. (**6**) While landing in a nearby pasture, he would offer to take them up for a few dollars.

(**6**) Evidently, danger excited him, although stories are told of other daredevil exploits he tried even before he became a pilot. (**6**) Before the war, because he was working in Idaho at a lumber mill, he supposedly rode the logs down a flume just for the thrill of it. (**6**) While the logs turned a blind corner and shot down a steep chute at a mile a minute, he landed in a holding pond.

(**7**) He developed flying circuses that were bigger and more famous than other pilots of the time. (**7**) One of his most favorite stunts was flying upside down; in fact, this trick earned him the nickname "Upside-Down Pangborn." (**8**) Another stunt he was noted for went as follows: He would climb out of the front cockpit of his two-seater and walk around on the lower wing while another pilot took control. (**9**) Flying over a racetrack, a crowd would form before he landed next door in a field to sell tickets to his air show. (**10**) But because public excitement about such tricks faded quickly caused Pangborn to think of other attention getters. (**10**) By shooting fireworks from the air at night, doing parachute jumps, and transferring wing walkers from one aircraft to another would help sell tickets. (**9**) Being so dangerous, men were frequently killed during the last two tricks.

(**11**) Pangborn's luck being legendary, he once survived a tumble from a speeding car at sixty miles per hour while attempting to grab a ladder attached to a plane. (**9**) Another time flying in Illinois, his engine threw a rod during a thunderstorm and caught fire. (**10**) By side-slipping to keep the fire from the cockpit and managing to touch down in a creek into which he and his co-pilot jumped minutes before the plane flipped over and exploded saved his life. (**9**) While taking shelter under a tree, a light-ning bolt struck a limb above their heads a few seconds later. (**9**) Fleeing to a ditch as they dodged the shower of bark and sparks, Pangborn's only comment was reportedly: "I knew we should have overhauled that engine."

(**5**) By the early '30s, the barnstorming fad had faded, as flying had ceased to be a novelty. (**7**) Even Pangborn got more serious than before: He made the first nonstop flight across the Pacific from Japan to the United States. (**2**) He was 14,000 feet above the ocean when he had to climb out of the cabin to fix his landing gear to ensure a safe landing and when his old wing-walking days came in handy.

(**8**) Barnstormers as these were a valuable group of trained pilots in the United States when World War II arrived. (**9**) Flying military planes or becoming flight instructors, their daring attitude and expertise was passed on. (**4**) This daredevil attitude appears to be an aviation tradition, and even today, if we would refer to the astronauts, we speak of their having "the right stuff."

WRITING ASSIGNMENTS

Write at least two pages about one or both of the following topics, using the guidelines of your teacher. Check your paper for all of the kinds of errors listed on the proofreading checklist at the end of Unit 4 (p. 322).

1. What reasons prompt a person to choose a risky occupation?

2. Vividly describe the incident in which Pangborn's engine caught fire as if you were his co-pilot.

CHAPTER 13
Adjective Clauses and Adjective Phrases

In this chapter, after briefly reviewing the previously discussed material concerning adjectives, you will see how ideas can be combined with adjective clauses and adjective phrases to help you subordinate less important ideas and add variety to your sentences.

FORMS, FUNCTIONS, AND POSITIONS OF ADJECTIVES

As you already know, adjectives modify nouns and pronouns. They answer questions like *how many, which, whose, what kind, which color, what size,* and *what shape.*

Single-word adjectives usually occur before the word they modify or after a linking verb.

The HEART of *a normal* MAN will beat

thirty-eight million TIMES *each* YEAR.

The MUSIC sounded *good.*

Adjective phrases and adjective clauses usually follow the noun they modify.

adjective phrase follows noun

The longest human BEARD *ever recorded* was seventeen feet, six inches.

The DEFINITION *of an anecdote* is a short, interesting or amusing NARRATIVE *about an event or a person.*

IRON *that has been protected by a thin layer of zinc* is called galvanized iron.

Exercise 1

Indicate with a separate caret (∧) where in the sentence *each* of the individual adjective structures in parentheses should be placed.

1. Art expresses the ideas. (that artists have about their world)

2. Painting is one of the arts. (oldest and grandest)

3. The paintings are prehistoric ones. (oldest known; that date back over 20,000 years before Christ)

4. Humans recorded their stories on the walls of caves. (Prehistoric; life)

5. Artists painted scenes on walls and ceilings. (Renaissance; grand; church)

6. Artists may paint on glass or concrete walls. (modern; fragile; sturdy)

7. Critics even believe that graffiti is art. (many; on subways and bathroom walls)

8. The styles have made art lovers of many people and art haters of a few. (different; that artists created through the centuries)

9. But people can find some style to appreciate. (most; of painting)

10. Your library offers books to introduce you to art movements. (many; famous; such as expressionism, impressionism, and pop art)

SUBORDINATORS FOR ADJECTIVE CLAUSES

There are seven subordinators for adjective clauses: *who, whom, whose, which, that, where,* and *when.* These subordinators (called **relatives**, and shown here in angle brackets) are unique. They do two things at one time: They connect the dependent clause (in parentheses here) to the main clause, and each functions as a subject, an object, an adjective, or an adverb in the dependent clause.

subject
An object (⟨that⟩ weighs five pounds on earth) would weigh two pounds on the planet Mercury.

object
All men (⟨whom⟩ the citizens of the United States have elected as president) have been native-born.

adjective
Mark Twain, (⟨whose⟩ real name was Samuel Clemens), grew up in Hannibal, Missouri.

Airplane-passenger service was begun on May 3, 1919, (⟨when⟩ a *adverb* pilot <u>flew</u> two women to New Jersey).

At the common meeting point/of Utah, Colorado, Arizona, and *adverb* New Mexico is a spot (⟨where⟩ a house <u>could be built</u> with each of its corners in a different state).

Exercise 2

In the following sentences, set off relative pronouns with ⟨angle brackets⟩, put parentheses around the adjective clause, and circle the noun that is being modified, as has been done in the first sentence.

1. (Edouard Manet) (1832–1883), (⟨who was an attractive, well-dressed, charming Parisian,) was not the stereotypical bohemian (artist)⟨that⟩ starved in a garret.)

2. The painters whom Manet studied with were traditionalists who usually rounded figures in paintings to give them a realistic sculpturelike quality.

3. Manet, whose art contrasted sharply with the art of his contemporaries, painted flat figures in jewel-bright colors without shadows or shading.

4. This approach, which left an "unfinished" look, tried to capture what the eye momentarily saw.

5. Manet's painting that most shocked the French people was *Luncheon in the Grass*, which pictured a nude woman at a picnic with two fully dressed men.

6. In Manet's time, paintings were usually judged by a prestigious art establishment in Paris that was known as the Salon.

7. The Judges of the Salon, who held an annual showcase of the Academy of Fine Arts, only included work that conformed to their standards.

8. The Salon always rejected Manet's paintings, which were full of color and light, but "approved" of works that were dark and alike.

9. Now his paintings, which were so badly received during his lifetime, hang in the Louvre and the New York Metropolitan Museum of Art.

NONRESTRICTIVE VS. RESTRICTIVE ADJECTIVE CLAUSES AND ADJECTIVE PHRASES

You may have noticed in the previous examples that some adjective clauses and adjective phrases require commas while others don't. Commas indicate that the adjective clause is not really needed in order to understand the sentence. The absence of commas indicates that the adjective clause *is* needed in order to understand the sentence. We will first look at clauses that are set off with commas.

Nonrestrictive Adjective Clauses and Adjective Phrases

Commas set off a **nonrestrictive** adjective clause or phrase, that is, a clause or phrase that is not really needed to identify the noun being modified.

In the following example, the clause *who was assassinated in 1963* adds some information about the modified noun, *John F. Kennedy*, but even without this extra information we would understand who he is. In other words, when we leave off the adjective clause, the sentence still makes good sense.

> *comma*   *comma*
> John F. Kennedy , *who was assassinated in 1963* , was the first Catholic president.
> *date of his death unnecessary to identify him*
> John F. Kennedy was the first Catholic president.

Note: A comma must be put before and after the nonrestrictive adjective clause or phrase, unless of course it is at the end of a sentence.

Only two types of nouns are followed by nonrestrictive clauses or phrases: proper nouns and nouns already familiar to the reader.

Proper Nouns: **Proper nouns** (which name specific persons, places, or things, including dates) are followed by nonrestrictive adjective clauses or adjective phrases.

specific person

Mr. Johnson , who is my math teacher , is very kind.

specific place

In the *Netherlands* , also called Holland , people speak Dutch.

specific date

December 24, 1814 , the date of the treaty , ended the war between England and the United States.

Nouns Already Familiar: A noun already familiar to the reader because (a) it has been mentioned earlier, (b) it is the only one of its kind, or (c) its reference is general and commonly known is also followed by a nonrestrictive adjective clause or adjective phrase.

mentioned before

I went to the movies last night. *The movie* , which was about Gandhi , was fascinating.

the only one

The highest mountain in the world , Mount Everest , is located in Asia.

general reference

A popular Indonesian dish is *nasi goreng* , which literally means "fried rice."

commonly known

Tennis , which is a popular sport , is not difficult to learn.

Note: When a noun like *tennis* is followed by a clause or phrase that narrows the noun to a specific type, the clause or phrase is *not* set off with commas.

specific types of tennis

Tennis that is played on grass is usually faster than *tennis* that is played on clay courts.

Exercise 3

In the following sentences, modified noun phrases have been capitalized. Add commas only when the adjective clause modifies a proper noun or a noun already familiar to the reader.

1. ANDREW WYETH who was the son of an illustrator of children's books is probably the most popular U.S. painter of the twentieth century.

2. N. C. WYETH who was Andrew Wyeth's father taught his son to pay attention to detail in his painting.

3. THE ART OF ANDREW WYETH which is both realistic and emotional shows rural America at its best.

4. HIS WORK which follows the style of earlier American realists has so much detail that it is almost like a photograph.

5. THE PEOPLE who appear in his paintings are THOSE that Wyeth knew.

6. HIS RECENTLY REVEALED "HELGA" SERIES which are nude studies of his neighbor has been critically acclaimed.

Restrictive Adjective Clauses and Adjective Phrases

When the adjective clause or adjective phrase is needed to understand which specific person or thing the modified noun is, it is called a **restrictive** clause or phrase. A restrictive adjective phrase or clause is *not* set off with commas.

In the first example that follows, the clause *who came by yesterday* "restricts" or "limits" the meaning of the noun *man*. It tells you *which* man *of all* men is my professor. Without the clause, the sentence would not make much sense because the reader wouldn't know which man is my professor.

no comma   *no comma*

The man *who came by yesterday* is my professor.

WHICH *man* ?

The man is my professor.

The movie *I saw yesterday* was fascinating.

WHICH *movie* ?

The movie was fascinating.

The house *on the corner* belongs to him.

WHICH *house* ?

The house belongs to him.

Note: An adjective clause beginning with *that* is always restrictive and is therefore never set off with commas.

Exercise 4

In the following sentences, modified nouns have been capitalized. Add commas before and after the adjective clause only if this modified noun is a proper noun or one already familiar to the reader.

1. MICHELANGELO BUONARROTI (1475–1564) a short and skinny man was one of the most famous ARTISTS that we have ever known.

2. Michelangelo was a MAN who never married, lived alone, ate frugally, and worked long hours.

3. On the DAYS that he had worked all day, he had no energy left at day's end to undress for bed.

4. When eighteen years old, he was a SCULPTOR who was ranked foremost in his city, Florence, Italy.

5. At twenty-one he completed his famous *PIETA* which now stands in St. Peter's in Rome.

6. *Pieta* is a NAME that is usually given to any picture or statue of the dead Christ held in his mother's arms.

7. Michelangelo's sculptures usually present FIGURES that seem larger than life.

8. MICHELANGELO whose first love was sculpture also was an architect and a painter.

Exercise 5

Add commas only where needed.

1. Not all artists who become famous have spent years studying.

2. Anna Robertson Moses also known as Grandma Moses is considered the Grande Dame of U.S. art.

3. Grandma Moses who started painting when she was seventy-six never had an art lesson.

4. Her realistic yet simple scenes depicting American rural life have been praised by critics and spectators alike.

5. These colorful pictures called "primitives" are based on her early life in rural New York.

6. She began to paint at the time when her arthritis made her pastime of embroidering too painful.

7. This energetic woman who lived to be 101 continued to create works of wonder and charm until shortly before her death.

8. Grandma Moses who painted without any formal training remains one of the twentieth century's most famous primitive artists.

Exercise 6

Punctuate and capitalize the following passage correctly.

Matisse was a French artist who was born in the 1900s he was a lawyer by training and started painting as a hobby Matisse was the best known of a group of artists whom critics at one of their exhibits labeled "Fauves" or "wild beasts" Matisse simplified his subjects and chose vivid colors that were not necessarily true to nature but reflected his sensations besides being famous for his paintings Matisse was well known for several other forms of art: sculpture book illustrations and tapestry design.

FORMATION OF ADJECTIVE CLAUSES

As you saw at the beginning of this chapter, the relative pronouns *who, whom, which*, and *that*, the relative adjective *whose*, and the relative adverbs *where* and *when* function as subordinator and subject, object, or adjective/adverb at the same time. In the next sections you will see how these pronouns and adverbs help form adjective clauses.

The Relative Pronoun as Subject

When you want to combine two sentences into a more effective one containing an adjective clause, remember the following:

1. The sentence that will be the adjective clause needs to go right after the noun or pronoun that it modifies.

2. The adjective clause must begin with a relative.

3. The relative pronoun must be an appropriate one for the noun modified.

who   for persons
which   for things
that (in restrictive clauses only)   for persons or things

King George I of England, (~~he~~ *who* was a native German), could not speak English.

Assembly line production, (~~it~~ *which* was adopted by Henry Ford in his Detroit auto factory), was first used effectively on June 6, 1913.

Raw material for shellac comes from an insect (t~~his~~ ~~insect~~ *that* lives in some of the Oriental countries).

Exercise 7

As in the preceding examples, change the sentence in parentheses to an adjective clause.

1. Virginia Dare, (she was born August 18, 1587), was the first child born of English parents on American soil.

2. The longest sentence (it was ever published) contained 823 words, 93 commas, 51 semicolons, and 4 dashes.

3. Children sometimes instinctively eat dirt in search of potassium, (this potassium is very necessary for their body growth).

4. Gypsum is a crystalline rock (the rock is made up of calcium and sulphur).

5. Captain Robert Gray, (he discovered the Columbia River), was the first man (this man circumnavigated the globe under the United States flag).

The Relative Pronoun as Object

Remember, the adjective clause can begin with a relative pronoun that functions as an object in that clause.

whom	for persons
which	for things
that or understood *that* (in restrictive clauses only)	for persons or things

Omar Khayyam, (most people know H̶I̶M̶ *whom* as a poet), was also a mathematician and astronomer.

One out of ten trucks (we meet T̶H̶E̶S̶E̶ ̶T̶R̶U̶C̶K̶S̶ *that* on our highways) carries explosives, flammables, or poisons.

A state of intoxication is a noticeable condition (there is disturbance in intellectual function and muscle coordination I̶N̶ *in which* T̶H̶I̶S̶ ̶C̶O̶N̶D̶I̶T̶I̶O̶N̶).

Note: If the relative pronoun functions as the object of a preposition, the preposition may occur either at the end or at the beginning of the adjective clause. Good writing usually has no prepositions at the end of clauses.

One famous Roman historian was Tacitus, (we learned much about *whom* first century Europe from H̶I̶M̶).

or   *whom*

(from H̶I̶M̶ we learned much about first century Europe).

Exercise 8

As in the preceding examples, change the sentence in parentheses to an adjective clause.

1. Pope Julius II, (no one dared defy Pope Julius), ordered Michelangelo to paint the entire ceiling of the Sistine Chapel in the Vatican.

2. So this world-famous art work, (Michelangelo began this art work only under protest), was created.

3. The fresco painting represents a History of the World, (this History of the World is from the Creation to the Deluge).

4. At the center of the fresco painting is *The Creation of Man*, (many critics consider *The Creation of Man* "a sublime moment in art.")

5. Michelangelo, (he took four years to complete this project), worked alone, usually on his back, atop a high scaffold.

6. In fresco painting, the artist could only plaster the piece of the wall or ceiling (he could finish that piece in one day).

7. Paint would not hold on plaster (this plaster was too wet) and would flake or crumble off plaster (this plaster was too dry).

8. The paint (it had dried on the plaster) could not be changed.

9. Therefore, the painter always had to keep in mind the difference in color of the wet paint (he was applying it) and the paint (he had applied it the day before).

10. Also, Michelangelo, (he could only work on a small part of the ceiling at a time), had to keep in mind the entire scene (it would cover the enormous curved ceiling).

11. Michelangelo, (he had to look up constantly for four years), injured his eyes, and for months thereafter he could read letters only if he held them above his head.

12. The year (Shakespeare was born that year), Michelangelo died in Rome, but his body, (the citizens of Florence had to smuggle his body from Rome), was buried in Florence.

Relative Pronouns Showing Possession

The relative pronoun or adjective that begins an adjective clause may also show possession.

whose   for persons
. . . of which   for things

The Greek philosopher Socrates, (~~his~~ *whose* philosophy is known only through the writings of his pupil Plato), left no writings of his own.

Corn whiskey is made of grain mash, (two-fifths of ~~the~~ *which* mash is corn).

However, the *of which* constructions are usually so awkward that we may substitute the adjective *whose*, even though the modified noun is not a person.

The albatross, (~~its~~ *whose* wingspread has been known to reach up to seventeen feet) , is an exceedingly large and strong seabird.

Exercise 9

As in the preceding example, change the sentence in parentheses to an adjective clause.

1. Andy Warhol, (his paintings are classified as "pop art,") was a modern artist.

2. A modern artist is a contemporary artist (such an artist has been painting from the 1950s on).

3. Pop artists, (their style was similar to Warhol's) were popular in America during the 1950s and 1960s.

4. Warhol, (his art did not show obvious emotion or feeling), used a stenciling process.

5. Warhol's art—(the subjects of his art included soup cans, car wrecks, and famous people)—was thought strange by many people.

6. Salvador Dali, (he favored objects that functioned symbolically), was another modern artist.

7. His sculpture of a giant spider (the center of the spider is a huge aquamarine) has legs of thin gold rods with stones on the ends.

8. Pablo Picasso, (Picasso began painting at an early age), was another modern painter (his art went through many phases).

9. His painting *Guernica*, (the intent of *Guernica* was to protest the atrocities of war), shows a distorted horse and below the horse disfigured people (they are in various states of despair).

10. This style, (it consists of oddly shaped, distorted figures), became known as "cubism"; in later years he also created pictures of people (they were painted from the inside out).

SUBJECT–VERB AGREEMENT IN ADJECTIVE CLAUSES

Remember, you must look at the modified noun to decide whether the relative pronoun should be replaced by either *he, she, it,* or *they* before you choose the correct form of the first verb.

It is the DOCTOR ⟨who⟩ often <u>suggests</u> a change in diet.

Note: One tricky subject–verb agreement exception occurs when the modified noun is preceded by *the only one*. Compare the sentences below.

they
many cities

Baton Rouge is one of many CITIES ⟨that⟩ <u>are located</u> on the Mississippi River.

he/she
only one student

He is the ONLY ONE of the students ⟨who⟩ <u>has brought</u> his assignment.

Exercise 10

Circle the correct verb of the pair of verbs in parentheses in each of the following sentences.

1. One of the great American architects who (was, were) known in the early 1900s was Frank Lloyd Wright.

2. At nineteen years old, he was the chief designer for one of the leading architectural firms that (was, were) in Chicago.

3. He was an artist who (was, were) a boldly original rebel against the ornate neoclassical and Victorian styles that (was, were) favored in his day.

4. Wright is the only architect among his contemporaries who (was, were) known to let the form of a building be determined by its function, environment, and construction materials.

5. He was a pioneer whose philosophy (was, were) that a building should appear to grow out of its natural surroundings.

6. As early as 1905, with this "organic architecture," he designed houses that (was, were) built around waterfalls or indoor gardens.

7. Wright felt that the two qualities that (was, were) to be satisfied in a design (was, were) color and texture.

8. At first, he was the only one of the architects of his time who (was, were) using precast concrete blocks reinforced with steel rods in his designs.

9. He introduced many innovations that (is, are) taken for granted today: double glass windows, all glass doors, metal furniture, indirect lighting, air conditioning, and panel heating.

10. Frank Lloyd Wright was the only rebel among his peers who (have, has) had a lasting influence on his field.

Exercise 11

Rewrite each of the following sets of short, choppy sentences into an effective sentence. You may use adjective clauses, adverbial clauses, or any other type of structure.

1. Imagine the earth as a perfect sphere. The sphere's mass spreads out evenly in all directions. In such a condition, the pull of gravity is the same in all directions.

_____

_____

_____

_____

2. But the earth is not a perfect sphere. It is flattened slightly at the poles. It bulges out at the equator.

_____

_____

_____

3. Actually, the earth is like a man. This man has a big roll of fat on his belly.

_____

_____

4. The earth has an irregular surface. It has continents and oceans. Its mass does not spread out evenly.

_____

_____

5. The rocks in some places are heavy. The rocks in others are light. The pull of gravity is not the same in all directions.

_____

_____

_____

6. Communication satellites pass over different regions of the earth often. These satellites experience different strengths of gravity in different places.

_____

_____

_____

7. These different strengths affect the way the satellites move. Their orbits are disturbed.

_____

_____

8. Astronomers study the effects of such disturbances. They call the effects of such disturbances "aberrations."

_____

_____

9. Astronomers analyze these aberrations. They get information about the shape of the earth.

_____

_____

10. From the data, they are able to figure out the shape of the earth. They can recreate the shape on computer screens.

_____

_____

Exercise 12

Write five sentences about the state or country you live in. Use an adjective clause in each sentence.

1. _____

_____

2. _____

_____

3. _____

_____

4. _____

_____

5. _____

_____

ADJECTIVE PHRASES

To add variety to your sentences or to eliminate wordiness, you can often shorten an adjective clause (in parentheses here) by taking out the relative pronoun subject (*who*, *which*, or *that*) and a *be* verb (in any tense).

The architecture (that is of a particular period) often affects other forms of art.

One main quality, (which is artistic attractiveness), must be satisfied in architectural design.

Architecture is a profession (that has been closely tied to art).

If there is no *be* verb, the first verb can often be changed to an *-ing* form or a *to*-infinitive.

An architect is a person (who designs buildings). *designing*

Wright was one of the first architects (who used concrete for buildings). *to use*

Exercise 13

As in the preceding examples, change each adjective clause in parentheses to a phrase.

[1]Mount Everest, (which is generally considered the highest mountain in the world), was once just an unknown, unnamed peak (that juts from the Himalayas). [2]In 1852, the British survey of India included its measurements for the first time. [3]At that time, this mountain, (which was located in the barely accessible Kingdom of Nepal), was identified simply with the Roman numeral XV.

[4]Not until 1852 were measurements of XV, (which had been taken before that time), interpreted. [5]Before that time, scientists (who were at

the surveyor's stations) had not really paid attention to this peak, (which had always been hidden from them by intervening mountains). ⁶The computations revealed that XV was an astounding 29,002 feet above sea level, and a more recent survey in 1975 sets it at 29,029 feet.

⁷By 1856, the British survey, (which had been completed and checked), showed that XV was in fact the highest mountain (that is in the world). ⁸The Surveyor General named the peak in honor of his predecessor, (who was Sir George Everest), but the Tibetans (who lived to the north of the mountain) already had a number of names for it, among them Chomolungma, (which means "Goddess Mother.")

⁹On May 29, 1953, (which was more than a hundred years after its official measurement), and after fifteen men (who were from thirteen separate expeditions) had died trying to conquer Everest, a New Zealander (who was named Edmund Hillary) and his Nepalese partner, (who was Tenzing Norgay), became the first (who reached its summit).

SUMMARY

Fill in the blanks with the appropriate response, to show your understanding of the principles in this chapter.

1. Adjectives answer questions like *how many*, _____,

   _____, _____, _____, and _____.

2. Single-word adjectives usually occur _____ a noun or after a _____ verb, but adjective clauses and adjective phrases usually occur _____ a noun.

3. Subordinators that introduce adjective clauses are called _____.

4. There are two types of adjective clauses and adjective phrases: restrictive and nonrestrictive. Only _____ adjective clauses or adjective phrases require commas. _____ clauses or phrases do *not* require commas.

5. A _____ adjective clause or adjective phrase adds extra information that is not needed to identify the specific person or thing it modifies.

6. Nonrestrictive clauses or phrases follow either _____ nouns or nouns already _____.

7. Put a check by those nouns and noun phrases that would be followed by a nonrestrictive adjective clause or adjective phrase.

   a. football

   b. Mr. Perry

   c. a woman

   d. my car

   e. the tallest person in the world

   f. a chair

   g. the upholstered chair in the corner

8. An adjective clause begins with an appropriate relative. Change the sentences in parentheses to adjective clauses.

   a. The man (he came by yesterday) is my friend.

   b. The man (you met him yesterday) is my friend.

   c. The man (we talked about him yesterday) is my friend.

   d. The man (his wife came by yesterday) is my friend.

9. Remember, to form adjective phrases from adjective clauses, you can delete the subject pronoun and either take out the *be* verb or change the first verb. Demonstrate this procedure using the following sentences.

   a. Gypsum is a crystalline rock that is made up of calcium and sulphur.

   b. Anne Boleyn, who was the second wife of Henry VIII, had six fingers on each hand.

   c. Harry S. Truman was the first president who vetoed a tax reduction bill.

Summary Exercise

Rewrite the following passage containing short, choppy sentences so that it will be more effective. You may use any of the structures that have been discussed in this book.

[1]In 1986, there was a mountain-climbing expedition. [2]This mountain-climbing expedition collected more data. [3]The data suggest that another peak may be the highest in the world. [4]This peak is located 800 miles

northwest of Everest. ⁵This peak is known as K2. ⁶It is also known as Godwin Austen. ⁷This peak may actually be 29,064 feet high. ⁸This is thirty-five feet higher than Everest. ⁹Several groups have expressed an interest. ¹⁰Their intent is to resurvey both mountains. ¹¹They are planning to do this in the next few years.

¹²Will K2 be proven higher? ¹³If so, the honors for reaching the highest peak will belong to two Italians. ¹⁴The Italians were the first to climb K2. ¹⁵These people will be famous. ¹⁶The two Italians reached the summit of K2 in 1954. ¹⁷Their names are Lino Lacedelli and Achille Compagnoni. ¹⁸Perhaps these two were the very first to climb the world's highest mountain.

¹⁹How could this mountain be ignored for fifty years? ²⁰This mountain is so vast. ²¹Both mountains have been surveyed numerous times. ²²But the process is elaborate. ²³There are many opportunities for error. ²⁴The errors may be caused by equipment failure. ²⁵Errors can also be made by human miscalculation. ²⁶In 1988 an expedition will measure K2. ²⁷It will also measure Mt. Everest again. ²⁸The expedition will use many sophisticated measuring devices. ²⁹They will even use satellites to measure these mountains. ³⁰This expedition should finally answer the question of which is higher.

WRITING PRACTICE

Write ten sentences or a short passage about one or more of the following topics, using the guidelines of your teacher. Make sure you have combined ideas effectively.

1. some of the unusual art styles discussed in this chapter

2. a specific building with an unusual structure

3. how you would design the perfect home

4. the validity of the statement that achievement results from "1% inspiration and 99% perspiration"

5. how you would teach someone a skill you are good at

REVIEW
Avoiding Ineffective Sentences

In this chapter you have seen how ideas can be combined to create more interesting and varied sentences. Avoiding ineffective sentences enables you to communicate better with your reader and to improve the style of your writing. In this review you will learn to recognize and improve ineffective sentences.

GUIDELINES

1. Avoid Awkward Strings of Adjective Clauses

Replacing some of the adjective clauses with adjective phrases may solve the problem.

Stringy: In 1923, Doane Robinson, who was a South Dakota state historian who proposed plans that were for Mount Rushmore, originally had an entirely different landmark in the Black Hills in mind.

Better: In 1923, Doan Robinson, a South Dakota state historian who proposed plans for Mount Rushmore, originally had in mind an entirely different landmark in the Black Hills.

2. Don't Misplace Adjective Clauses and Adjective Phrases

Remember, adjective clauses and adjective phrases must follow the word they modify as closely as possible.

Misplaced: Robinson had dreamed of Western heroes carved on the face of the mountain such as Kit Carson and John Colter.

(handwritten note: Kit Carson and John Colter aren't mountains)

Correct: Robinson had dreamed of Western heroes such as Kit Carson and John Colter carved on the face of the mountain.

3. Form the Main Clause and Adjective Clause Correctly

Do not forget to delete repeated nouns or pronouns.

Incorrect: However, Gutzon Borglum, the sculptor he invited ~~him~~ to survey the site, had other plans.

Incorrect: However, Gutzon Borglum, the sculptor he invited to survey the site, ~~he~~ had other plans.

Correct: However, Gutzon Borglum, the sculptor he invited to survey the site, had other plans.

4. Avoid Wordy Structures Such as *the reason why* . . .

Wordy: ~~The reason why was that~~ he felt that a plan on so large a scale needed appropriate subjects.

Better: He felt that a plan on so large a scale needed appropriate subjects.

5. Add Commas Before and After the Nonrestrictive Element After a Proper Noun or One Familiar to the Reader

Commas are used to set off an adjective clause or phrase only when the modified word is a proper noun or a noun familiar to the reader. When commas are needed there, be sure to punctuate.

Incorrect: He envisioned the faces of George Washington, Thomas Jefferson, Abraham Lincoln, and Theodore Roosevelt̸who were four great presidents.

Correct: He envisioned the faces of George Washington, Thomas Jefferson, Abraham Lincoln, and Theodore Roosevelt, who were four great presidents.

6. Don't Use Commas to Set Off Restrictive Adjective Clauses or Adjective Phrases

Remember that most adjective clauses, such as *that* clauses, and adjective phrases do not use commas.

Incorrect: Construction started in 1927, but problems̸that were caused by bad weather and lack of funding̸often stalled the project.

Correct: Construction started in 1927, but problems that were caused by bad weather and lack of funding often stalled the project.

Correct: Construction started in 1927, but problems caused by bad weather and lack of funding often stalled the project.

7. Avoid "Broad Reference"

Avoid using *which* to refer to a whole clause instead of to a specific noun, especially if it is unclear whether the pronoun refers to the preceding noun or the whole clause.

> *Unclear:*   Borglum, who died in 1941, did not live to finish the project, which was unfortunate.
>
> *Better:*   Unfortunately, Borglum, who died in 1941, did not live to finish the project.

8. Don't Use *who* for Things, *which* for Persons, or *that* in Nonrestrictive Clauses

Use the appropriate relative: *who, whom,* or *whose* for persons, *which* for animals or things, and *that* (in restrictive clauses only) for persons, animals, or things.

> *Incorrect:*   The stone portraits, ~~who~~ measured sixty feet from head to chin, required engineering instead of the usual sculpting techniques.
>
> *Correct:*   The stone portraits, which measured sixty feet from head to chin, required engineering instead of the usual sculpting techniques.
>
> *commas indicate nonrestrictive*
>
> *Incorrect:*   His entire budget for the project, ~~that~~ included the salaries of the 300 workers, was not quite one million dollars.
>
> *Correct:*   His entire budget for the project, which included the salaries of the 300 workers, was not quite one million dollars.

9. Avoid Strings of Main Clauses

Effective sentences have main ideas in main clauses, ideas of equal rank in coordinate structures, and ideas of less importance in dependent structures.

Stringy: The basic shape of each head was established through blasting away rock at least 120 feet thick, and the features were first carved from the surface by jackhammer, drill, or chisel, and finally the features were smoothed out with air guns and drill bits. Even with such rough methods, Borglum succeeded in adding ingenious details and he added a twinkle in the eye, for he put a granite shaft inside a hollowed pupil of the eye. The project was not finished, but Borglum died in 1941, and his son took it over, for he wanted to finish it, but he had to abandon it a year later because it lacked support again.

Better: After the basic shape of each head was established through blasting away rock at least 120 feet thick, the features—first carved from the surface by jackhammer, drill, or chisel—were smoothed out with air guns and drill bits. Even with such rough methods, Borglum succeeded in adding ingenious details, such as a twinkle in the eye by putting a granite shaft inside a hollowed pupil of the eye. The project wasn't finished yet when Borglum died in 1951, and his son, who took over, had to abandon the work a year later because of lack of support again.

10. Avoid Obscuring the Main Idea with Too Many Adjective Clauses or Adjective Phrases

Excessive Detail: Today, the stone portraits on Mount Rushmore, an imposing landmark in the Black Hills, proposed originally by Doane Robinson, a South Dakota state historian, and admired by visitors every day, are still not as Borglum had envisioned them.

Better: Today, the stone portraits on Mount Rushmore, admired by visitors every day, are still not as Borglum had envisioned them.

Summary of Guidelines from the Review

Here is a quick list of things to avoid if you wish to write more effective sentences. The list summarizes all of the points just covered in the review and is a handy reference for the editing exercise that follows.

1. Avoid awkward strings of adjective clauses.

2. Avoid placing an adjective clause or adjective phrase too far from the word it modifies.

3. Don't forget to delete repeated nouns or pronouns when forming adjective clauses.

4. Avoid wordy structures such as *the reason why* . . .

5. Don't forget the commas needed to set off nonrestrictive adjective structures after a proper noun or one familiar to the reader.

6. Don't use commas to set off restrictive adjective phrases or adjective clauses.

7. Avoid using *which* when it's unclear whether it refers to a specific noun or pronoun or the whole previous clause.

8. Don't use *who* for things, *which* for persons, or *that* in nonrestrictive clauses.

9. Avoid strings of main clauses.

10. Avoid using so many dependent clauses and phrases that the main idea is not clear.

EDITING EXERCISE

The following paragraphs contain some correct and many incorrect and ineffective sentences. The number enclosed in parentheses in front of a sentence or passage (keyed to the numbered list just discussed) identifies the problem to be corrected. On a separate sheet of paper rewrite the passage correctly and more effectively, using your sentence-combining skills.

(**9**—entire paragraph) The Taj Mahal was built during the seventeenth century. It was built in India. It is an architectural wonder. Twenty-two thousand workers worked twenty-four hours a day. Its construction took over twenty-two years.

(**1**) The Taj Mahal is a memorial that was built for the wife of an Indian emperor who was the fifth emperor of the Mughal dynasty and whose name was Shan Jahan. (**8**) He and his wife, Mumtaz Mahal, which he loved very much, had been married for nineteen years when she died giving birth to their fourteenth child.

(**2**) The Shah was almost destroyed by her death, who locked himself in his room. His followers feared he would die. (**4**) The reason why was that he would neither eat nor drink. They only knew he was alive because they could hear him moaning in his grief. (**8**) When he came out on the ninth day, his hair, that had been dark eight days before, was now totally white.

(**1**) Shah Jahan decided that the capital city, which was Agra, which was on the Jumna River, would be the perfect place for her tomb. (**1**) He chose a site along the river bank which was close to the palace which he could see from his windows. He designed the most fabulous memorial he could think of. For the walls of the building, the workmen used over twenty-eight kinds of gem stones. (**9**) A sheet of pearls was spread over the coffin, the doors were made of solid silver, and they had large arches, and the arches were of solid gold. (**2**) Many of these beautiful touches did not last, however, because foreign soldiers destroyed them that came to India during the eighteenth century. (**6**) But the beauty, that had been created, could not be destroyed.

(**3**) Later the Shah, who had planned a tomb for himself just like his wife's, he never got a chance to build it. (**7**) His son was an evil man which became clear when he took the throne and locked his father in the palace. (**10**) The Shah, who died after eight days of imprisonment, at 74, was found with eyes open staring out the window at the beautiful Taj Mahal, the architectural wonder built during the seventeenth century in the capital city, Agra, on the Jumna River.

WRITING ASSIGNMENTS

Write at least two pages about one or both of the following topics, using the guidelines of your teacher. Check your paper for all of the kinds of errors listed on the proofreading checklist at the end of Unit 4 (p. 322).

1. Describe in detail what you would create to "immortalize" a person who is special to you.

2. Using specific examples from this book, illustrate the truth of this proverb: "A man's reach should exceed his grasp."

CHAPTER 14
Noun Clauses and Noun Phrases

In this chapter we will combine ideas by using nominals—words, phrases, and clauses that function as nouns. Before going on, we will briefly review pertinent materials.

FORMS AND FUNCTIONS OF NOMINALS

Nominals are words (nouns, pronouns, gerunds, and infinitives), phrases, or clauses that answer the question *who, whom,* or *what*.

Words:	*Paris* is the capital city of France.
	It is in Europe.
	Reading is a way to learn about other countries.
	To learn broadens one's horizons.
Phrases:	I like *the new book.*
	I like *the book about Paris.*
	I like *reading about Paris.*
	I like *to read about Paris.*
	I don't know *how to speak French.*
Clauses:	I believe *that I will visit Paris soon.*
	When I will go there is not certain yet.

Remember, nominals are subjects or objects, or they rename subjects and objects.

Subject:	*The person sitting there* is my friend.
Object:	
of a verb:	I don't know *what he said.*
	He said, "*It takes more sugar to sweeten a cold beverage than a hot one.*"
	Give *him* the sugar bowl.
of an infinitive:	He can now try to prove *his statement.*
of a gerund:	He enjoys writing *letters.*
of a preposition:	He is annoyed because of *what you said.*

Structure that renames:
a subject: My friend, *a student teacher*, is talking about
                          sweeteners.

a subject after   Seeing is *believing*.
a linking verb:

an object: He can now prove one thing: *that the world
                          is not exactly round*.

Note: A nominal structure that immediately follows the subject or object and renames it is called an **appositive**.

Exercise 1

Write above each italicized nominal whether it is a subject (*S*), object (*O*), or structure that renames a subject or object (*R*).

1. You may wonder *what purposes the holly plant has today*.

2. Are there any other uses for holly besides *being a decoration at Christmas?*

3. *Eating the berries* is definitely not advisable for people.

4. The reason is *that they make some people vomit*.

5. The Brazilians, however, make *a popular tea* from its leaves.

6. Some people also use this plant for *medicine*.

7. In fact, the berries, leaves, and bark all have *medicinal applications*.

8. One use of the berries is *to stop the bleeding of a cut*.

9. Powder that is made from the berries is applied to *the cut*.

10. Liquid brewed from the leaves and bark can speed *the healing of broken bones*.

11. *Bandages* are first steeped in this liquid before the bones are bound in them.

12. In England, tea made from the leaves alone may be given to *patients* to bring down a fever.

13. *It* is also believed to be good for the liver.

14. A supply of holly leaves is harvested yearly in many countries to ensure *freshness*.

15. The leaves are then dried for *medicinal use*.

PUNCTUATION RULES FOR NOMINALS

As the following sentences show, nothing separates subjects, objects, or complements from the verb.

> That the same amount of sweetening tastes sweeter at higher temperatures <u>is</u> a fact.
>
> An ear of corn always <u>has</u> an even number of rows of kernels.
>
> Rhode Island <u>was</u> the first of the original American colonies to declare independence from Great Britain.

Remember, however, that nonrestrictive (unnecessary) modifiers or structures that rename within a complete subject or object may be set off by commas or sometimes with dashes.

> Three different kinds of sugar—dextrose, fructose, and levulose—are found in honey.
>
> Grover Cleveland held the office of sheriff of Erie County, New York, before becoming president of the United States.

Exercise 2

Punctuate the following passage and capitalize where necessary. Punctuation rules previously studied also apply.

A few years ago Gwynne Giles a University of Toronto pharmacologist began a search for an alternative to breath tests that detect levels of alcohol in the body these so-called "Breathalyzer" tests are typically used by law-enforcement personnel to ticket drunk drivers the result of his research is a device measuring alcohol vapors that are emitted from the eyes.

Giles' "Eyelyzer" is a clear plastic cone placed over the eye for about fifteen seconds the device contains a sensor at the cone's apex that measures any flammable vapors such as ethanol.

The "Eyelyzer" test is very accurate and versatile in fact it is more so than breath tests when Giles compared blood breath and eye measurements of alcohol levels he found that the blood and eye test results matched 95% of the time while breath tests boasted only an 85% correlation. The "Eyelyzer" test is very versatile for it can be given to anyone conscious or unconscious whereas the Breathalyzer can only be administered to those able to take a deep breath and exhale it into that device.

A problem with the accuracy of the Breathalyzer test is that for about a quarter of an hour after a drink has been swallowed some vapors on one's breath actually result from a small amount of liquor still on the tongue law officers obviously cannot prove that a person is indeed legally drunk based solely on a Breathalyzer test the results of the "Eyelyzer" test in contrast cannot be skewed by a last-minute drink.

Exercise 3

Combine each of the following wordy statements into one effective sentence, using all your sentence-combining skills. Remember to punctuate correctly.

1. The seeds of holly bushes provide food for some animals. The holly leaves are also food for certain animals.

   _____

   _____

   _____

2. Cows eat the holly's prickly leaves. Rabbits do too.

   _____

   _____

3. These animals have a thick pad in the roof of their mouths. This pad protects them from the sharp pointed edges.

   _____

   _____

   _____

4. In addition, wild fowl love to eat the bright red berries, or seeds. Blackbirds especially love to eat them.

   _____

   _____

5. Holly berries sprout in almost any type of soil. This natural process is inefficient for two reasons.

   _____

   _____

6. First, there is the appetite of the birds. This eliminates many of the berries before or after they fall.

_____

_____

7. A second drawback is this. The seed takes two years to germinate after it has fallen.

_____

_____

8. Therefore, holly growers periodically make cuttings from 4- to 5-year-old plants. Growers do this so that they can start new holly bushes.

_____

_____

_____

9. In effect, people have substituted a more efficient system. It is more efficient than waiting for those slow seeds to sprout.

_____

_____

_____

10. What holly growers have done is simple. They have ensured a faster way to propagate this beautiful plant. It is also a less chancy way.

_____

_____

_____

Punctuating Quotations

When you want to report what someone said or thought, you usually say, "He said . . . " or "She thought . . . " The objects after these verbs sometimes have special punctuation rules.

There are two ways to report what a person said: You can either repeat the words exactly the way they were said (a **direct quotation**) or *paraphrase* them (an **indirect quotation**).

direct quotation
He said, "I am going to travel to the Sahara."

indirect quotation
He said that he was going to travel to the Sahara.

As you can see, you need quotation marks in direct quotations but not in indirect quotations.

When you use quotation marks, you must pay attention to where capital letters, periods, commas, and other punctuation marks go. Here are several helpful rules.

First Word of Quote Is Capitalized If It Is a Complete Sentence:

complete sentence
He said, "We are going to the movies."

dependent clause
"We are going to the movies," he said, "if we have time."

"We are going to the movies," he said. "Then we are going out to eat."

Comma or Period Goes *Before* End Quotation Mark:

"We are going to the mall tonight," he said.
He said, "We are going to the mall tonight."

Semicolon Goes *After* End Quotation Mark:

She added, "The movie is a classic"; however, she didn't like it.

Question Mark or Exclamation Mark Goes *Before* End Quotation Mark If Only the Quoted Material Is a Question or an Exclamation:

question

"Was the movie any good?" he asked.

exclamation

She answered, "It was terrific!"

Question Mark or Exclamation Mark Goes *After* End Quotation Mark If the Complete Sentence Is a Question or an Exclamation:

question

Did he say, "The movie was terrific"?

exclamation

What a stupid question, "Why should I take another English course?"!

Exercise 4

In each of the following historical quotes, add appropriate punctuation before and/or after each quotation mark (when necessary).

1. According to Mason Locke Weems, the man responsible for the apocryphal cherry tree myth, the young George Washington said "I can't tell a lie, Pa; you know I can't tell a lie. I did it with my hatchet "

2. "Run to my arms, you dearest boy " cried his father "Glad am I that you killed my tree, for you have paid me a thousandfold "

3. The crowd at Washington's inauguration was absolutely silent until Chancellor Robert R. Livingston, who administered the oath, shouted "Long live George Washington, President of the United States "

4. When James Hoban's design for the White House was selected over his own, Thomas Jefferson reportedly criticized it by saying "It is big enough for two emperors, one Pope, and the Grand Lama "

5. The official report of Major S. H. Long's two-year expedition to explore the Great Plains stated "This area is almost wholly unfit for cultivation " however this report did not stop western-moving pioneers.

6. After the newspapers had announced the name of the Democratic nominee for president in 1844, the opposing Whig party leaders sarcastically asked "Who is James K. Polk "

7. One American historian answered this question years later by asserting "He was the least conspicuous man who had ever been nominated for President "

8. Henry Clay of Kentucky, a compromiser who struggled to avoid the Civil War by trying to please both North and South, was twice defeated for the presidency but fervently exclaimed "I would rather be right than president "

9. "Whatever you say, tell the truth " Grover Cleveland instructed his campaign managers following the Republicans' charge that he had once fathered an illegitimate child. This honesty won him the presidency in 1885 despite the truth of the accusation.

10. Because he weighed over 300 pounds, William Taft was the butt of many jokes; once, after the President told his friend Elihu Root that he had just ridden twenty-five miles on horseback, Root asked "How is the horse "

FORMATION OF NOUN CLAUSES

Forming Noun Clauses from Statements

When you paraphrase what someone has said, you may have to add or change some words. You usually add the connector *that* (in angle brackets here), and often you must change the pronouns.

direct quotation

My parents said, "WE are sure that OUR car was stolen."

paraphrase

My parents said ⟨*that*⟩ THEY were sure that THEIR car was stolen.

Sometimes the verb in the dependent clause must be changed, too. Remember that, according to the sequence-of-tense rule, the first verbs in the main and the dependent clauses usually are in the same tense.

"I <u>am</u> hungry!"

Charles *says* that he <u>is</u> hungry.

Charles *said* that he <u>was</u> hungry.

However, if the independent clause states something that is still true or occurs regularly, the tenses do not have to agree.

"Water <u>freezes</u> at 32° Fahrenheit."

He *explained* that water <u>freezes</u> at 32° Fahrenheit.

Exercise 5

Read the passage. Then finish the dependent clauses begun for you in the numbered sentences that follow it.

Good manners and ideas about what constitutes proper behavior aren't the same everywhere in the world. In France, Austria, Germany, Switzerland, and West Africa, you are being rude if you ask directions or ask a salesperson anything without first saying "Bon jour," "hello," or some other polite greeting. In Southeast Asia and parts of Africa, exposing the sole of the foot or of the shoe or sitting with your toes pointing toward someone is considered rude. Touching a person's head is not acceptable in Thailand, for the head is thought to be sacred.

Etiquette at the dining table also differs from country to country. When should a person begin to eat if she is seated at the table with a group, but her food arrives before theirs? In England it is customary to begin eating as soon as your food arrives, even if others are waiting; in Holland the proper thing would be to wait for the others to be served; in Korea it is impolite to start before the oldest person present eats.

1. The passage states that in several European countries and in West

   Africa _____

   _____.

2. In response to a question about dining, the passage explained that

   _____

   in Holland.

3. On the other hand, it said that _____

   _____ when dining in Korea.

4. The passage also mentions that in Thailand _____

   _____.

5. Apparently, many Southeast Asians and Africans feel that _____

   _____

   _____ is rude.

6. Before reading this passage you might have thought that _____

   _____,

   but now you know that _____

   _____.

Forming Noun Clauses from Wishes, Demands, Suggestions, and Formal Requests

When you express a wish, you express something that is unreal. To show that the wish is unreal, you must use a past tense for a "now" situation and a past perfect tense for a "before" situation. (Remember that the *be* verb has a special past form for unreal situations—see p. 338.)

he isn't a better friend

I wish John <u>were</u> a better friend.

he wasn't a better friend

I wished that John <u>had been</u> a better friend.

When you express a demand, a suggestion, or a formal request with a verb like *move* or *request*, the first verb in the dependent clause also has a special form—it is always the base form.

base form

He *moves* that the meeting <u>be</u> adjourned.

base form

The audience *requested* that she <u>perform</u> another encore.

Note: Other verbs that are like *move* and *request* include the following: *demand, command, order, require, stipulate, insist, forbid, suggest, advise, recommend, urge, propose, desire, prefer, beg,* and *ask.*

Exercise 6

Read the following passage. Then finish the dependent clauses begun for you in the sentences that follow it. Your answers should be true according to the information in the passage and grammatically correct.

If you are offered refreshments in an Arabic country, you should politely refuse at first but accept when the host coaxes you. In Moslem lands a person should never use his left hand—even if that person is left-handed—to give or receive items, to eat, or to hold a cigarette, because Moslems reserve that hand for bathroom functions. Also, a tourist should always ask permission to take pictures, since Moslems usually object on religious grounds.

In the Islamic culture a woman is required to dress modestly, and some countries take an extremely strict interpretation of "modest." Basically, a woman needs to cover most of her skin and wear loose clothes. Sleeveless dresses, scooped necklines, and even skirts just below the knee are considered immodest.

When visiting religious sites in most countries, women should generally avoid wearing pants, and all tourists should beware of touching the statues or acting irreverently. In some countries tourists might be arrested and fined for sacrilege.

Fortunately, the majority of social and cultural mistakes made by foreigners are forgiven or excused because most governments believe that the tourists were simply ignorant and not intentionally offensive. Nevertheless, it is a good idea to study the culture of the places you plan to visit to avoid impoliteness and misunderstandings.

1. This passage recommends that a person _____

   _____

   if offered refreshments in an Arabic country.

2. One thing it stipulates is that left-handed people _____

   _____.

3. Of course, in most countries people are forgiving because they believe that tourists _____

   _____.

4. However, there is a possibility that a person _____

   _____.

5. Many Moslem countries require that a woman _____

   _____

6. In a number of countries, custom forbids that tourists _____

   _____.

7. I wish that traveling to other lands _____ not so expensive, for

   it is the best way to learn about other cultures.

Exercise 7

Complete the sentences that follow this passage. Your answers should be true according to the information in the story and grammatically correct. Pay special attention to verb tenses in combining dependent and main clauses.

Mary, a high school drama teacher, and her fiance made an appointment to be married at the county courthouse. Everything went according to schedule until the judge asked, "Will you take this man to be your wedded husband?"

"I do," said Mary.

"The proper response," whispered the judge, "is *I will.*"

"But in all the shows that I have seen and been in," Mary insisted, "they always say *I do.*"

The judge and Mary stared at each other, and the groom grew increasingly nervous. The impasse was broken when the witness, an elderly English teacher, announced in an authoritative voice that could be heard at the rear of the chamber, "If you wish to be absolutely correct, the response should be *I shall.*"

The judge searched the room in an appeal for help. Finding none, he snapped his book shut and declared, "Whatever, I now pronounce you husband and wife."

1. Mary and her husband-to-be were at the county courthouse because

   _____.

2. Everything _____

   during the first part of the ceremony.

3. Then the judge asked if Mary _____

   _____.

4. Mary answered that she _____.

5. The judge thought that the proper response _____.

6. However, Mary answered that in all the shows she _____

   _____.

7. While the judge and Mary _____ ,

   the groom _____ .

8. The witness, an English teacher, broke the impasse when she an-

   nounced that the correct _____ .

9. As the judge searched the room, he obviously wished that _____

   _____ .

10. Since _____ ,

    he snapped his book shut and declared that he _____

    them husband and wife.

11. Although the judge had at first demanded that _____

    _____ ,

    he capitulated in the end.

Forming Noun Clauses from Questions

When you paraphrase a question someone asked, you have to do even more than change pronouns and verbs.

As the following examples show, there are several differences between a direct question and a paraphrased question. If the question starts with a question word (such as *where, when, why, how, who,* or *whose*), it becomes the connector (in angle brackets here).

He asked, "What movie do you want to see?"

He asked ⟨*what*⟩ movie I wanted to see.

But if the direct question does not start with a question word, you must add *if* or *whether*.

He asked, "Are you going out tonight?"

He asked ⟨*if*⟩ I was going out tonight.

He asked ⟨*whether*⟩ I was going out tonight.

Another important change involves word order. In a direct question the first verb usually comes before the subject (circled here), but in a paraphrased question the subject comes first.

He asked, "Whom shall (we) invite?"
He wanted to know whom (we) should invite.

John asked, "Have (you) seen my math book?"
John asked if (I) had seen his math book.

Also, in a direct question we often need the *do* helping verb, but in a paraphrased question we do not.

He asked, "What movie do (you) want to see?"
He asked what movie (I) wanted to see.

Remember, a direct question ends with a question mark, but a paraphrased question does not (unless, of course, the whole sentence is a question).

He asked, "When did you leave?"
He asked when I had left.
Did he want to know when I had left?

Exercise 8

In the following passage, change the direct questions in parentheses to paraphrased questions. Make sure you have a connector, and make all appropriate changes in tense, word order, and punctuation. The pronouns have already been changed for you. The first sentence has been done as an example.

Heredity and You

[1]When you were born, your parents had no idea *whom you would* (Whom will you look *look like or what you would grow up to be.* like?) or (What will you grow up to be?). [2]From the first moments of your

life they probably argued about (Whom in your family do you look like?)

and (What abilities may you have inherited?).

³Think about appearance for a moment, and ask yourself (Are you light-haired like your father when he was young?) or (Is your hair curly like your mother's?). ⁴In considering your abilities, have you ever wondered (Do you have a talent for music or mathematics? Are you strong and well coordinated? Are you good in sports? Do you learn things easily?), or (Are you good in some subjects but not so good in others?).

⁵All of these traits, and many, many more, are at least partly the result of your *heredity*.

⁶But what about the world around you? ⁷How do you think it has affected you? ⁸Ask yourself (Where do you live?) and (Do you live in a small town, in the country, or in a suburb of a large city?). ⁹(Where do you live?) and (Whom do you live with?) are part of your *environment*. ¹⁰So are your friends, your school, your place of worship, the country you live in, the books you read, the movies you see, and the shows you watch on television. ¹¹All of these things have an influence on (Who are you?).

Exercise 9

Go back to Exercise 4 (p. 404) and rewrite sentences 1, 4, 6, 8, and 10 by changing the direct quotation to an indirect quotation.

1. _____

_____

_____

_____

_____

4. _____

_____

_____

_____

_____

6. _____

_____

_____

_____

8. _____

_____

_____

_____

10. _____

_____

_____

_____

_____

GERUNDS, INFINITIVES, AND OTHER TYPES OF NOUN PHRASES

You can vary your sentences or eliminate wordiness by using phrases instead of clauses to express the same thoughts. Instead of a noun clause, you can use infinitives, gerunds, or other types of noun phrases.

As the following examples show, a *that* clause can be replaced with (1) an infinitive, (2) a gerund, or (3) some other type of noun phrase.

To transport
That we transport the goods quickly is necessary.

Transporting
That we transport the goods quickly is necessary.

Quick transportation of
That we transport the goods quickly is necessary.

Note: Often, all three structures are possible, but, depending on the sentence, usually one sounds better than the others.

Exercise 10

Create a gerund phrase, a *to*-infinitive phrase, or some other noun phrase, as in the preceding examples, from each underlined verb in parentheses. The first three have been done for you. *Note*: A verb may be identical to its corresponding noun form and not need changing in a few cases.

[1]According to one researcher's theory, lead (*poisoning*) (poison) may have made a *contribution* (contribute) to the Rome *fall of Rome* (fall). [2]Their custom was (cook) a special grape syrup in lead pots or in copper utensils lined with lead. [3](Flavor) their wine with this syrup and (use) such wine in many recipes probably provided their daily diet with a toxic amount of lead. [4]Because the syrup was a staple in the Roman diet, this researcher's (estimate) is that the Romans ingested more than five times the lead that modern health experts consider acceptable.

[5]Scientists now know that a heavy lead (<u>concentrate</u>) in one's environment results in lead (<u>poison</u>). [6](<u>Absorb</u>) toxic levels of lead into the body is possible a number of ways: through skin (<u>contact</u>), (<u>inhale</u>), or (<u>ingest</u>) with food or drink. [7](<u>Convulse</u>), a coma, or mental retardation may follow in children and infants after (<u>expose</u>). [8]Adults after chronic (<u>expose</u>) may have noticeable personality (<u>change</u>).

[9]No wonder so many Roman emperors with their lavish style of (<u>live</u>) had such erratic (<u>behave</u>)! [10]Their mental capacity was probably undermined by their (<u>glut</u>). [11]Ironically, the fall of the Roman Empire was perhaps caused not by outside enemies' (<u>attack</u>) Rome, but by a silent enemy's (<u>strike</u>) from within at the very core of the empire—its leadership.

SUMMARY

Fill in the blanks with the appropriate response, to show your understanding of the principles in this chapter.

1. **Nominals** are words, _____, or _____ used as nouns.

2. Nominals can function as _subject_ or _____, and structures that

   _____.

3. Capitalize the following direct quotations, and add quotation or other punctuation marks.

   a. He said   we are going to New York tomorrow

   b. He asked   will you feed my cat for me

   c. When I agreed he exclaimed   you are great

4. Paraphrase the following direct questions. Make sure you have a connector, and be certain to make all appropriate changes in pronouns, tense, word order, and punctuation.

"I am talking on the phone." He said _____

_____.

"Life is beautiful." She felt _____

_____.

"I own three Cadillacs." I wish _____

_____.

"The meeting is adjourned." He moved _____

_____.

"Will you go to the movies with us?" They asked _____

_____.

"What does he want to eat for breakfast? She wanted to know _____

_____.

Summary Exercise

On a separate sheet of paper, rewrite the following passage using all of your sentence-combining skills (use adverbial, adjective, and nominal structures). Try to vary your sentences and avoid wordiness.

We hear the word *twins*. Immediately, one reaction is normal. We picture two people. These people are exactly alike. But then we think about it further. We may recall something important. There are some boy/girl sets of twins. There are sometimes two of the same sex, but they do not really look alike. The latest research suggests something surprising. Scientifically, at least four types of twins exist. Most of us are familiar with only two types.

First, everyone knows about identical twins. These result when a single egg is fertilized. It then splits in two. Each section develops into a separate fetus. These fetuses have identical genes. Identical twins occur once out of every 250 births. However, to predict identical twins is not easy. They seem to occur at random.

Fraternal twins result from two eggs. These eggs are released at the same time. They are fertilized by separate sperm. Again, both eggs develop into fetuses. They are born from the same parents, so genetically they are alike. Any siblings born from the same parents are alike for the same reason. By now you are probably thinking of one obvious question. "Are all boy/girl sets of twins fraternal?" The correct response follows. "Yes, but a lot of twins of the same sex are fraternal as well." Fraternal twins are born minutes apart, but they may look nothing alike. Statistics about fraternal twins are very specific. Fraternal twins occur often. In fact, fraternal sets are twice as likely to occur as identical sets. They also run in families.

Scientists have now identified half-identical twins. They have even identified twins of different fathers.

The half-identical group is rare. A pre-ovum (not a true egg yet) divides itself into two equal halves. Then it is fertilized by two separate sperm. These twins have identical genes from their mother's egg. They have different genes from the father, however. Two sperm were involved rather than one. These twins look very much alike, but they are not "mirrors" of one another. Identical twins are.

Last, there are twins from different fathers. This group is even more rare. A new egg is somehow released. Subsequently it is fertilized by another man. However, the previous month's fertilized egg is already present. These facts seem to account for this phenomenon. These babies are basically step-siblings. They just happen to be born at the same time.

WRITING PRACTICE

Write ten sentences or a short passage about one or more of the following topics, using the guidelines of your teacher. Make sure you have combined ideas effectively.

1. a folk remedy with which you are familiar

2. the things eyes can tell

3. the traits you hope your children will or will not inherit from you

4. the advantages or disadvantages of being a twin

5. how you would prepare an alien to behave properly at a party

REVIEW
Avoiding Ineffective Sentences

In this chapter you have seen how ideas can be combined to create more interesting and varied sentences. Avoiding ineffective sentences enables you to communicate better with your reader and to improve the style of your writing. In this review you will learn to recognize and improve ineffective sentences.

GUIDELINES

1. Avoid Strings of Brief, Simple Sentences or Main Clauses

Use dependent structures to subordinate ideas.

Stringy: The U.S. Capitol is a building. This building may never be finished. William Thornton was an architect. He drew the plans for the U.S. Capitol. George Washington was president at the time. President Washington laid the cornerstone for the building. This was done in 1793. Congress required changes. Architect William Thornton's plan was not satisfactory to them. The problem needed to be solved immediately. His plans were changed immediately after that. The building was changed at that time. It has been changed many times since. The U.S. Capitol has had many wings added on. This building also has been remodeled. Both have happened a lot.

Better: The U.S. Capitol building may never be finished. In 1793, immediately after President Washington had laid the cornerstone, Congress asked the architect, William Thornton, to change the plans. Since that time, the U.S. Capitol building has been frequently remodeled.

2. Avoid Faulty or Excessive Subordination

Make sure main ideas are properly emphasized and not obscured by too much loosely related detail.

Faulty
subordination: What Thornton drew a plan for was a building that had two wings, one for each house of Congress. What the building was designed to be was a type of structure that would be joined at the center which had a chamber topped by a dome that would be modest and that would be at the center. What was planned was that the wing that was situated to the north would be finished by 1800, and it was.

Better: Thornton originally designed a building with two wings, one for each house of Congress, joined at the center by a chamber topped by a modest dome. The north wing was finished by 1800, according to plan.

3. Avoid Mixing Direct and Paraphrased Statements

Indirect quotes must start with a connector and have subject–verb word order.

Mixed direct/
indirect: In 1803, President Thomas Jefferson asked Benjamin Latrobe ~~would he~~ continue William Thornton's work and when ~~could he~~ finish the south wing?

Better: In 1803, President Thomas Jefferson asked Benjamin Latrobe if he would continue William Thornton's work and finish the south wing.

4. Avoid Wordy or Faulty *is when, is why,* or *is because* Constructions

Wordy: In 1807 ~~is when~~ Latrobe finished the south wing.
Better: Latrobe finished the south wing in 1807.

Wordy: Because the center chamber was not built yet ~~was why~~ a wooden walkway joined the two wings.
Better: Because the center chamber was not yet built, a wooden walkway joined the two wings.

5. Avoid Dependent-clause Verb Errors

Remember that after verbs such as *move, request,* and *order* in the main clause, the verb in the dependent clause has a base form.

Incorrect: Then came the War of 1812, and the British ordered that the Capitol ~~was~~ burned.

Correct: Then came the War of 1812, and the British ordered that the Capitol be burned.

6. Avoid Unnecessary Shifts in Voice, Pronoun, or Tense

a. *Active/passive shift:*   Latrobe's replacement, Charles Bulfinch, finally completed the midsection in 1827. Thornton's original plans were followed and the midsection was capped with a low, copper-sheathed dome.

Better: Latrobe's replacement, Charles Bulfinch, who finally completed the midsection in 1827, followed Thornton's original plans and capped the midsection with a low, copper-sheathed dome.

b. *Pronoun shift:*   In 1851, however, because of the expanding government, the officials felt everyone needed more room, and they had plans drawn up for two more chambers extending the Capitol to the north and south. For this work, we hired Thomas Walter, the fourth architect.

Better: In 1851, however, because of the expanding government, the officials felt they needed more room and had plans drawn up for two more chambers extending the Capitol to the north and south. For this work, they hired Thomas Walter, the fourth architect.

c. *Tense shift:*   He drew plans for additions that harmonize in style with the existing structure. But now that the bottom level was to be so large, the small dome seems out of scale.

Better: He drew plans for additions that were in harmony with the existing structure. But the bottom level was now so large, the small dome seemed out of scale.

7. Avoid Wordy Structures

Try to be concise.

Wordy: Therefore, Walter designed a new dome made from cast iron. He cleverly combined two shells that were separate. These were called the inner and the outer domes. He explained his work by saying that these shells allowed the mass that was so huge to expand and contract. These expansions and contractions were caused by temperature changes caused by the weather. Then when the Civil War began, they thought that construction would stop because the Union Army needed the iron. They needed the nine million pounds of iron that were supposed to go into the dome. Fortunately, President Lincoln, who noted this problem, decided to help and rescue the project. He decided the work would continue and everything went on as planned.

Better: Walter then decided to build a new cast-iron dome. He cleverly combined two separate shells, the inner and the outer domes, which would allow the huge mass to expand and contract with temperature changes. At the outbreak of the Civil War, construction almost stopped because the Union army needed the nine million pounds of iron that were to go into the dome. President Lincoln rescued the project, and work continued as planned.

Summary of Guidelines from the Review

Use this list as a handy reference for the editing exercise that follows.

1. Avoid strings of simple sentences.

2. Avoid too many dependent clauses.

3. Don't put the subject after the verb in a paraphrased question.

4. Don't use *is when, is why,* or *is because.*

5. Don't forget to use special verb forms after a wish or verbs like *move.*

6. Avoid unnecessary changes in (a) voice, (b) pronoun, or (c) tense.

7. Avoid wordy structures.

EDITING EXERCISE

The following paragraphs contain many incorrect and ineffective sentences. The number enclosed in parentheses in front of a sentence or passage, keyed to the preceding numbered list, identifies the problem to be corrected. On a separate sheet of paper rewrite the passage correctly and more effectively, using your sentence-combining skills.

(**1**—entire paragraph) Do you know something? You think you use soap, but the "soap" you use may not be soap. This soap might be detergent. People think they use lots of "soap." In fact, they use less real soap now. The use has declined in the last three or four decades. Most manufacturers make synthetic soap or a manmade kind. They prefer to use that kind of soap. They think it is better than the real thing.

(**2**—entire paragraph) That detergents were invented in the 1930s to work with water that was named "hard" because of its qualities was a result of the fact that hard water has a mineral content that is higher than water that is called "soft," and that most soaps that are pure don't lather with water that is hard. The result is that we notice that the soap that is "real" soap just doesn't clean in a way that we consider effective.

(**4**) "Real" soap is when a blend of fat and alkali is made to lather. (**4**) The reason this blend, when rubbed in water, produces a lather is because it breaks dirt into particles. (**4**) The fact that this lather lifts dirt to be rinsed off later is why soap cleans.

(**6c**) Early soaps consisted of an alkali, like wood ashes, that people rub on the skin with water. (**6a**) Then oil or fat would often be rubbed on by bathers to soften their skin. (**3**) Eventually, someone wondered how could he combine ashes and oil. (**3**) He then discovered how did this blend make a better lather and did it prove more effective. (**3**) Historians are not sure when did humans first use "soap" to clean themselves, but its use was first recorded by Galen, a Greek doctor in the second century A.D. (**4**) Galen noted that when the patient bathed was why skin diseases he was treating seemed to heal more rapidly.

(**6a**) The Romans, who were introduced to real soap by the "barbaric" Gauls, were the first to manufacture large amounts of soap, and perfume was added to the soap by them. But after the fall of Rome, soap and bathing fell into general disfavor in Europe. (**5**) In fact, doctors advised that people bathed less because they believed that frequent bathing was bad for one's health. (**4**) In the sixteenth century, at most once a month is when most people, including Queen Elizabeth I of England, took a bath.

(**4**) Not until 300 years later was when Louis Pasteur, among others, proved that using soap actually prevented infection by eliminating undesirable bacteria from the skin. (**5**) Thereafter, scientists suggested that soap was used in disease control.

(**6a**) Early British colonists showed the first signs of what some people consider to be an obsession with the use of soap, for a strong soap from lye and fat was usually made by colonial housewives. (**6c**) Soon soap factories with kettles so large that each of them can produce 150 tons were built. (**3**) What did such a massive production of soap indicate was that many people used soap.

(**6b**) Today, a typical health aid aisle in a U.S. supermarket holds hundreds of soaps one can buy to cleanse your body, hair, and teeth. (**6b**) Other aisles are devoted to products that help us clean dishes, floors, clothes, cars, and even one's pets.

(**7**) As of today it is apparent that in the United States, soap, whether it is considered to be "real" or is labeled as "manmade," is being considered to be of great importance in cosmetic use. (**7**) Many people who are consumers probably use more soap of any kind than is actually necessary or believed to be necessary for eliminating bacteria that are considered undesirable from the skin and other body parts because it is apparent from statistics that are currently used in detecting who buys soap and other health products that the person considered to be average by these experts and who lives in the United States uses about twenty-seven pounds of soap and soap products each year that he or she is alive.

WRITING ASSIGNMENTS

Write at least two pages about one or both of the following topics, using the guidelines of your teacher. Check your paper for all of the kinds of errors listed on the proofreading checklist at the end of Unit 4 (p. 322).

1. Write a commercial for a new cleansing product (use specific detail).

2. Write about an obsession (other than one for cleanliness) you have noticed in American life.

Writing an Essay

At the end of each unit has been a section called "The Writing Process." The cumulative purpose of these sections has been to show you the four essential steps in writing: developing ideas, adding and selecting details, polishing, and proofreading. Here we will briefly summarize the main points made in those sections and add a few more suggestions. But first we will discuss the characteristics of the end product—the essay.

WHAT IS AN ESSAY?

An **essay** is a short piece of writing (anywhere from 200 to 2000 words) that exposes the truth, persuades, or explains in a clear, thoughtful, and interesting fashion. An essay may also entertain the reader, but its entertainment value is not as important as its main purpose: to give the reader specific information so that he or she will understand the writer's point of view about an issue, event, person, or place.

An essay focuses on a main idea: the point that the writer is making. A good essay does not stray from this idea. The writer is like a person traveling from one place to another: Although there are many side roads and intersections, the traveler journeys over only those that lead to the destination.

PARTS OF AN ESSAY

Just as a journey has a starting point and an end point, an essay has a beginning—an introduction—and a conclusion. The body of the essay is like the journey itself.

Introduction

An essay needs a good start. A good essay introduction is like a good takeoff of an airplane, a fast start in a swimming race, or a strong and well-aimed kickoff in a football game. The introduction lets the reader know the direction the essay will take and what to expect from it. The introduction also tries to capture interest and motivate the reader to continue reading.

Body

The body of an essay, which may consist of one or several paragraphs, is its main part. Even without an introduction and conclusion, the body would make sense. It may tell a story or several anecdotes; it may give examples, reasons, and facts. Most important, the body gives a great deal of specific information that helps make the essay's point.

Conclusion

The essay conclusion is like the landing of an airplane, bringing the reader down from mid-air. There are different ways to "land" an essay. The conclusion may remind the reader of the essay's main point without repeating exactly what has already been said. Or the conclusion may explain what the author has learned through writing the essay. A conclusion could be a personal observation, evaluation, or insight.

Many inexperienced writers have trouble composing an essay because they think their first draft has to be a finished one—with an introduction, a body, and a conclusion. But, as you saw in the writing sections, writing is a process. Most experienced authors take their essay through several drafts before they consider it finished. Let's review the process.

THE WRITING PROCESS

Developing Ideas

Once you have a topic in mind, an assigned one or your own, you need to develop ideas. You may already know what your main point is going to be, or you may simply jot down some notes. If you lack a main idea, you can, as you practiced earlier, write freely whatever comes to mind, to discover what it is you have to say. The free writing will give you materials to use for the body of the essay. If you write four or five pages' worth, there is probably going to be some material that will be useful in a later draft. Then you need to read over your notes or pages of free writing and isolate a main idea. Set it down in one sentence—your thesis statement. It is not important whether you actually use that sentence in your later drafts; at this point it gives you a goal, just like the destination of a journey.

Selecting and Adding Detail

Having settled on a main idea, you can start organizing. At this point you can add an introduction and a conclusion. Read over your notes or pages of free writing, particularly those passages that have something to do with your main idea. It is most important to read critically. If an anecdote, a story, or a fact has nothing to do with your main idea, either change it or take it out. Divide the passages into clear paragraphs, each with its own point.

   Then you need to select or add details. Critically examine the sentences and words you want to keep. Are they relevant? Are there any details that should be added? Your reader is not interested in general opinions, but in facts and specifics from which to learn.

Polishing

Good writing, as you may remember, requires revision. Once you have a rough draft to work with, read it aloud. Make sure that all the pieces fit together logically. And remember, writing is very different from speaking. In a conversation, your listeners may show with facial expressions or questions when they don't understand you, whereas in writing you must *anticipate* your readers' questions. Does each sentence flow logically into the next, or are there abrupt changes of thought that might confuse the reader?

Just as when you decorate a room you try various items in different places, you might try reorganizing your essay material to see where it works best. Write more than one draft, making each version clearer, possibly including better examples, and improving your introduction or conclusion.

Style

In "To the Student," at this book's opening, we pointed out the differences between spoken English and educated written English. Keeping your reader in mind, adapt the language you use, the kinds of details you give, and even your choice of subject to suit your reader. Ask yourself, "Who will read this essay?" Would you go to a job interview in a bathing suit, or to the beach in a tuxedo or cocktail dress? Like your choice of clothes, your language should be adapted to the occasion. Avoid slang words or words that may be offensive to your readers.

Good writing is clear and concise. Imagine how difficult it would be to appreciate a beautiful piece of furniture in a room full of magazines, newspapers, unfolded laundry, and leftover TV dinners. Similarly, you shouldn't hide what you mean behind an abundance of empty words. Use only those words you need—no more—to make your point. Also, avoid standard phrases like "he was there for me" that have lost their literal meaning (clichés) and vague, wordy, passive constructions such as "it is believed by this author." Select words that carry a strong, vivid image. Don't repeat yourself. If you feel it necessary to stress a point, then say it again, but in different words.

Proofreading

Finally, good writing contains few grammatical and mechanical errors. You should eliminate errors because they may confuse the reader or detract from the quality of your ideas.

WRITING ASSIGNMENT

First select a writing assignment you have done previously in this course, one about a topic you are very familiar with and that contains a lot of specific detail and facts. Then revise that earlier draft into an essay.

Checklist for Essays

The following list may be useful for checking your essay before you hand it in. Read each of the listed parts of your essay separately.

1. TOTAL ESSAY
   Does the essay make a point?

2. INTRODUCTION
   Does the introduction prepare the reader for what is ahead? Does the first sentence make the reader interested in your essay?

3. BODY
   Does each paragraph discuss only one topic? Does each paragraph add to the essay's main idea? Are arguments, statements, or generalizations supported with specific facts, illustrations, or examples? Are sentences and paragraphs ordered in such a way that the reader can easily follow your thoughts?

4. CONCLUSION
   Does the conclusion either restate the main idea of the essay or add a personal observation, evaluation, or insight?

5. STYLE
   Is the writing concise and to the point, or is it wordy? Is the writing detailed, concrete, and exciting, or is it vague, abstract, and difficult to understand? Are sentences varied and interesting or short, choppy, and boring?

6. WORD CHOICE
   Is the language appropriate, or does it contain slang words or words that may offend? Are words used appropriately, or are they misused or overused?

7. PROOFREADING
   Does the essay contain errors in grammar, punctuation, or spelling?

Appendix 1
Common Irregular Verbs

Base Form	Past Form	Past Participle
arise	arose	arisen
awake	awoke, awaked	awoke, awaked
be	was/were	been
beat	beat	beaten
begin	began	begun
bid	bid	bid
bite	bit	bitten
blow	blew	blown
break	broke	broken
bring	brought	brought
build	built	built
burst	burst	burst
buy	bought	bought
catch	caught	caught
choose	chose	chosen
come	came	come
creep	crept	crept
cut	cut	cut
dive	dove, dived	dived
do	did	done
draw	drew	drawn
dream	dreamed, dreamt	dreamed, dreamt
drink	drank	drunk
drive	drove	driven
eat	ate	eaten
fall	fell	fallen
find	found	found
flee	fled	fled
fly	flew	flown
forget	forgot	forgotten, forgot
freeze	froze	frozen
get	got	gotten, got
give	gave	given
go	went	gone
grow	grew	grown
hang ("suspend")	hung	hung

	Base Form	Past Form	Past Participle
But	hang ("execute")	hanged	hanged
	hear	heard	heard
	hide	hid	hidden
	know	knew	known
	lay	laid	laid
	lead	led	led
	let	let	let
	lie	lay	lain
	lose	lost	lost
	mean	meant	meant
	pay	paid	paid
	prove	proved	proved, proven
	ride	rode	ridden
	ring	rang, rung	rung
	rise	rose	risen
	run	ran	run
	say	said	said
	see	saw	seen
	send	sent	sent
	set	set	set
	shake	shook	shaken
	shine (as with light)	shone	shone
But	shine ("polish")	shined	shined
	show	showed	shown, showed
	shrink	shrank, shrunk	shrunk, shrunken
	sing	sang, sung	sung
	sink	sank, sunk	sunk
	sit	sat	sat
	slide	slid	slid
	speak	spoke	spoken
	spin	spun	spun
	spring	sprang, sprung	sprung
	stand	stood	stood
	steal	stole	stolen
	stink	stank, stunk	stunk
	swear	swore	sworn
	swim	swam	swum
	swing	swung	swung
	take	took	taken
	tear	tore	torn
	throw	threw	thrown
	wear	wore	worn
	wind	wound	wound
	write	wrote	written

Appendix 2
Mechanics and Punctuation

ABBREVIATIONS

Standard Abbreviations Are Acceptable in:

Titles used before or after proper names

Clarifying words that accompany times, dates, or numerals

Names of publications, organizations, or government agencies commonly known by their initials (NYU, FBI, etc.)

Representing certain widely recognized Latin phrases, such as *i.e.* ("that is"), *e.g.* ("for example"), *etc.* ("and so forth"), and *vs.* ("versus"); however, in formal writing the English equivalents are preferred

APOSTROPHES

Use Apostrophes:

To show ownership with nouns and with some pronouns (*Jack's, everyone's*)

To form contractions showing the omission of letters or numerals, as in *don't* or '89

Before *s* to make the plural of alphabetical letters, numerals, symbols, and terms referred to as terms, such as *A*'s, +'s, 5's, and *and*'s

Do Not Abbreviate:

Titles that do *not* accompany proper names

Clarifying words (such as A.M. and P.M.) that are *not* accompanying times, dates, and numerals as usual

Words such as *street, avenue, road, park, company*, and *high school* when used apart from a proper name

Names of states, countries, months, or days

Personal names

The word *Christmas*

Words referring to school subjects (like *gym* and *math*)

The words *volume, chapter*, and *page*, unless used in technical writing

The words *and* (&) and *junior* (as in jr. high)

Do Not Use Apostrophes:

To form the possessive of personal pronouns or of the pronoun *who*

To make inanimate objects show ownership, like "the building's front" (say instead, "the front of the building")

To form the plural of common or proper nouns or of any pronouns (remember: to become plural, most words add -*s* or -*es* endings, or change their spelling—*child/children*)

When adding the -*s* ending on present tense verbs

CAPITALIZATION

Capitalize:

The first word of any sentence, including quoted sentences

The first and last words of a title, plus all important words in between except small prepositions and conjunctions (*to, or, and,* etc.) and the adjectives *a, an, the*

All proper nouns and words derived from them, such as these:

1. Specific persons, races, nationalities, languages, places, organizations, and the like

2. Days of the week, months, and holidays

3. Historical periods, documents, and events

4. Specific educational institutions, academic degrees, and departments

5. Specific geographical areas (for example, the Orient, the Middle East, the South)

6. Names of planets and stars

7. Titles preceding a name (or after if a title of high distinction like Chief Justice)

8. Abbreviations for time (like A.D.), government divisions (like FHA), titles before or after a name, and call letters for radio and television stations

9. The pronoun *I*

10. *Mother, Father, Grampa,* and the like only if used in front of the person's name or in place of that person's name

11. The second part of a split quotation only if that part is a complete sentence ("I can't go," she said. "You go instead.")

12. Words referring to God

All words in the greeting of a letter, plus the first word in the closing phrase before your signature

Do Not Capitalize:

The first word after a semicolon

Common nouns

Seasons of the year

Names of academic studies, unless followed by a specific course number or unless derived from a proper noun ("Economics 101"; French)

Directions or compass points

The words *earth*, *moon*, and *sun*

Words like *mother* and *father* when preceded by a possessive ("my mother")

The second part of a split quotation if it is *not* a complete sentence ("I can't go," she said, "not until after work, anyway.")

COLONS

Use Colons:

To introduce lists preceded by a phrase such as *the following* or *as follows*

Between independent clauses with no conjunction between them only if the second statement explains a word in the first ("I only have one complaint: I can't get my new phone to work.")

After the greetings of business letters

Between the numerals referring to chapters and verses in the Bible

Between numerals indicating clock time (3:30 P.M.)

To formally set off appositives at the ends of sentences ("She brought the thing I love the most: chocolate-filled donuts."); however, in informal writing a comma or dash is common

Do Not Use Colons:

To introduce listings after verbs ("The three appointees are: Sally, Joe, and Sara.")

To introduce listings or explanations after the phrase *such as* ("The cake recipe contained errors, such as: no eggs, no sugar, and not enough milk.")

In front of subordinators introducing dependent clauses ("He promised to come: because I insisted.")

COMMAS

Use Commas:

Before coordinate conjunctions that link two independent clauses

After introductory dependent adverb clauses

After long introductory phrases and even short ones if there is a chance of misreading the sentence without punctuation there

Between items in a series of three or more (a listing)

In pairs to set off unessential appositives, phrases, or dependent clauses that add interesting detail not needed to understand the main clause

In pairs to set off unnecessary interruptions within the main clause, especially between the subject and verb or between the verb and its object or complement

Between the city and the state in addresses

Between the day and the year in dates

To separate coordinate (equal) adjectives modifying the same word ("I prefer simple, low-calorie recipes.")

After the words *yes* and *no* when they begin a sentence

To set off mild outcries of emotion, such as "oh"

To set off direct quotations from the phrases introducing them that announce who is speaking (for example, *he said* or *she asked*)

Before the words *such as* and *especially* when they introduce an example ("Making a good impression is important, especially at a job interview.")

Before contrasted elements introduced by the word *not* ("You should eat nutritious foods, not junk food.")

To separate two verbs back to back so that the reader won't misread ("The question is, was that a good example?")

Before questions tacked onto the end of statements, asking your response ("You are coming to the party later, aren't you?")

After the greetings of friendly letters and the closing words or phrases that precede your signature in all letters

Do Not Use Commas:

To join two independent clauses *not* joined by a coordinator ("comma splice")

Between the two parts of a compound predicate, subject, or complement

Before the first item in a listing or after the last item

In a series that repeats *and* or *or* between each item

To set off appositives, phrases, or dependent clauses needed to understand the main clause

To separate subjects from their verbs or the verbs from their objects or complements if no interruption appears

After phrases like *he said* if what follows is an indirect quotation beginning with the word *that*

To set off dependent clauses beginning with *that*

DASHES

Use Dashes:

To dramatically set off interruptions you wish to stress

To emphasize or call special attention to appositives at the end of statements ("It was the last person I wished to see—my boss.")

In pairs to set off an unnecessary interruption or appositive that already contains commas ("The three of us—Susan, Robert, and I—were happy to be home.")

EXCLAMATION MARKS

Use Exclamation Marks:

Following words, phrases, or statements showing strong emotion

HYPHENS

Use Hyphens:

To form compound nouns such as *commander-in-chief*

To write out numbers from twenty-one to ninety-nine and, of course, fractions (one-half)

After the prefixes *ex-*, *self-*, and *all-* (consult a dictionary about other such prefixes)

Before the suffix *-elect*, as in "president-elect"

To join words into a single adjective that precedes a noun ("space-oriented program")

To avoid misinterpreting a word like *re-covered* versus *recovered*

At the end of a line to show a division between syllables of a word that must be continued onto the next line

Do Not Use Dashes:

To avoid deciding what punctuation is needed between clauses, especially independent clauses

Do Not Use Exclamation Marks:

After mild expressions of emotion

One after another for emphasis (One exclamation mark is as emphatic as is needed!)

Do Not Use Hyphens:

To split a one-syllable word

To split a compound noun anywhere except where the hyphens already exist

To split a word anywhere but at a natural break in pronunciation (between syllables)

To split a word so that only a single syllable is placed at the end of a line or is carried over to the next line

NUMBERS

Write Out Numbers in Words:

Whenever the number can be expressed in one or two words

Whenever the number begins the sentence

PARENTHESES

Use Parentheses:

To set off any comment that is either really unimportant or highly unrelated to the main thought (like an "aside" in drama)

PERIODS

Use Periods:

Following sentences that make a statement or give a command

After indirect questions (statements about a question)

After most abbreviations, unless the abbreviation is a substitute for the name, such as *NATO*, or is an often-used, informal form of a name, such as *math* or *Ed* (for Edward)

Do Not Write Out Numbers in Words:

Whenever the number must be expressed in more than two words
Whenever the number is part of one of the following:

1. date

2. street, apartment, or room number

3. road number

4. chapter or page number, or numbered line of printed matter

5. decimal, percentage, fraction, or measurement

6. the hour, if followed by the abbreviation A.M. or P.M.

Do Not Use Parentheses:

In addition to a pair of commas to set off unnecessary elements in
the sentence (any unessential interruption may be set off by pairs
of commas, dashes, or parentheses)

Do Not Use Periods:

After phrases or dependent clauses ("fragments")
With other end punctuation marks (one punctuation mark is
sufficient!)

QUESTION MARKS

Use Question Marks:

Following direct questions

Inside end quotation marks if the quotation itself is a question (Gary asked, "Is that your brother?")

Outside end quotation marks if the entire sentence is a question, not just the quoted part (Did you ask, "Who should leave first"?)

QUOTATION MARKS

Use Quotation Marks:

To enclose direct quotations (exact words of a speaker or writer), including dictionary definitions of words

To enclose titles of any smaller work published within a larger work, such as titles of chapters, newspaper or magazine articles, essays or short stories, and poems

Special Note

Periods and commas go *inside* end quotation marks.

Semicolons and colons go *outside* end quotation marks.

Question marks, exclamation marks, and dashes go *inside* end quotation marks when they punctuate only the quoted material but *outside* when they punctuate the entire sentence or parts of the sentence not quoted.

Quotation marks go only around quoted material. A phrase of interruption would thus split a quotation into two separate parts. ("I guess it's okay," she said, "to leave early.")

Quotation marks belong at the beginning and end of the whole passage if the quoted material consists of several sentences.

Beginning quotation marks are the only punctuation marks ever placed at the start of a written line (never start a line with a comma or the like).

Do Not Use Question Marks:

After indirect questions (statements about questions)

After polite requests, even if they sound like questions
(Would you please answer the phone.)

Do Not Use Quotation Marks:

To set off indirect quotations (what somebody said that someone
else said)

To enclose the titles of book-length, separately published works
(these titles are underlined)

To set off your own title (unless it is a quotation)

SEMICOLONS

Use Semicolons:

Between independent clauses that are related in meaning but are *not* joined by any conjunctions

Between independent clauses joined by a conjunctive adverb; also, in formal writing a comma after the conjunctive adverb is preferred

Before coordinate conjunctions joining two main clauses *only if* either of the independent clauses already contains commas ("The three nominees were Jan, Sam, and Mark; but Mark declined.")

To separate items in a series *only if* one or more of those items already contain commas for another reason ("Miami, Florida; Dallas, Texas; and Denver, Colorado, are our company's shipping centers.")

UNDERLINING

Underline:

Titles of books, plays, magazines, newspapers, movies, pamphlets, musicals, record albums, etc. (any separately published work)

Names of ships, trains, aircraft, or spacecraft

Titles of paintings, sculptures, or other art works

Foreign words or phrases (*fait accompli*—French for "accomplished fact")

Terms referred to as terms, letters of the alphabet, or symbols referred to in a sentence ("Avoid using the word *and* so often, and never use the abbreviation *&* in formal writing." *Note:* In informal writing, the terms and alphabet letters in this example would be set off with quotation marks.)

Do Not Use Semicolons:

Between an independent and a dependent clause ("fragments")

Before conjunctive adverbs if they are *not* joining two main clauses ("fragments")

Before coordinate conjunctions joining two main clauses, *unless* one main clause already contains commas

To separate a *listing, unless* one or more of the listed items already contain commas

Do Not Underline:

Your own title (unless you have used the title of a published work that would normally be underlined)

Foreign words that have been "adopted" into English (check your dictionary)

Too often, for emphasis (underlining for emphasis is effective only if used sparingly)

Acknowledgments

Acknowledgments

Exercises on pages 10–11, 15–16, 18, 19–20, 21–22, 217–220, 252–253, and 314–316 taken from *Stories Behind Everyday Things* (Pleasantville, New York: Reader's Digest Association, 1980). Copyright 1980 by the Reader's Digest Association, Inc. Used with permission of the Reader's Digest Association, Inc., Pleasantville, New York.

Exercises on pages 105–106, 125, 132–133, 140–141, 158–159, 174, 270–271, 281–282, 283–284, 285, 287, 291–292, 292–293, and 297 taken from *Strange Stories, Amazing Facts* (Pleasantville, New York: Reader's Digest Association, 1976). Copyright 1976 by the Reader's Digest Association, Inc. Used with permission of the Reader's Digest Association, Inc. Pleasantville, New York.

Exercise on pages 77–78 taken from "Men losing distinction as rarer sex," *News Star-World*, 25 May 1987. Used with permission of The Associated Press.

Exercise on page 98 taken from *Illustrated World Encyclopedia* (Woodbury, New York: Bobley Publishing Co., 1981). Used with permission of Bobley Publishing Co.

Exercise on page 186 taken from Chuck Stewart, "Let's get on with the game," *News Star-World*, 9 August 1987. Used with permission.

Exercise on pages 191–192 taken from Sue MacDonald, "Prosthetic devices step closer to bionics," *News Star-World*, 3 August 1987. Used with permission of Gannett News Service.

Exercise on pages 194–195 taken from Paul Hoffman, "Triskaidekaphobia Can Strike When You're Most Expecting It," *Smithsonian* 17, no. 11 (February 1987): 124, 126. Copyright © 1987 by Paul Hoffman. Reprinted by permission of Sterling Lord Literistic, Inc.

Exercise on pages 195–196 taken from Lionel Casson, "'It would be very nice if you sent me 200 drachmas,'" *Smithsonian* 14, no. 1 (April 1983): 124. Used with permission.

Exercise on pages 196–197 taken from George B. Schaller, "Secrets of the Wild Panda," *National Geographic* 169, no. 3 (March 1986): 287, 290. Used with permission.

Exercise on pages 200–201 taken from Eunice Minn, "Name book spells out meanings," *News Star-World*, 13 July 1987. Used with permission of Gannett News Service.

Exercise on page 215 taken from *Illustrated World Encyclopedia* (Woodbury, New York: Bobley Publishing Co., 1981). Used with permission of Bobley Publishing Co.

Exercise on pages 220–225 taken from *Illustrated World Encyclopedia* (Woodbury, New York: Bobley Publishing Co., 1981). Used with permission of Bobley Publishing Co.

Exercise on pages 227–228 taken from *Electronics*, Irving Adler (New York: Alfred A. Knopf, Inc., 1981). Copyright © 1961 by Irving Adler. Reprinted by permission of Alfred A. Knopf, Inc.

Exercise on pages 233–235 taken from "Lies run the gamut in complexity," *News Star-World*, 18 July 1987. Used with permission of The Associated Press.

Exercises on pages 249, 266–267, and 274–275 taken from *The Literary Life and Other Curiosities*, Robert Hendrickson (New York: Penguin Books, 1981). Copyright © 1981 by Robert Hendrickson. Used with permission by Robert Hendrickson.

Exercise on pages 254–255 taken from Tom Pedulla, "Cheating isn't rare; catching 'em is," *News Star-World*, 9 August 1987. Used with permission by Gannett News Service.

Index

Index